Microsoft® Office® 2021 For Macs®

by Bob LeVitus

Houston Chronicle "Dr. Mac" columnist

and Dwight Spivey

for dummies®

A Wiley Brand

Microsoft® Office® 2021 For Macs® For Dummies®

Published by: **John Wiley & Sons, Inc.,** 111 River Street, Hoboken, NJ 07030-5774, www.wiley.com

Copyright © 2022 by John Wiley & Sons, Inc., Hoboken, New Jersey

Published simultaneously in Canada

For general information on our other products and services, please contact our Customer Care Department within the U.S. at 877-762-2974, outside the U.S. at 317-572-3993, or fax 317-572-4002. For technical support, please visit https://hub.wiley.com/community/support/dummies.

Wiley publishes in a variety of print and electronic formats and by print-on-demand. Some material included with standard print versions of this book may not be included in e-books or in print-on-demand. If this book refers to media such as a CD or DVD that is not included in the version you purchased, you may download this material at http://booksupport.wiley.com. For more information about Wiley products, visit www.wiley.com.

Library of Congress Control Number: 2022934336

ISBN 978-1-119-84044-2 (pbk); ISBN 978-1-119-84046-6 (ebk); ISBN 978-1-119-84047-3 (ebk)

SKY10033835_032522

Table of Contents

Introduction

You made the right choice twice: Microsoft Office for Mac and this book.

Take a deep breath and get ready to have a rollicking good time. That's right — this is a computer book, but it's fun. What a concept! Whether you're brand-spanking new to the Office suite or a grizzled Office veteran, we guarantee that reading this book to discover the ins and outs of Office for Mac is fun and easy.

About This Book

Why write a *For Dummies* book about Office for Mac? Well, Office for Mac is a big, somewhat complicated suite of productivity applications, so we made *Office 2021 For Macs For Dummies* a not-so-big, not-so-complicated book that shows you how to perform the most common tasks you're likely to perform using Office for Mac, all without boring you to tears, confusing you, or poking you with sharp objects.

In fact, we think you'll be so darned comfortable that we wanted the title to be *Office For Macs without Discomfort, the Very Comfortable 2021 Edition*, but the publisher wouldn't allow it. Apparently, we *For Dummies* authors have to follow some rules, and using *For Dummies* and *Office For Macs* in this book's title are among them.

Speaking of dummies, we don't think you're dumb — quite the opposite! Our second choice for this book's title was *Office For Macs For People Smart Enough to Know That They Need Help Using It*, but you can just imagine what the Wiley folks thought of that. ("C'mon, that's the whole point of the name!" they insisted. "Besides, it's shorter this way.")

Anyway, the book is chock-full of information and advice, explaining everything you need to know about Office for Mac in language you can understand — along with giving you timesaving tips, tricks, techniques, and step-by-step instructions, all served up in generous quantities.

Foolish Assumptions

Although we know what happens when you make assumptions, we've made a few, anyway. First, we assume that you, gentle reader, know nothing about using Office — beyond knowing what it is, that you want to use it, that you want to understand it without digesting an incomprehensible technical manual, and that you made the right choice by selecting this particular book.

And so we do our best to explain each new concept in full and loving detail. Maybe that's foolish, but, so be it.

Oh, and we also assume that you can read. If you can't, just ignore this paragraph.

Icons Used in This Book

Little round pictures (icons) appear to the left side of the text throughout this book. Consider these icons miniature road signs, telling you a little something extra about the subject at hand. Here's what the different icons look like and what they all mean:

TIP

Look for Tip icons to find the juiciest morsels: shortcuts, tips, and undocumented secrets about Office for Mac. Try them all and impress your friends!

REMEMBER

When you see this icon, you know that this particular bit is something we think you should memorize (or at least write on your shirt cuff).

TECHNICAL STUFF

Put on your propeller-head beanie and pocket protector; these tidbits include the truly geeky stuff. They're certainly not required reading, but they must be interesting or informative or else we wouldn't have wasted your time with them.

WARNING

Read these notes very, very, very carefully. (Did we say *very?*) Warning icons flag important information. Neither the authors nor the publisher is responsible if your Mac explodes or spews flaming parts because you ignored a Warning icon. (Just kidding — that type of catastrophe won't happen.) Macs don't explode or spew (with the exception of a few choice Michael Spindler–era models — true Apple aficionados will know what we're talking about). But we got your attention, didn't we? We tell you again: Read the Warning notes very carefully.

Beyond the Book

There's even more Office for Mac information on www.dummies.com. This book's cheat sheet shows you how to create automatic replies to senders in Outlook, check documents for accessibility problems, embed fonts in your Word documents and PowerPoint presentations when sharing, and even check the current weather when viewing your Outlook Calendar. To get to the cheat sheet, go to www.dummies.com, and type *Office 2021 for Macs For Dummies Cheat Sheet* in the Search box. You'll see not only the cheat sheet but any significant updates or changes that occur between editions of this book.

Where to Go from Here

Go to a comfortable spot (preferably not far from a Mac) and look through this book.

In the first few chapters, we describe the basic everyday topics you need to understand to operate your Mac effectively. If you're new to Macs and Office for Mac, start with Chapters 1–3, which make up Part 1. The discussion in Part 1 is so basic that if you've been using Office awhile, you might think you know it all — and you might know most of it. But, hey! Not-so-old-timers need a solid foundation. So read what you need and skip the rest.

What are you waiting for? Go — enjoy the book!

1

Introduction to Microsoft Office for Mac

IN THIS PART . . .

Get an overview of the various versions of Office for Mac as well as how to install and set them up.

Become acquainted with the four major apps in the Office suite: Word, PowerPoint, Excel, and Outlook.

Explore Office features that work the same way in all four apps, such as menus, toolbars, preferences, and help.

Chapter **1**

Overview from 10,000 Feet

O ver the next several hundred pages, you can find out in detail about the apps that make up the Microsoft Office for Mac suite. But first you must decide which version of the suite you want or need, acquire a copy of it, and then install it and find out how to update it to ensure that you're always running the latest and greatest (not to mention most stable) version.

So, without further ado, dig in!

The Many Faces of Office for Mac

When it comes to choices, it seems Microsoft wants to make sure you have a veritable cornucopia of them for Office apps. Combining the number of packages available for individual and business use, there are roughly a dozen to choose from. For simplicity's sake, we focus on the several tasty flavors of Office for Mac for individuals and home users:

>> Office for Mac Home & Student

>> Office for Mac Home & Business

>> Microsoft 365 Personal

>> Microsoft 365 Family

Office for Mac Home & Student and Office for Mac Home & Business are both one-off purchases; you pay one price up front and then own it forever. Microsoft 365 Personal and Microsoft 365 Family offer a subscription model, in which you pay a monthly or yearly fee, with access halting only when you choose to cancel or you miss a payment.

The four editions all provide the big three apps — Word, Excel, and PowerPoint — with variations based on whether you selected the Office or Microsoft 365 version. The Microsoft 365 editions of the big three apps provide the latest features and updates on a continual basis — Microsoft calls these premium versions. When Microsoft develops and implements a new feature, you get it automatically, so you apps are always up to date. The Office editions provide classic versions of the big three — what you see is what you get, with no additions or updates except security and bug fixes. You can't take advantage of new features and products unless you purchase the next Office edition Microsoft releases (they're usually several years apart).

Here's the skinny on each of the four editions:

>> **Office for Mac Home & Student :** The retail price is $149.99 for a single installation. As the least expensive edition, it includes the big three apps and OneNote. Many users need nothing more.

Note that this edition does *not* include Microsoft Outlook. Outlook, which is sometimes called the Swiss army knife of personal communications software, combines an email client with an address book, a calendar, to-do lists, and searchable notes in a single app.

Unless you dislike the Mail, Contacts, and Calendar apps that are included with macOS, you probably won't miss Outlook much.

TIP

>> **Office for Mac Home & Business:** The retail price is $249.99 for a single installation. What do you get for the additional dough (along with the big three and OneNote)? In two words: Microsoft Outlook.

What's that, you say? You don't know whether you need Outlook? Well then, we suggest that you save yourself a bundle and start with the Home & Student Edition.

Does your organization require or prefer that you use Outlook? It's best to find out before you make a purchase. You can't simply pay a few more dollars to upgrade from Office Home & Student to Office Home & Business; you'd have to pay the full price of Office Home & Business to gain access to Outlook.

>> **Microsoft 365 Personal:** For the price of $69.99 annually or $6.99 monthly, you get access for one person to premium versions of the big three, OneNote, Teams, and Outlook, 1TB of OneDrive online storage (more on OneDrive in the next chapter), and the ability to install and use your subscription on up to five devices — Macs, PCs, iOS devices, and Android. That's right: five devices with support for a variety of desktop and mobile operating systems!

>> **Microsoft 365 Family:** The price is $99.99 annually or $9.99 monthly for access to everything in Microsoft 365 Personal. Plus up to six people can use the subscription instead of one. You can also try it for free for one month.

So there you have it — four editions for four budgets.

Installing Office

Regardless of which edition you decide to buy, you'll need a Microsoft account and an internet connection to download the installation package for your apps.

Getting a Microsoft account

A Microsoft account is similar to your Apple ID; it's an account for you to manage your Microsoft apps and purchases. To download and install your Office apps, your purchase of Office for Mac must be associated with a Microsoft account (personal, business, or school account).

If you don't have a Microsoft account, go to `https://office.com/setup` **to** create one.

Downloading and installing Office

To install Microsoft Office, you need the username and password for an administrator account on this Mac. If you don't have an administrator account and password handy, it would behoove you to get one now.

After you have that detail settled, here's how to download and install your Office apps:

1. **Go to** `https://office.com` **and sign in to the Microsoft account associated with your Microsoft 365 or Office purchase.**

2. **Click the Install Office button and download the installer package.**

3. **Locate and double-click the installer package to launch the installer app.**

4. **Click Continue on the first screen.**

   The screen displays the license terms.

5. **Read every word of the license terms, and then click Continue.**

TECHNICAL
STUFF

   We're only half kidding — we know that no one reads the licensing information. But because you're about to enter into a legally binding agreement, we would be remiss not to at least pretend to urge you to read every word.

6. **On the next screen, click Agree.**

   The Select a Destination screen appears.

7. **Choose the destination disk for the software installation and then click Continue.**

   The Standard Install on *your hard drive's name* screen appears.

8. **If you want to install the Office apps somewhere other than the Applications folder, click the Change Install Location button and select another destination.**

TIP

   In the next step, you click Install. But if you're short on disk space, consider not installing some of the apps. To do so, click the Customize button before you click the Install button and then deselect any items you don't want to install.

9. **Click the Install button to open an authentication window, enter an administrator name and password, and then click OK.**

   Go get yourself some coffee or a soft drink — the installation takes a bit of time.

10. **When the screen informs you that the installation is complete, click the Close button and you're ready to go.**

Head on over to your Applications folder and double-click one of the newly installed Office apps to get started.

DEALING WITH MULTIPLE VERSIONS OF OFFICE

If you have an earlier version of Office on your hard drive when you install Office, the older version isn't touched. You now have two (or possibly even three or more) Office versions in your Applications folder.

In a perfect world, all your Office documents, both new and old, would launch the current versions of Word (or other Office apps) when you open them. But in the real world, this may or may not be your experience.

So, we offer you this little lesson in macOS file-opening mastery. You can cause a single file or all files to open in a specific app in two ways. The first method is to right-click the document, choose Open With from the contextual menu, and select an app. The second method is to set a single file or all files of its type to open in a specific app, as follows:

1. To specify which version of Word, Excel, or PowerPoint opens when you double-click one of its document files, single-click that document file and then choose File ⇨ Get Info (or press ⌘+I).

   A drop-down Open With menu appears. If you don't see the Open With menu, click the small, gray disclosure triangle next to the words Open With.

2. Click the Open With menu and select the version of the app you want to open when you double-click this document.

3. If you want all documents of this type to launch this version of Word, click the Change All button.

There you have it — if the wrong version of an Office app launches when you open a document, you now know how to fix it.

Keeping Your Apps Up-to-Date

Microsoft AutoUpdate is a nifty app that's installed along with your other Office apps (although you won't find it in your Applications folder). AutoUpdate does what its name implies: It automatically searches for updates to your Office apps and installs them.

To open AutoUpdate:

1. **Open an Office app (such as Word or Excel).**

2. **Choose Help ➪ Check for Updates from the menu at the top of the screen.**

   The AutoUpdate app launches and scans Microsoft's servers to check for updates to any Microsoft apps you have installed (even apps that don't come with Office, such as Microsoft's web browser, Edge).

3. **When updates are found, click the Update All button to download and install all available updates, or click the Update button to the right of the app's name to only update that app.**

4. **(Optional) If you want AutoUpdate to periodically check for and install updates automatically, select the box labeled Automatically Keep Microsoft Apps up to Date.**

5. **Quit AutoUpdate when you're finished.**

TIP

If you don't elect to have AutoUpdate work automatically, be sure to check every few weeks to a month to make sure you have the latest updates and fixes.

Chapter **2**

A Sweet Suite: Introducing the Office Apps

Microsoft Office for Mac isn't a single, monolithic app that processes words and numbers, creates slide shows, manages your email, calendar, and contact database, and more. No, Office is a suite of programs that share numerous interface characteristics so that many functions are the same across all apps, making it easier for you to seamlessly move between them. The programs are designed to work together harmoniously, adding up to a sum that's greater than its parts.

When you install the software, you don't create a single app named Microsoft Office for Mac, nor is there a single folder that houses all the installed apps. Rather, you'll find that each app is installed separately (in the *Applications* folder, by default); they're easy to find, though, because each starts with the word *Microsoft* (Microsoft Word, Microsoft Excel, and so on). The lone exception is One-Drive, which is simply named *OneDrive.*

TECHNICAL
STUFF

You may have more or fewer Microsoft Office apps in your Applications folder. The number depends on which edition of Office you purchased and which options you choose during installation.

The following list briefly describes the items that matter, focusing on what each one is or does. Note that some of these may not be in your installer package, depending on which version of Office you've purchased or subscribed to:

>> **Microsoft OneNote:** OneNote is a free-form digital note-taking app that can be used to house those great inspirations that pop into your brilliant mind from time to time.

>> **Microsoft Excel:** Excel is the number-crunching member of the Office family. You use this program to create spreadsheet documents.

>> **Microsoft Teams:** Teams is a video-conferencing and collaboration tool designed for organizational communications. It's very much like Zoom and other such apps, but with a familiar Microsoft flair.

>> **Microsoft Outlook:** Microsoft Outlook is the Swiss army knife of Microsoft Office apps — it includes not one, not two, but *five* separate functions. It's

- An email client

- An address book

- An appointment calendar

- A task and to-do list manager

- A repository for notes

>> **Microsoft PowerPoint:** PowerPoint is the presentation-creating member of the Office family. You use it to create slide shows.

>> **Microsoft Word:** Word is, of course, the Office word processing program. But it's much more than that these days because you can use it to create almost any document that contains text or images or both.

>> **OneDrive:** It seems that more and more apps and traditionally computer-focused functions are taking place in the cloud these days, meaning these things are web-based (living on the internet). OneDrive is Microsoft's version of cloud-based storage and is similar to Apple's own iCloud service.

TIP

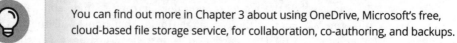

You can find out more in Chapter 3 about using OneDrive, Microsoft's free, cloud-based file storage service, for collaboration, co-authoring, and backups.

>> **Microsoft AutoUpdate:** It's important to keep your Microsoft apps updated and in tip-top shape. AutoUpdate keeps you in the update loop by automatically checking for updates periodically and even updating apps automatically, if you so choose.

What's New and Good

Microsoft Office for Mac has many new or improved features, but perhaps the most important one is that the suite is now coded to run natively (although thankfully not exclusively) on Macs that have Apple Silicon processors. Office apps are also built for Macs with Intel processors. The installer app will know which version your computer needs during installation.

The system requirements have changed, too. Microsoft supports the three most recent versions of macOS. When a new major version (not an incremental update) of macOS is released, Microsoft picks up support for it and drops support for the oldest. As of this writing, Office for Mac is supported for macOS Monterey, Big Sur, and Catalina. When a newer version of macOS is released (a major version is typically released on an annual basis in the fall), Microsoft will support it, Monterey, and Big Sur, and drop support for Catalina.

We'll stop calling the suite *Office for Mac* now and refer to it as just plain ol' *Office.* Because you're reading this book, you *should* be using Office on a Mac. If you aren't a Mac user, you're reading the wrong book.

There's a lot more to Office, so let's get to it. We start by describing what's new and good in the latest version of Office and continue with major new features common to most or all of the programs that make up the suite. After that, you look at new features and improvements specific to Word, PowerPoint, Excel, and Outlook. The section concludes with a short rant on what's bad or ugly in this release.

The suite life

All Office apps have received facelifts, so that's a good thing all around. They still look very macOS-like but incorporate the coloring and themes of their Windows counterparts to make it easy to switch between platforms and still feel a sense of familiarity. Figure 2-1 shows you the ribbon's Home tab for Excel, Outlook, PowerPoint, and Word. Note the color assigned to the Quick Access toolbar for each; these are the same colors used for each app in Windows, iOS, and Android.

TIP

You can enable or disable certain ribbon features or change the order of its tabs by choosing *App Name* ⇨ Preferences ⇨ Ribbon & Toolbar from the menu at the top of the screen in every app.

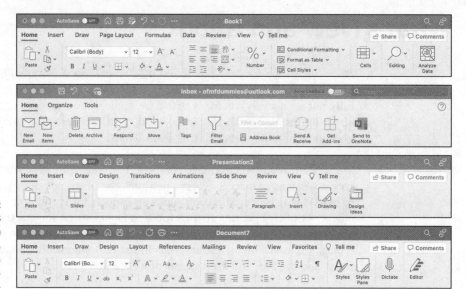

FIGURE 2-1:
The ribbon's
Home tab as seen
in Excel, Outlook,
PowerPoint,
and Word,
respectively.

Throughout this book, we examine some of the new features available throughout Office. For now, here's an overview :

>> **Co-authoring:** Now multiple users can collaborate simultaneously on a single Office document using different computers (Macs or PCs). Updates made by other people appear on your screen in real time, and you can choose to be alerted whenever other document collaborators are present. To use real-time co-authoring, you and your collaborators must store shared files in OneDrive. This feature doesn't work with the LTSC version of Office. LTSC, which stands for Long Term Servicing Channel, is available only for commercial or government clients.

>> **SharePoint and OneDrive:** All Office apps support not just one but *two* Microsoft cloud storage services. You can open and save documents stored on either cloud from a Mac or a PC or one of the Office web apps.

TIP

Microsoft offers 5 gigabytes of free online storage space when you sign up for its free OneDrive service at `https://onedrive.com/`. (This is the same amount as Apple's basic version of iCloud but a mere bagatelle compared to Google Drive's 15GB for a basic free account.) When you store documents on your free OneDrive, you can not only open them using Office on a Mac or PC but also edit them in a web browser using one of the Office web apps. If you need more than 5GB of storage, you'll need to sign up for Microsoft 365, where you can get up to 1TB (or 1,000GB!) of storage.

>> **Office for the web apps:** Open an Office document without a copy of Office? You betcha. If the file is stored on your (free) OneDrive, you can open and edit it in a web browser, as shown in Figure 2-2. This feature isn't exactly new but has been updated immensely.

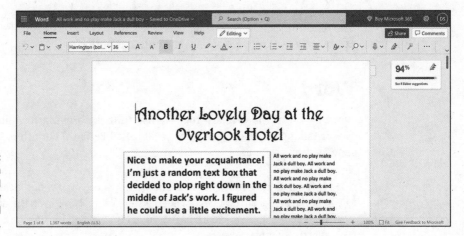

>> **AutoSave:** If your document is stored in OneDrive, you can use the AutoSave feature to instantly save any changes you've made, as well as make those changes visible in real-time on other devices. This feature doesn't work on the LTSC version of Office.

Many features mentioned in this section are available in Word, PowerPoint, and Excel but not in Outlook. That's because many of these new features are document oriented and Outlook is the only one of the four that doesn't create its own documents.

>> **Graphics galore:** Office offers a slew of new images, icons, and other graphics, particularly via the web, to beautifully adorn your documents, spreadsheets, and presentations.

>> **Improved new document experience:** Excel Workbook gallery, PowerPoint Presentation gallery, and Word Document gallery provide quick access to themes, templates, and recently used documents. Browse great-looking previews to see what your document will look like before you start working on it.

>> **Improved performance:** Don't expect the Office apps to launch in under .005 seconds or to fetch your groceries, but they have been updated to open faster and to work more efficiently than previous versions.

Office has hundreds of other tweaks, fixes, new features, and improvements, including many streamlined dialog boxes, toolbars, and panes, and better media integration (with your pictures, movies, and music). We could probably write an entire book about all the new and improved capabilities in Office. But the boss says that we have to show you how to use everything, too, so we had best move along now.

The following sections provide overviews of new features specific to the big four Office apps — Word, Excel, PowerPoint, and Outlook.

Word

Word has been the primary tool we use to make a living for quite a while now (we're talking decades here). Word still feels like Word but offers several enticing new features, such as

>> **Enhanced dark mode:** Dark mode was a feature in previous incarnations, but the actual document remained a stark white. Now, even the documents themselves utilize the dark background and themes, making dark mode that much easier on the eyes.

>> **More colors in immersive reader view:** The immersive reader view now supports several colors to help make things more interesting and allow for customization.

>> **Better voices in read aloud mode:** You now have more lifelike and natural-sounding voices to grace your ears when listening to Word read back the text of your documents while using read aloud mode.

PowerPoint

Among the new features in PowerPoint, a few stand apart from the rest:

>> **Animated GIFs of slide shows:** The latest version of PowerPoint for Mac allows you to save your presentations as animated GIFs, which make it easy to share via platforms such as social media.

>> **Ink replay:** Sometimes it's fun (and even necessary) to use the Draw tab to draw on your slides to emphasize something. Wouldn't it be cool if your audience could watch replays of you drawing (or "inking" as Microsoft calls it) on your slides? With ink replay, you can incrementally show how your inkings progress during the slide show, kind of like watching a mini-movie of you as you made the drawings in real time.

>> **Scalable Vector Graphic image format:** You have the option of saving images and other graphics in your slides as separate images. For example, if you've received a presentation that contains a graphic you'd like to save, you can do so as a separate file. The new format for saving images in PowerPoint (as well as Word and Outlook) is called SVG, or Scalable Vector Graphics. SVG files are able to maintain their quality, even when resized.

Excel

Excel users will be delighted by the following features, new to Excel :

>> **Sheet views:** When collaborating with others on a spreadsheet, your view may be altered from time to time by someone else if they're filtering or sorting. Sheet views allows you to create a custom view so that the actions of others don't affect what you're seeing.

>> **XLOOKUP function:** XLOOKUP is a new function that allows you to search and find anything in a table or range in a spreadsheet. You can look for info in one row of a column and have the result appear in the same row of another column.

>> **Updated Draw tab:** The ribbon's Draw tab provides better functionality than previous iterations, making it super-simple to add compelling graphics and notations to spreadsheets.

>> **Watch window:** The new Watch window allows you to keep an eye on multiple cells in multiple worksheets, all within a single window. This way, you can see how changes you make in the cells of one worksheet affect those in your Watch window.

>> **Dynamic arrays:** Dynamic array is a new way that Excel calculates data, enabling you to do quickly what used to be time-consuming. Dynamic array functions make it easy to place a formula in one cell and have it return multiple values in multiple cells. According to all the Excel gurus we know, this feature is a game-changer.

Outlook

Outlook is the venerable email, calendar, and note-taking tool that Microsoft Office for Windows users have used for decades now; it's a staple for many a Windows user. Mac users used to have their own Microsoft tool with similar functionality called Entourage, but Microsoft (wisely, in our opinion) decided to port Outlook to macOS back in 2011, and the Mac Office suite has been the better for it.

However, we have to say that there's not much new here in the latest version, save for the SVG feature mentioned in the PowerPoint section and a new, refreshed interface that looks very nice next to its Office counterparts and macOS itself.

TECHNICAL STUFF

We told a wee fib. There is something new for Outlook, namely a new Outlook called "New Outlook"! When you view the Quick Access toolbar at the top of a window in Outlook, you'll probably note a switch near the upper-right called New Outlook. If you click that switch, you'll be greeted by New Outlook. However, there's a reason that New Outlook isn't the default; Microsoft doesn't think it's quite ready for prime time, because many features in the old Outlook haven't been moved to New Outlook. We bet that by the next version of Office for Mac, the New Outlook switch will be a relic of the past, but for now it's something you can use to get a feel for what's to come. Don't worry — you can click the switch to return to old Outlook as quickly and easily as you switched to the New.

What's New but Bad

We wish we could tell you that everything new in Office is an improvement, but we'd be lying. The bad news is that each of the four main Office apps has at least a dozen known issues, even as we write these words.

Because Microsoft will likely issue an update and fix some or all of these issues before you read this book, we don't list them here. Instead, to find out more about outstanding issues today, follow these steps:

1. **Choose Help ⇨ Word (or Excel, PowerPoint, or Outlook) Help.**

2. **Type** known issues **in the Search field on the toolbar of the Help window, as shown in Figure 2-3, and then press Return.**

3. **Click one of the known issue results, as shown in Figure 2-3.**

The other aspect that we consider bad, or at least not that good, is that a handful of features found in Office for Windows didn't make it into Office for Mac. The most egregious is that Windows Outlook supports Visual Basic for Applications (VBA) but Mac Outlook does not.

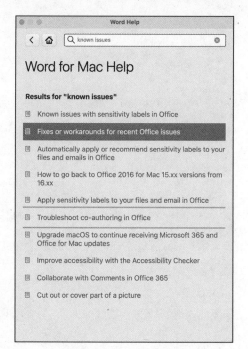

FIGURE 2-3:
Find out about
known issues via
Help in all four
main Office apps.

Together, They're Better

The individual apps work with each other to form a whole that's greater than the sum of its parts. For example, if you choose the same theme for your documents in Word, PowerPoint, and Excel, all documents in all three apps will use the same consistent color scheme and fonts. It's like having a graphic designer on your staff without the overhead or drama.

Another example: You can link information from one document to another so that when information in the first document changes, the change is reflected in the second document automatically.

Chapter **3**

Common Features in All Office Apps

The Office apps share elements that are similar or the same in most or all of its programs. For example, the gallery appears by default whenever you launch any of the three major apps (Word, PowerPoint, or Excel) and works the same in all three. Opening and saving files works the same everywhere. Menus, ribbons, and toolbars work much the same in all apps they appear in. And so on.

In this chapter, you'll find tips, techniques, and how-to's that you can apply to all Office apps.

Using Menus in Office Apps

Each Office app has around a dozen menus in its menu bar. Some, such as the Apple, File, Edit, View, Window, and Help menus, are mostly the same as their namesakes in other Office programs (and macOS) and contain the usual commands. Others, such as the Format, Tools, and Insert (Word, Excel, and PowerPoint) menus, offer different options in different programs. And some menus, such as Word's Table menu, Excel's Data menu, and PowerPoint's Arrange and Slide Show menus, are exclusive to a particular app.

We discuss many of the commands on these menus throughout the rest of this book; in this chapter, we cover some general information about using commands and features that are mostly the same in all Office apps.

First, although many menu commands work only after you've selected (highlighted) some text or another object, a number of menu commands *don't* require text selection. For example, all items on the View menu work, regardless of whether text is selected when you choose them. Many items on the Insert menu operate based on the location of the insertion point in your document and, in fact, blow away any text that's selected when you choose them.

WARNING

Be careful about selecting text. Although many commands require you to select text first, other commands replace the selected text with something completely different. For example, if you choose Insert ⇨ Chart (or one of many other items on the Insert menu) while text is selected, the selected text is replaced by the chart. (Chapter 5 covers text selection in more detail.)

TIP

Fortunately, the Office apps let you perform an almost unlimited number of undo actions, so you can undo what you did even after you've performed other actions in the meantime. Just choose Edit ⇨ Undo as many times as necessary to restore the text you just replaced. It wouldn't hurt to memorize its keyboard shortcut, ⌘+Z. By the way, this shortcut for Undo works in almost every program on your Mac.

Another thing to know about Office app menus is that an item that ends with an ellipsis (. . .) opens a dialog rather than performs an action immediately. Nothing happens unless or until you click OK or another action button. When you click OK, the appropriate action is performed either on the selected text, at the insertion point, or to the entire document, depending on the menu command.

TIP

If you accidentally choose a menu item that opens a dialog, either click the Cancel button or press the Esc key on your keyboard to dismiss the dialog without making any changes to your document.

An arrow on the right side of a menu item, such as the ones next to Insert, Delete, and Select on Word's Table menu, shown in Figure 3-1, means that you see a submenu when you select that item.

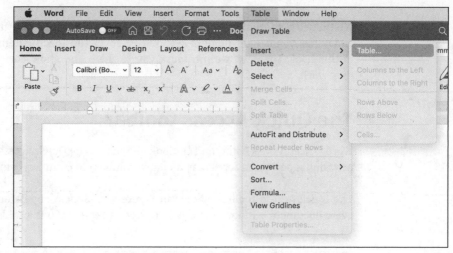

When an item on a menu is dimmed, such as Split Table, Merge Cells, and Split Cells on the Table menu (refer to Figure 3-1), you can't select the item because that command isn't available at this time.

Why would an item be unavailable? In Figure 3-1, the items that are dimmed are available only when you've placed a table in your document and either the table is selected or the insertion point is somewhere in the table.

TIP

If you see a dimmed menu command, look at your document and ask yourself why it's dim. Usually, the answer is a logical one, such as the command works only on a table or requires a text selection.

Toolbars, Ribbons, and Panes: Think "Visual" Menus

The big three Office apps (Word, Excel, and PowerPoint) offer at least one toolbar, one pane, and the ribbon (Outlook employs only a toolbar and the ribbon). Think of all three as visual menus. They make tasks easier and more convenient because you don't have to remember a command name or which menu it's on. Instead, you click a button or pull down a menu to execute the command.

Furthermore, some items on ribbons, toolbars, and panes can do more than meets the eye. You start with a look at how some of these items which may appear on ribbons, toolbars, and panes, work.

We flipped a coin and PowerPoint won, so it's the PowerPoint ribbons, toolbars, and panes you see in the next section. We cover the specific items in them later in this book; for now, we introduce you to them and show you a bit about how they work.

The Quick Access toolbar

Word, Excel, PowerPoint, and Outlook all include the Quick Access toolbar, which provides super quick access (as its name implies) to common commands.

The Quick Access toolbar, shown in Figure 3-2, appears by default at the top of every document window. It can't be moved or resized, so it's said to be *docked*.

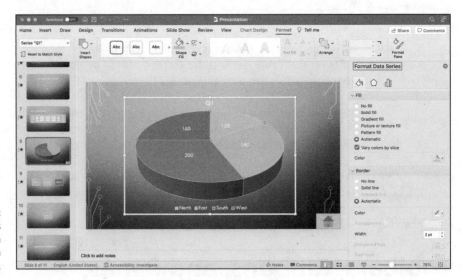

FIGURE 3-2:
The Quick Access toolbar, shown here in PowerPoint.

TIP

To find out what any button on a toolbar does (or on a ribbon or pane, for that matter), move the mouse cursor directly over it and then don't move the cursor for a few seconds. The button's name then appears in the little *tooltip* box.

Reveling in the ribbon

Think of a *ribbon* as a group of context-sensitive toolbars designed to make your life easier. Each ribbon has multiple tabs; each tab contains tools suited for specific tasks.

You can, of course, click any tab to activate it, but the ribbon is context-sensitive. Note in Figure 3-2 that the PowerPoint ribbon has 11 tabs, including Home, Transitions, Animations, Chart Design, and Format. That's because a chart in one of the slides is selected; were the chart not selected, you wouldn't see the Chart Design and Format tabs.

Compare this ribbon with the one shown in Figure 3-3, where we've selected a text box instead of a chart. Note that the new tab, Shape Format, now appears on the ribbon and that the Format tab and the Chart Design tab have been removed, indicating that we're no longer working with a selected chart but are working with a text box.

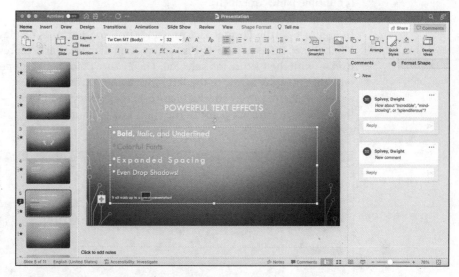

FIGURE 3-3: Notice the Chart Design and Format tabs on the ribbon have been replaced with the Shape Format tab.

Click the tab that's already selected on the ribbon to hide it and leave only its tabs showing. You can also choose View ⇨ Ribbon on the menu at the top of the screen to toggle between hiding and showing ribbon tabs.

That's really all you need to know to get started with ribbons. Trust us, there's much more to come throughout the rest of the book.

TIP

You can add or delete commands from the preconfigured tabs and menus or create your own custom tabs from scratch. We show you just how to do so for each app in the coming chapters.

Panes are anything but a pain

In addition to toolbars, Word, Excel, and PowerPoint have numerous panes, which are basically like windows within the main window of your document, workbook, or slide. In PowerPoint, for example, some of these panes include Comments, Format Shape, Design Ideas, Format Picture, and Stock Images.

Each pane opens on the right side of the current window; you can have multiple panes open at once, with each one represented by a tab that you can select to navigate between them. Most panes have a number of panels, often nested within subtabs, that you can hide or disclose by clicking the little arrow to the left of their names. To close a pane, click the x in its upper-right corner (or on the pane's tab if multiple panes are open).

In Figure 3-4, the Format Picture pane (in PowerPoint) is displaying its tabs — Fill & Line, Effects, Size & Properties, and Picture, each represented with an icon — with the Picture tab selected. The Picture Color panel is open, or disclosed; note that the gray arrow to the left of its name points downward. The three other panels — Picture Corrections, Picture Transparency, and Crop — are closed, so their disclosure arrows point to the right rather than down.

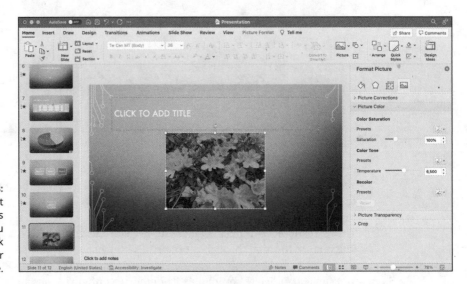

FIGURE 3-4:
The Format Picture pane has multiple tabs you can use to work with your selected image.

We discuss various panes, subtabs, and panels throughout the rest of this tome, but because describing every item on every menu, pane, or ribbon tab is beyond the purview of this book, we urge you to take a few minutes to familiarize yourself with the items on each one in all the Office apps.

Customizing the Quick Access Toolbar, Ribbon Tabs, and Keyboard Shortcuts

Customizing elements in the Office apps is something of a pastime for the aficionados we know; we'll admit, it can be fun and even empowering to make things appear and work the way you want (or need) them to. You can add, delete, and rearrange many items to your liking. You can even create ribbon tabs from scratch and add or change the keyboard shortcuts for most commands.

Customize the Quick Access toolbar

The Quick Access toolbar is a great place for tools you routinely need fast access to in any document, workbook, or slide, and it can be customized to suit your tastes.

TIP

Once you customize the tools in the Quick Access toolbar for one document, workbook, or slide, they're the same in every new window in that app going forward.

Follow these steps to customize the Quick Access toolbar in Word, Excel, or PowerPoint (Outlook doesn't apply here, we're afraid):

1. **Choose *App Name* ⇨ Preferences to open the Preferences dialog.**

2. **Click the Ribbon & Toolbar button.**

3. **Near the top of the Ribbon & Toolbar dialog, select the Quick Access Toolbar tab.**

4. **Select an option in the Choose Commands From pop-up menu, scroll through the list of available commands, and then click to select the one you want.**

5. **Click > in the middle of the dialog, shown in Figure 3-5, to add the selected command to the Customize Quick Access Toolbar commands list.**

TIP

To remove a command from the Quick Access Toolbar, select it under the Customize Quick Access Toolbar list and click < in the middle of the dialog.

6. **(Optional) Drag-and-drop commands in the order you would prefer them to appear in the Quick Access toolbar.**

TIP

If you want to revert to the original Quick Access toolbar, click the options icon (three dots in a circle) under the Customize Quick Access Toolbar list and select Reset Only Quick Access Toolbar.

7. **To save your changes, click Save in the lower right.**

Changes appear in the Quick Access toolbar immediately.

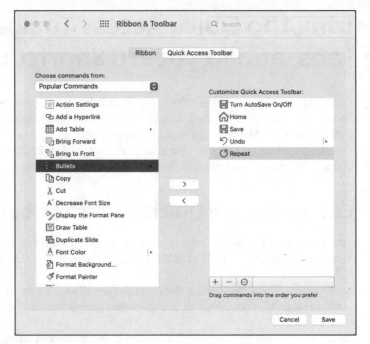

FIGURE 3-5:
The Quick Access
toolbar is highly
customizable in
Word, Excel, and
PowerPoint.

Customize ribbon tabs and menus

The Quick Access toolbar isn't the only way to have a whirlwind of a time customizing and modifying. The ribbon likes — one could almost say it begs — to be tinkered with, too.

To modify existing ribbon tabs and menus:

1. **Choose** *App Name* ⇨ **Preferences to open the Preferences dialog.**

2. **Click the Ribbon & Toolbar button.**

3. **Select the Ribbon tab near the top of the Ribbon & Toolbar dialog.**

4. **Select an option in the Choose Commands From pop-up menu, scroll through the list of available commands, and then click to select the one you want.**

5. **Select an option in the Customize the Ribbon pop-up menu, and then click to select the tab and tab group to which you want to add the command you chose in Step 4.**

6. **Click > in the middle of the dialog to add the selected command to the selected ribbon tab.**

To remove a command from a tab, select it under the Customize the Ribbon list and click < in the middle of the dialog to send it packing.

Show or hide ribbon tabs and tab groups by selecting or deselecting the check box to the left of their names.

7. **Click the Save button to save your changes.**

Your new command can now be found in the ribbon tab you added it to.

As shown in Figure 3-6, the main tabs in the tabs list often include tab groups, which are subcategories within the tab. (For example, the Edit Master subtab is listed under the Slide Master tab.) Click > next to a tab group to expand it. You can place commands within tab groups by selecting the tab group in Step 5 instead of the main tab itself.

FIGURE 3-6:
Ribbon tabs and menus just love to be modified in the Preferences dialog of Word, Excel, and PowerPoint.

As with commands in the Quick Access toolbar, you can drag and drop commands to customize their locations in the ribbon tab, too.

Creating ribbon tabs and tab groups

One feature we adore in the latest edition of Office for Mac is the ability to create ribbon tabs and tab groups, instead of being stuck with only the predefined tabs and groups. Why do this? Perhaps you use a set of commands all the time; instead of clicking various tabs and tab groups, keep them in one place for easier access and rejoice in the time you save.

Follow these steps:

1. **Choose *App Name* ⇨ Preferences to open the Preferences dialog.**

2. **Click the Ribbon & Toolbar button in the Preferences dialog.**

3. **Select the Ribbon tab near the top of the dialog.**

4. **Click the + button at the bottom of the tabs list on the right and choose New Tab from the menu that appears.**

5. **In the tabs list, select New Tab (Custom).**

6. **Click the options icon (three dots in a circle) at the bottom of the tabs list and then select Rename from the menu.**

7. **In the Display name field, enter the desired name and then click Save.**

Add new tab groups to your new tabs in the same way. Repeat Steps 4–7, but choose New Tab Group instead of New Tab in Step 4.

Customizing keyboard shortcuts

You add or change keyboard shortcuts for commonly used menu commands in Word and Excel. Follow these steps:

1. **Choose Tools ⇨ Customize Keyboard to open the Customize Keyboard dialog, shown in Figure 3-7.**

2. **Select a command to assign a keyboard shortcut to.**

   The Categories list (in the upper left) groups all menus and command categories that contain commands to which you can assign a keyboard shortcut. You can select a category and scroll through the list of commands it contains or you can search for a command by typing it in the search field.

   TIP

   If you're not sure which category to choose, choose the All Commands category, near the end of the scrolling Categories list, to display all available commands.

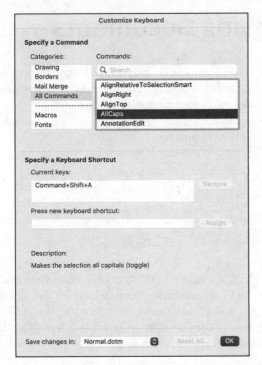

FIGURE 3-7:
Create your own
or modify existing
keyboard
shortcuts.

3. **In the Press New Keyboard shortcut box, enter the key combination you want for that command by pressing the keys on your keyboard.**

   As you press the keys, the box will populate with the new shortcut. If the shortcut you're trying to assign is in use by another command, you'll see which command it's assigned to just below the shortcut you typed.

4. **To assign the shortcut to the command, click the Assign button.**

5. **When you're finished, click OK.**

Clicking the Reset All button restores all shortcuts to their factory settings.

TIP

We advise against using a keyboard shortcut that's already in use by macOS. Check the Keyboard Shortcuts pane in the macOS Keyboard System Preferences pane to avoid conflicts. You can avoid most conflicts if you combine modifier keys. The ⌘ and Control keys combine well and avoid conflicts with most settings. Using ⌘ and Option works almost as well (though Microsoft already uses this combination for a few commands).

Creating and Saving Documents

Word, Excel, and PowerPoint are *document-centric* apps, which means that their main purpose is to create documents you save on your computer. These saved documents are known in computer parlance as *files*.

In this section, you discover how to

>> Create a new, blank document from scratch

>> Create a document from a template

>> Save a document to your computer in an appropriate file format

>> Turn on and manage the AutoRecover function

To create a new, blank document in Word choose File⇨New Document; in Excel choose File⇨New; and in PowerPoint choose File⇨New Presentation. To create a new, blank document in Outlook, choose File⇨New and then select E-Mail, Meeting, Appointment, Group, Contact, Contact List, Task, Note, Email from Template, Folder, or Main Window from the submenu.

You have three ways to open an existing Office document file:

>> **From Finder:** Double-click any document created by an Office app, and that app launches and opens the document.

>> **Choose File⇨Open:** Use this command after you've launched whichever Office app you want to work in. (You can also press ⌘+O.)

>> **Use the gallery:** The gallery multipurpose dialog can serve as the starting point for new Office documents and as a quick way to find documents you've worked on recently. To open the gallery, choose File⇨New from Template (or press ⌘+Shift+P).

Using the gallery to open templates or recent documents

The multipurpose *gallery* dialog, available in all Office apps, makes it easier than ever to choose a template for a new document or to open a recently used file. The Word Document gallery is shown in Figure 3-8, and the Excel and PowerPoint galleries look almost the same.

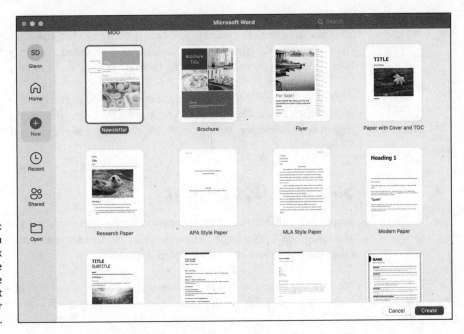

FIGURE 3-8:
You can start a new, blank document in the gallery or choose a document template or theme.

TIP

If the gallery doesn't appear automatically when you launch an Office app, choose File ⇨ New from Template (or press ⌘+Shift+P) to open it.

The gallery dialog contains the following elements:

>> **New:** Click New in the left pane to see templates and categories. In Figure 3-8, the selected category is Newsletter.

>> **Recent:** Click Recent in the left pane to see a list of the most recent documents you've opened, listed according to the last time they were opened.

Many users like to have the gallery open automatically when they launch an Office program, which is how its set by default. If for some strange reason the gallery doesn't always open automatically when you launch an Office app, here's what to do: Open the app's preferences, click the General icon at the top of the Preferences window, and then click the Show Document/Workbook/Presentation Gallery When Opening Word/Excel/PowerPoint check box.

>> **Shared:** Click Shared in the left pane to see documents, workbooks, or presentations that are being shared with you by others.

>> **Open:** Click Open to browse local and online storage to find and open documents quickly.

>> **Home:** Click Home to view a mashup of the New, Recent, and Shared tabs.

>> **Search field:** Type a word or words in the search field at the top right of the gallery window to find files that contain that word or those words.

To open an item in the gallery, you can, of course, select the item by clicking it and then click the Create (for new documents) or Open (for existing documents) button. But simply double-clicking the item is faster and easier.

Finally, if you don't see anything you want to open in the gallery, click Cancel. The gallery window disappears, but the app remains open (though it may have no document windows open at this time). To close the gallery and quit the app, choose File ⇨ Quit.

Saving a document

Saving a document in any Office app works the same way as in almost every other Mac program. The unique Office wrinkles involve saving files automatically and choosing a file format for your saved document.

We start by describing how to save a file. Saving a document file involves two tasks: saving the file for the first time and resaving the file every so often.

Part I: The initial save

For the first save, select a folder to save the file in and give the file a meaningful name. To do that, choose File ⇨ Save or File ⇨ Save As (or press ⌘+S). Either way, the standard macOS Save As dialog appears in front of your document, as shown in Figure 3-9.

If your Save As dialog doesn't look similar to Figure 3-9, click the disclosure arrow to the right of the current folder's name to expand it.

To save the file, navigate to the folder you want to save the document in (the current folder is Word Docs in Figure 3-9) and name the file (Getting Started in Figure 3-9).

Part II: The resave

After you save a file for the first time, you're not done with saving — not by a long shot. You still need to resave the document often so that if the app or your Mac crashes, you lose only the work you've done since the last time you saved.

This part is much easier than Part I. After you save and name a file, for subsequent saves, you merely need to choose File ⇨ Save or press ⌘+S.

Save your file. Do it early. Do it often. Just do it, and do it a lot.

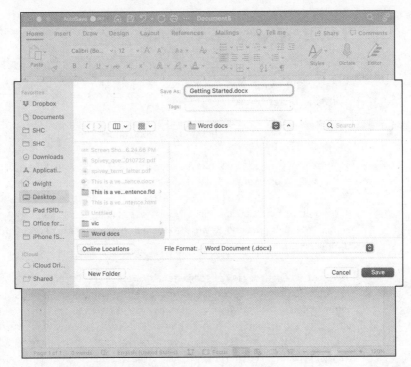

FIGURE 3-9:
The Save As
dialog for a Word
document.

DECIDING WHICH FILE FORMAT TO CHOOSE WHEN SAVING A DOCUMENT

The File Formats pop-up menu in the Save dialog lets you choose the file format for the file you're about to save. In Figure 3-9, Word is about to save this document in the default Word file format (.docx). The default format in Excel is .xlxs and for PowerPoint it's .pptx.

The default file formats for Office documents since 2007/2008 are four-letter acronyms (FLAs) that end with the letter *x*. Before that, they were three-letter acronyms (TLAs) that *did not* end with an *x* (for example, the default for Word was .doc). The *x* indicates that the newer format is based on eXtensible Markup Language, or XML, an open standard for encoding documents in a machine-readable form.

Those default formats are perfectly fine most of the time, but occasionally you may want (or need) to use a different format. If someone you're sending a document to is unable to open it, try saving a copy of the document in an older format, such as .doc, .xls, or .ppt. Or if the person doesn't need to edit the document, perhaps a PDF would work best.

SAVE VERSUS SAVE AS

In addition to letting you name and save a document that has never been saved, Save As has another reason to exist: It lets you resave a file that has already been saved by giving it a different name.

Why would you want to do that? Here's a good (albeit somewhat rude) example:

Suppose that you have two cousins: Kate and Nancy. You write Kate a long, chatty letter and save this document with the name Letter to Kate. At some point afterward, you decide to send almost the same letter to Nancy, but with a few changes. So you change the part about your date last night (Nancy isn't as liberated as Kate) and replace all references to Kate's husband, Kevin, with the name of Nancy's husband, Norman. (Aren't computers grand?)

So you make all these changes to Letter to Kate, but you haven't saved this document yet. And, although the document on your screen is a letter to *Nancy,* its filename is still Letter to Kate. Think of what would happen if you were to save the letter now without using the Save As feature: Letter to Kate reflects the changes you just made. (The material in the letter meant for Kate is blown away, replaced by the material you write to Nancy.) Thus, the filename Letter to Kate is inaccurate. Even worse, you would no longer have a copy of the letter you sent to Kate!

The solution? Just use Save As to rename this file Letter to Nancy by choosing File⇨Save As. A Save As dialog appears, in which you can type a different filename in the Save As field. You can also navigate to another folder, if you like, and save the newly named version of the file there.

Now you have two distinct files: Letter to Kate and Letter to Nancy. Both contain the material they should, but both started life from the same file. *That's* what Save As is for.

An even better idea is to choose Save As just before you begin modifying the document and give it the new name. That way, when you're done with your changes, you don't have to remember to choose Save As — you can just perform your habitual Save. It also protects you from accidentally saving part of the letter to Nancy without changing its name first (which you're likely to do if you're following our advice about saving often). So, when you decide you're going to reuse a document, choose Save As *before* you begin working on it, just to be safe.

A-U-T-O-matic Recovery

AutoRecover is a feature (enabled by default) in Word, Excel, and PowerPoint that attempts to preserve your document contents in the event of a catastrophic event (like a computer crash or power outage). You can disable this feature (don't do it, we implore you) or re-enable it by opening Preferences in the app, clicking the Save button in the Preferences dialog, and deselecting or selecting the Save AutoRecover Info box (it's labeled Enable AutoRecover in Excel).

TIP

When the Save AutoRecover Info setting is enabled, you usually don't lose any work after a crash. AutoRecover generally recovers all your work, right up to the moment of the crash, even if you haven't saved the document or haven't saved it in a while.

WARNING

Despite the preceding tip, be aware that AutoRecover doesn't always work. So, even if you enable it, resave your documents regularly. Train your fingers to issue the ⌘+S keyboard shortcut every few minutes, whether you think you need to or not.

Saving and Using Documents in the Cloud

In addition to saving files to your local hard disk(s), as we describe in the section "Creating and Saving Documents," earlier in this chapter, you can also save documents to a OneDrive or SharePoint location in the cloud. The service is especially useful for documents you'll be collaborating on with others, but you can also use it for backup copies of the file, just in case.

OneDrive and SharePoint are similar cloud-based file storage systems. The difference between them is that OneDrive is publicly available from Microsoft at no cost and SharePoint is privately maintained. If you work for an enterprise, your IT department may provide a SharePoint server. For everyone else, there's OneDrive.

TIP

The more important the file, the more places you should back it up.

WARNING

If you don't have a OneDrive (or SharePoint) service, this section may not make sense.

Saving a file on a OneDrive or SharePoint location

Saving a file using the OneDrive (or SharePoint) service is a little different than saving a file locally. To save a file in the cloud, choose File ➪ Save or File ➪ Save As.

A Save As dialog drops from the title bar. Click the Online Locations button in the dialog box, just to the left of the File Format menu (refer to Figure 3-9). The Save As field is now called Name; type a name for the document in that field. Select a OneDrive or SharePoint location on the left side of the dialog (as we did in Figure 3-10), choose a folder for saving the document, and then click the Save button.

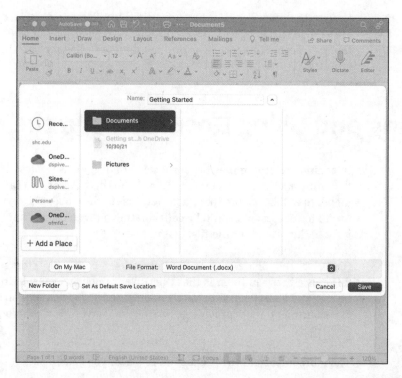

FIGURE 3-10:
Saving a Word document to OneDrive.

TIP

If you see an On My Mac button next to the File Format menu, you're already saving to an online location. If you want to save it locally (on your computer) instead, click the On My Mac button.

You may have noticed the AutoSave button in the upper-left corner of your documents. This feature saves documents you've stored in OneDrive or SharePoint automatically, preventing you from losing your precious content in the event something goes wrong. This button toggles to On automatically when you save a file to OneDrive or SharePoint.

TIP

By the way, OneDrive and SharePoint require the XML file formats .docx, .pptx, or .xlsx to use the AutoSave feature.

Sharing a file you've saved using OneDrive or SharePoint

To share a file you've saved using OneDrive or SharePoint, click the Share button in the upper right of any document window and choose either:

>> **Invite People:** Creates an email that you send to whomever you want to share the file with. You can also give them editing privileges.

>> **Copy Link:** Creates a link either allowing or not allowing editing privileges that you can then share with others.

>> **Send a Copy:** Creates a copy of the file in Word, PDF, or HTML format that you can then email to a recipient.

You can find out more about collaboration in later chapters, so we leave it at that for now.

Opening a file you've saved on your OneDrive or SharePoint location

Reopening a file from your OneDrive or SharePoint location is easy. Simply use the gallery's Recent list, as described earlier in this chapter. If you've used that file in the past, it's likely to be in Recent Documents.

TIP

When you use the gallery's Recent list, you might have difficulty discerning which documents are stored on your hard drive and which are stored in the cloud. Simply look at the line of text directly under a filename to see where it's stored.

The other way to open a file is to choose File ⇨ Open from the menu bar, select the file from the list, and then click the Open button.

Understanding App Preferences

All Office apps have app Preferences dialogs, and they all look and work much the same. Some items they contain are specific to the app, but they generally look and work alike.

Rather than burn up a lot of pages listing every preference option in every app, we give you the general information you need for setting app preferences, as well as the reasons you might want to do so.

App preferences: Why?

As you see in a moment, every Office app has dozens and dozens of different preference settings you can alter to suit your fancy or needs.

Most preference settings let you enable, disable, or specify values for the way features work in the program. The idea is that you choose the setting that makes the feature work the way you want it to work.

For example, Outlook allows you to set up and use multiple email accounts in the Accounts section of Outlook's Preferences dialog. Word and Excel allow you to choose the unit of measurement they use for their on-screen rulers and page measurements by default — inches, centimeters, points, or picas. The default is inches, but if you're more comfortable with one of the others, you can choose it in the app's Preferences, and all rulers and measurements in that app will be displayed in those units forever (or, at least, until you change the preference setting again).

TIP

We discuss some preferences in later chapters, but only ones that are pertinent to the discussion at hand. So, you might want to spend some time experimenting with the various preference settings and customizing your Office apps to work the way you prefer.

App preferences: How?

You open the Preferences dialog the same way in each Office app: Choose Preferences from the app's eponymous (Word, Excel, PowerPoint, or Outlook) menu or press ⌘+, (comma).

Although the four Preferences dialogs look slightly different, as shown in Figure 3-11, they all work much the same.

As you can see, each app's Preferences dialog has many categories, each represented by an icon.

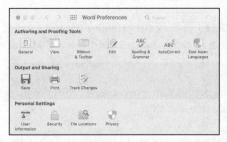

FIGURE 3-11:
The Word, Excel, Outlook, and PowerPoint Preferences dialogs.

TECHNICAL STUFF

When you click one of these icons, you're said to be using that category's preference pane. For example, Figure 3-12 displays Outlook's Notifications and Sounds preference pane, which offers most of the features — such as check boxes, radio buttons, buttons, and pop-up menus — that you're likely to encounter in preference panes.

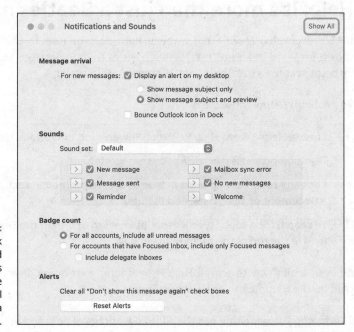

FIGURE 3-12:
The Outlook Notifications and Sounds pane has most of the features you'll find in a preference pane.

To see the items in a category, click the category's icon or name. When you do so, the Preferences dialog magically changes to display that category's preference pane.

Radio buttons are known by this name because, as with the preset buttons on a car radio, you can press only one at a time.

REMEMBER

The following three screen elements are in the Word, Excel, and PowerPoint Preferences dialogs but not in the Outlook Preferences dialog:

>> **Search field:** Search for a word or phrase, which is handy if you know of a preference you want to change but can't remember which pane it's in.

>> **Forward and back icons:** These icons work the same as the forward and back icons in Finder or a web browser. The back icon (<) displays in reverse chronological order the panes you've visited since you opened the Preferences dialog, and the forward icon (>) cycles through panes visited by pressing the back icon.

>> **The show all icon:** You can click this icon (which looks like 12 stacked dots and appears at the top of the window) when you're done with a preference pane and want to return to the main Preferences dialog with all the icons available.

Help: It's more than just a Beatles movie

If you're puzzled about what a menu item does or how to use it, Office Help, shown for Word in Figure 3-13, is much better than in previous versions, primarily because it uses the Apple (not Microsoft) Help system.

To get help, follow these steps:

1. **Choose Help⇨Word Help (or Excel, PowerPoint, or Outlook Help).**

   The appropriate Help window appears.

2. **Click any topic that appears in blue in the Help window, such as Creating a Document or Text, Lists, and Bullets.**

3. **To search for a topic, type a descriptive word or two in the Search Help field in the top of the main Help window.**

TIP

An even easier way to search Help is by typing your query directly in the search field on the Help menu, as shown in Figure 3-14.

This method of searching has the added advantage of pointing out the appropriate menu item, if there is one.

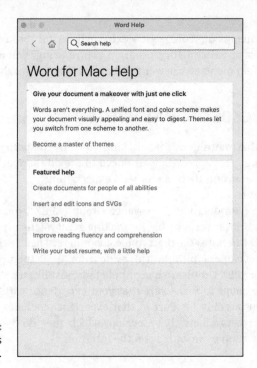

FIGURE 3-13:
Help in Office is
better than ever.

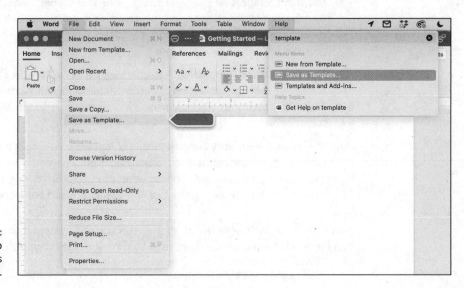

FIGURE 3-14:
Even the Help
menu in Office is
helpful.

Help isn't just for menus or Word — it's extremely useful throughout the Office suite. So, regardless of which Office program you're using, you can almost certainly find on its Help menu an answer to whatever issue is puzzling you.

Official Microsoft websites

Microsoft knows that more goes into making your user experience a great one than just developing great apps. They also need to provide support for those apps that goes above and beyond their customer's expectations.

The Microsoft Apple Productivity Experience Group (APEX), formerly known as their Mac Business Unit, is responsible for making great Microsoft apps (primarily the Office suite and OneNote) for their Apple customers. They're the second largest group of Mac developers in the world, aside from Apple themselves. The good folks in Microsoft's APEX Group are huge Apple fans, just like us, so they're jumping through all the hoops to make sure that your experience with Microsoft apps is as good as it can possibly be. Part of that experience includes providing top-notch support for the products they develop, which they do by contributing to Microsoft's various support resources on the internet:

>> **Microsoft Support** (https://support.microsoft.com): Find support for your favorite Microsoft apps, including training materials, contact numbers, cheat sheets and other helpful documentation, tips to make the most of what your app of choice offers, and more.

>> **Microsoft Office Templates** (https://templates.office.com): Peruse Microsoft's extensive collection of document templates for Word, Excel, and PowerPoint. Many are free to download, while others require a Microsoft 365 subscription.

>> **Microsoft Community Forums** (https://answers.microsoft.com): The Community forums connect Microsoft users from all over the world so they can share experiences, guide one another through projects, or just discuss how cool they think the marriage of Apple and Microsoft products is.

Don't be shy to avail yourself of Microsoft's support system if you need a helping hand or a bit of good advice from time to time (or every day, for that matter).

2

Mastering Microsoft Word

Start with the most basic of basics by navigating in a Word document by mouse and by keyboard and seeing how to best use Word's various views.

Practice the tasks most people spend the majority of their time performing in Word: formatting, moving, and modifying text and images.

Take advantage of Word's tools for making your work look better — spelling and grammar checkers, a dictionary, a thesaurus, and more.

Explore more advanced word processing features, such as templates, headers, footers, tabs, margins, and indents, plus columns, lists, tables, boxes, and styles.

Create a table of contents, collaborate with other Word users, and print envelopes and labels.

» Understanding the various ways to view your documents onscreen

» Navigating documents by mouse or keyboard

» Tips for shortening your learning curve

Chapter **4**

Getting to Know Microsoft Word

According to the dictionary built into Word's own Smart Lookup tool, a word processor is

. . . a program or machine for storing, manipulating, and formatting text entered from a keyboard and providing a printout.

We've come a long way from the days of typewriters, when ensuring that you had clean, error-free, *good-looking* documents took a great deal of time and labor (and a wee bit of luck).

The word processor changed all that. Using a word processor, you can go back and change anything you've typed at any time you like. You can save documents and reuse or modify them later. You can use dozens of different font faces, sizes, and weights (though you should probably limit yourself to no more than a handful per document). You can change the size of margins; add, resize, or modify pictures and drawings; and create multiple columns or tables (grids) in your documents with just a few clicks or keystrokes.

In other words, a word processor gives you nearly complete control over the contents of a document and the way the document looks. With a word processor, you can do all of this (and more):

>> Save, reuse, and print documents you create or receive from others

>> View and edit multipage documents

>> Make unlimited changes to the contents and formatting of documents

>> Add images to documents

>> Search for specific words or phrases in documents

>> Check the spelling of every word in documents

In this chapter, we introduce the basic aspects of Microsoft Word (which is itself the gold standard of word processors), starting with the various views you can switch among so that you can work most effectively depending on the task at hand. Then it's on to basic navigation using the mouse and keyboard. Finally, we share a pair of tips to make life easier when you add text and graphics to your documents in later chapters.

Using a Variety of Versatile Views

Word has many ways to look at your document: the print layout, web layout, outline, draft, focus, immersive reader, and full screen views. Word also has many ways to change the view, but some methods aren't available to all views:

>> **View tab:** Click an icon on the View tab to change to any of the views except full screen view.

>> **View menu:** Choose the View menu and then choose any view — except immersive reader view — by name. A check mark in front of a name indicates that the view is active.

>> **Icons at the bottom of a document window:** You can select five of these views — all except immersive reader and full screen — by clicking the appropriate icon at the bottom of any document window. See Figure 4-1.

To change the view of a document, choose the view by name from the View menu (a check mark in front of its name indicates that the view is active) or from the View tab.

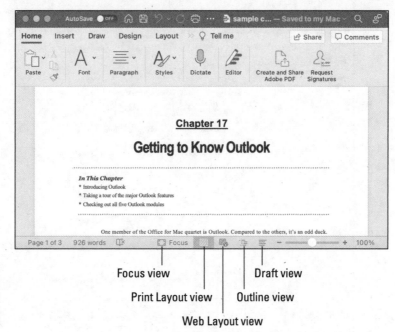

FIGURE 4-1:
You can switch among these views by clicking their icons.

Focus view

Print Layout view

Web Layout view

Draft view

Outline view

The following sections briefly describe each view.

Print layout view

Print layout view — which is Word's default — is a What You See Is What You Get (WYSIWYG, pronounced "wiz-ee-wig") view that shows you exactly what your printed document will look like, as shown in Figure 4-2.

Most users prefer to work in print layout view, but if your Mac is older or slower, you may be happier using draft view for composing and editing and then switching to print layout view just before printing a document.

Web layout view

Web layout view, shown in Figure 4-3, simulates the way your page will look when viewed in a web browser if you were to use Word's File ⇨ Save As ⇨ Web Page command to save the page as an HTML document. The document has no page breaks because web pages have no page breaks. The text continues until the end of the page, regardless of the amount of text.

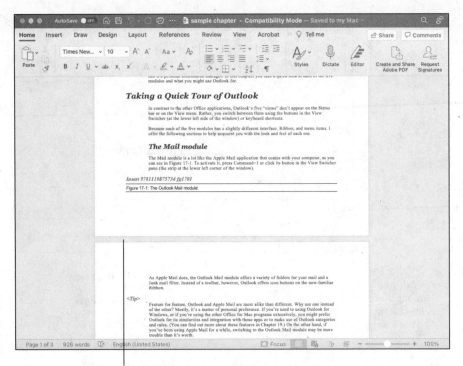

FIGURE 4-2:
Print layout view
shows exactly
what your
document will
look like when
printed.

Page break indicator

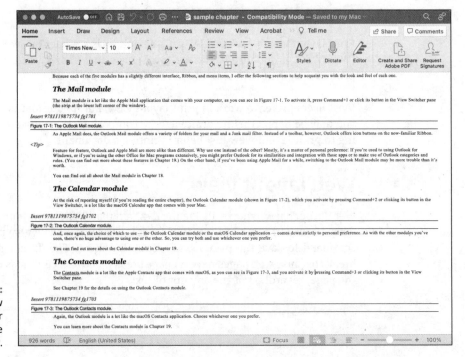

FIGURE 4-3:
Web layout view
displays your
page as if it were
in a web browser.

Also, note that the document in Figure 4-3 does not have left or right margins. That's because text on web pages saved by Word fills the page from left to right. If you were to resize this window, the text would reflow, expanding or contracting so that each line is exactly the width of the window.

Outline view

Outline view, shown in Figure 4-4, is helpful for creating an outline or organizing a long document.

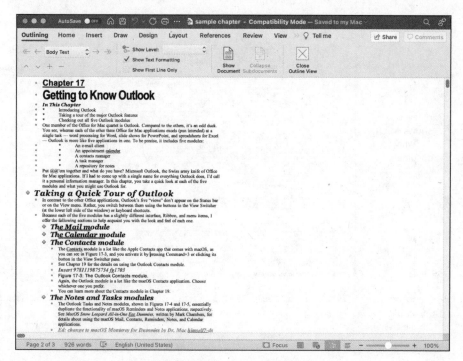

FIGURE 4-4:
Outline view
displays your
document as an
outline.

You can collapse and expand text below a heading or subheading in outline view by double-clicking the plus sign to its left; we've collapsed the text below the subheads "The Mail module" and "The Calendar module" in Figure 4-4. Note that these two subheads have plus signs to their left and are partially underlined. These visual cues indicate that both subheads have subordinate text or sub-subheads.

The other helpful feature of outline view is that you can drag a heading or sub-heading and the text below it to another location in your document by just clicking and dragging the plus sign, a feature that's particularly convenient in longer documents.

Draft view

Draft view, shown in Figure 4-5, is the view formerly known as normal view. It's your quick-and-dirty "just get it done" view, useful for basic typing and editing tasks, or for any time you don't need text to appear in What You See Is What You Get (WYSIWYG) form on your screen. This view is the one that many Word jockeys prefer for completing most tasks.

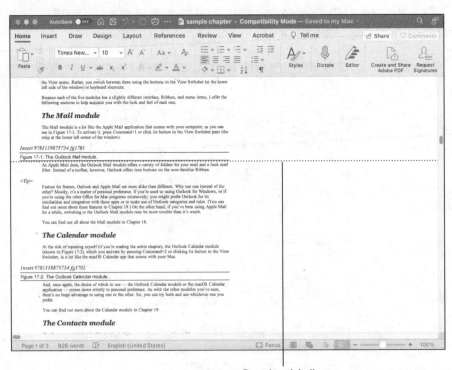

FIGURE 4-5:
Draft view is the simplest view.

Page break indicator

Note that the page break between pages 1 and 2 is denoted only by a thin dotted line. Compare Figure 4-5 to Figure 4-2, which also shows a WYSIWYG view.

TIP

The older and slower your Mac's processor, the faster draft view feels in comparison with layout views like Print Layout — *another* reason to consider using this view most of the time.

Focus view

We've tested word-processing and other types of writing programs that help people focus on work by blacking out everything on the screen except the document. We like the feature, but after using Word for so long, no other writing program felt right.

So you can understand why Word's focus view, shown in Figure 4-6, has become a favorite view for many Word aficionados.

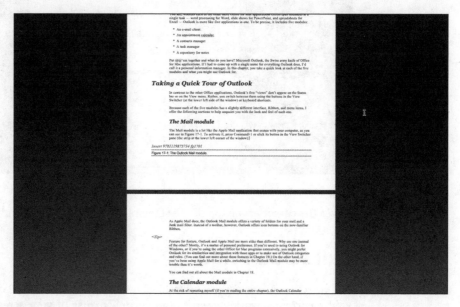

FIGURE 4-6:
Focus view shows your document and little to nothing else.

See what we mean? You see nothing but the document — as shown in Figure 4-6. And as you can see, Word uses dark mode when in focus view.

Plus, the focus view is available in combination with other viewing formats. Simply select Draft, Outline, Web Layout, or Print Layout by clicking their respective icons in the bottom right of the window or by selecting them from the View menu or View tab on the ribbon. While in focus view, you'll need to hover your cursor near the very bottom of the screen to see the view icons (see Figure 4-7).

You can enable or disable Focus in the following ways:

>> Press ⌘+Control+Shift+F on your keyboard (you might find it easier to use two hands).

>> Click the Focus icon at the bottom of your document window.

>> Press the Escape (esc) key on your keyboard.

>> Click the Exit button in the upper left of the document window.

>> Choose View ➪ Focus.

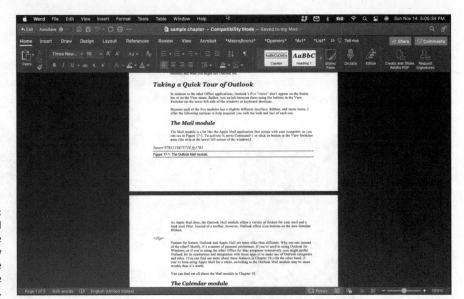

FIGURE 4-7:
The toolbar and ribbon are accessed by hovering the cursor near the top of the screen.

REMEMBER

Hover the cursor at the top of the screen to reveal the toolbar and ribbon.

Full screen view

Full screen view is exactly as advertised — it displays the Word document in which you're currently working across the entire expanse of your screen's real estate. This view removes any other distractions on your screen, such as the dock or the Music app's MiniPlayer.

You can enable or disable full screen view by

>> Pressing Fn F on your keyboard (or ⌘+Control+F if your keyboard doesn't have Fn keys)

>> Clicking the green dot in the upper-left corner of the document window

>> Pressing the Escape (esc) key on your keyboard

>> Choosing View⇨ Enter (or Exit) Full Screen

REMEMBER

If you need to see the items and menus in the toolbar, hover the cursor at the top of the screen to reveal them.

Immersive reader view

Immersive reader view is a unique reading and listening experience with several tools and tricks to help you access a document's contents with ease. Options such as Column Width and Read Aloud make it simple (and dare we say a bit fun) to read documents in Word.

To enable immersive reader view, which is shown in Figure 4-8, click the View tab on the ribbon and then click the Immersive Reader icon.

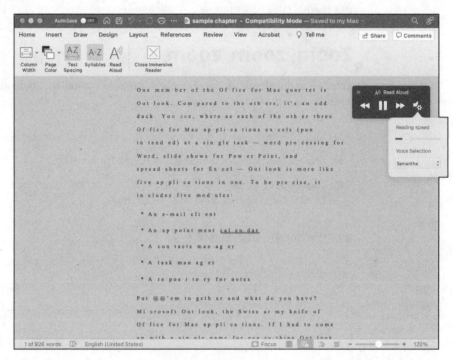

FIGURE 4-8:
Immersive reader
view with several
of its tools
activated.

The Immersive Reader tab on the ribbon has the following tools:

>> **Column Width:** Select the column width. Figure 4-8 displays a Moderate column width.

>> **Page Color:** Select from a range of page background colors. Orchid was selected for Figure 4-8.

>> **Text Spacing:** Increase the text's legibility by adding extra space between the characters and using a clean font. Enable Text Spacing is shown in Figure 4-8.

>> **Syllables:** Display break points in words to indicate syllables, as shown in Figure 4-8.

>> **Read Aloud:** Click to have Word read the text aloud and open the Read Aloud playback controls, shown in Figure 4-8. Click the gear icon to select a different playback speed and use a different voice. The word being read is highlighted as the reading progresses so that you can follow along visually.

>> **Close Immersive Reader:** Exit immersive reader view and return to the previous view you were using.

Remember that immersive reader view is meant to be a help, not a hindrance. If some of its options or tools disrupt your reading experience, you aren't obliged to use them.

Zoom, zoom, zoom

You can make elements onscreen look bigger or smaller. There are three ways to zoom in or out of your document:

>> Click the Zoom icon in the View ribbon to open the Zoom dialog.

>> Choose View⇨Zoom and select an option from the list.

>> Use the zoom slide control in the lower-right corner of windows in Draft, Outline, Web Layout, and Print Layout mode.

All three are shown in Figure 4-9.

FIGURE 4-9: Use the Zoom dialog (left), Zoom menu (middle), or zoom slide control (right) all to enlarge or reduce onscreen elements.

 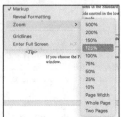 

TIP

If you choose the Page Width option in the Zoom dialog or Zoom menu, your text grows and shrinks automatically as you resize the window. Remember, though, that it's the zoom that's changing, not your font size.

Getting around in Your Document

When you begin filling your formerly blank Word document with text and images, which you can find out how to do in Chapter 5, it's good to know how to move around effectively within the file. This section tells you how to do just that, using the mouse, trackpad, and keyboard keys. (Most people use a combination.)

A scroll new world: Navigating by using the mouse or trackpad

One way to move around in your document is to use the scroll bars and scroll arrows that appear at the sides and bottom of the Word window, as shown in Figure 4-10.

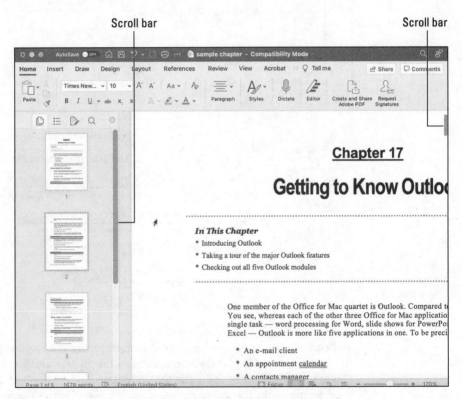

FIGURE 4-10:
Use scroll bars to get around in your document.

If your mouse has a scroll wheel, scroll ball, or Multi-Touch surface (like Apple's Magic Mouse), you can also use it to navigate your document.

TIP

Using the wheel or ball scrolls your document vertically (up or down). If you press the Shift key before you turn the wheel or ball, some mice then scroll horizontally (left or right). Try it with your mouse to see whether this method works for you.

Another way to move in your document is to use the Thumbnail pane (shown in Figure 4-11), which you display or hide by choosing View⇨Sidebar⇨Thumbnail. This action (or selecting anything else in View⇨Sidebar) also displays the sidebar on the left side of the document window.

Thumbnail tab   Selected page

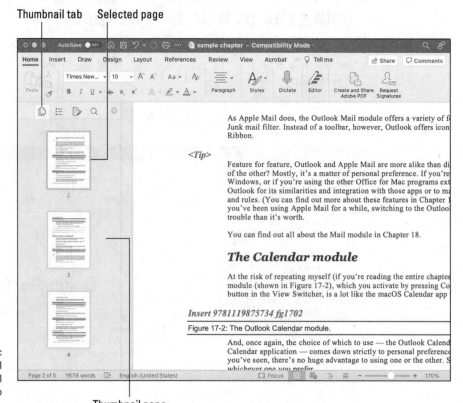

FIGURE 4-11:
Click a thumbnail in the Thumbnail pane to move to that page.

Thumbnail pane

You can also move around in your document using the Document Map (shown in Figure 4-12). Click the Document Map tab in the sidebar or select View⇨Sidebar⇨Navigation to open the tool. The Document Map lists the headings in your document in the sidebar; simply click a heading to jump right to the page it's on.

Document Map tab   Selected page

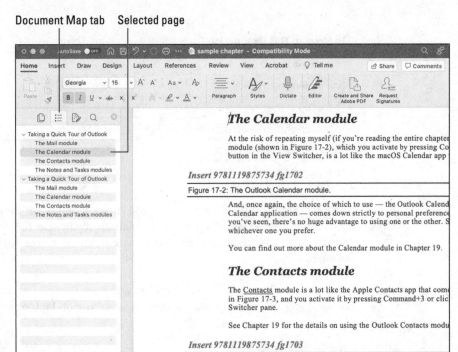

FIGURE 4-12:
View and
navigate your
document by
using headings
in the
Document Map.

Navigating by using keyboard navigation

You can move the cursor around a document without even touching the mouse, if you want. And, if you *really* want to become a whiz in Word, memorize most or all of the shortcuts in the following table, which shows how to move the cursor around a document by using only the keyboard.

To Move to This Destination	Press This
One character to the left	Left arrow
One character to the right	Right arrow
One word to the left	Option+left arrow
One word to the right	Option+right arrow
One line up	Up arrow
One line down	Down arrow
To the end of a line	⌘+right arrow or End
To the beginning of a line	⌘+left arrow or Home
One paragraph up	⌘+up arrow
One paragraph down	⌘+down arrow

To Move to This Destination	Press This
One screen up (scroll)	Page Up
One screen down (scroll)	Page Down
To the top of the next page	⌘+Page Down
To the top of the previous page	⌘+Page Up
To the end of the document	⌘+End
To the beginning of the document	⌘+Home

TIP

To select (highlight) text as you move the cursor using these shortcuts, just hold down the Shift or ⌘ key. Chapter 5 tells you more about selecting text and why you need to do so to format text, copy and paste it, and perform other tasks in your document.

REMEMBER

Some keys, such as End, Home, Page Up, and Page Down, may not be on all keyboards, especially small profile keyboards like those on laptops or iMacs.

MAKING THINGS EVEN EASIER

As former Apple CEO Steve Jobs was famous for saying, "One more thing." The following three tips should help you get the hang of using Word. All three work in all Office apps, not just Word.

Tip 1: Display icon labels on the ribbon.

Although icons help illustrate their functions, some are straight up cryptic. Labels be helpful but most icons on the ribbon don't have them. Thankfully, it's easy to display the labels temporarily — simply hover your mouse pointer over an icon, hold for just a moment, and the label will pop up on screen. The label disappears when you move your mouse pointer again.

Tip 2: Find icons that disappear from the ribbon when the document window is too narrow.

No worries: Just click the gray angle brackets (>>) on the right side of the ribbon (in this example, they appear to the right of layout view) and the missing items appear on a menu.

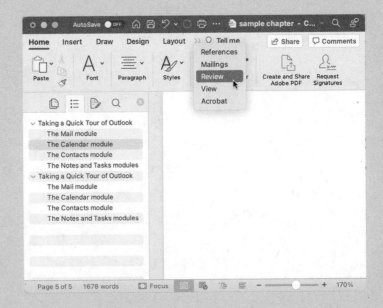

Tip 3: If you prefer not to use focus view but want to gain document space, minimize the ribbon.

This last tip is especially handy if you're a MacBook user. To hide or display the ribbon, simply click the name of the currently selected tab on the ribbon, or select View⇨Ribbon in the menu. The newly created space may not seem like much, but if your screen measures only 11 or 13 inches, it may make a difference.

Chapter **5**

Creating Documents

Chapter 4 introduces you to Word and tells you a bit about what the program is and what it does. In this chapter, you see how to use it. What do we mean by *it?* We're glad you asked. In this chapter, you find out the basics of creating documents and how to select text, change the appearance of text and images, and add text and graphics from other sources, such as web pages or documents created in other apps. We also show you how to use the ribbon's References tab to add elements such as footnotes, citations, and tables of contents, quickly and easily.

Adding Text and Graphics to Your Document

In this section you learn how to process words, but first you need a blank document to work with. To create one, choose File⇨New Document or use the keyboard shortcut ⌘+N.

Now put some stuff — namely, text and graphics — in your document so that it's not blank any more.

Because draft view displays only text, you have to switch to print layout view to work with images or graphical objects.

If pictures, charts, shapes, or other objects don't appear in your document where you expect them, the document is probably in draft view. Switch to print layout view by choosing View ➪ Print Layout or by clicking the Print Layout icon in the lower-right corner of the document window.

Entering text in your document

When you first stare into a blank Word document screen, you should see the insertion point cursor blinking on and off in the upper-left corner. This cursor indicates that whatever you type will appear right there.

To add text, merely start typing. When you're finished with a paragraph, press the Return or Enter key to start a new one and repeat this process until you've had your say.

Inserting an image in your document

Inserting an image into a document is almost as easy as typing text. Office for Mac comes with an extensive collection of clip art images that you can use in Word, Excel, and PowerPoint documents. In fact, the collection of art is so extensive that it's found in two different places in each app — some in the Stock Images gallery and the rest in the Online Images browser. And, if none of the included art suits your needs, you can just as easily insert your own images.

Stock Images gallery

To insert art from the Stock Images gallery, click where you want the image to appear in your document and then choose Insert ➪ Pictures ➪ Stock Images on the menu at the top of the screen.

The Stock Images pane opens on the right side of the document window, as shown in Figure 5-1.

You can browse the Stock Images gallery by clicking different categories and subcategories at the top of the pane on the right. Or to search the Stock Images gallery, type one or more words in the search field near the top.

FIGURE 5-1:
The Stock Images
gallery contains
hundreds of
images.

To place an image from the Stock Images gallery into your document:

1. **Make sure that the insertion point (the blinking cursor) is exactly where you want the image to appear.**

2. **At the top of the Stock Images pane, click Images.**

3. **Click the images you want to add.**

   Each image displays a check mark to denote that it's selected.

4. **Click the Insert button.**

   In Figure 5-2, we've inserted two images in the document.

The Stock Images gallery also provides access to four other categories, each with their own set of subcategories: Icons, Stickers, Illustrations, and Cutout People. If you don't see some of these subcategories, click the arrow to the right of Icons. In Figure 5-3, we've inserted three examples from Education Subcategory of the Icons category.

TIP

If you forget to put the insertion point where you want the image to appear, have no fear. Simply drag the image where you'd like it to appear in the document.

FIGURE 5-2:
We've selected and inserted two images from the Stock Images gallery.

FIGURE 5-3:
A document with icons from the Education subcategory.

Online Pictures browser

The Stock Images gallery contains the majority of artwork that comes with Office, but you'll find a veritable cornucopia of additional art and images in the Online Pictures browser. As its name indicates, this browser allows you to search for images stored on the web.

To insert art from Online Pictures, click where you want the image to appear in your document and then choose Insert ➪ Pictures ➪ Online Pictures.

The Online Pictures pane, shown in Figure 5-4, opens on the right side of the document window, just like the Stock Images pane before.

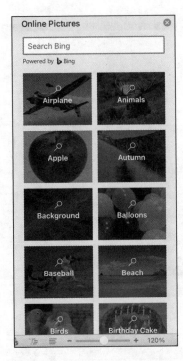

FIGURE 5-4:
Search Online Pictures for images to add to your document.

You can browse the Online Pictures offerings by clicking one of the predefined search topics. Or search for an image by typing one or more words in the search field near the top. To place an image from the Online Pictures browser into your document:

1. **Make sure that the insertion point (the blinking cursor) is exactly where you want the image to appear.**

2. **Click a predefined search topic from the list or enter a search term in the search field.**

   The Online Pictures pane appears.

3. **Click the images you want to add.**

   Each selected image sports a check mark.

TIP

   Click the filter icon to the left of the Creative Commons Only option to narrow your search based on criteria such as image size or layout.

4. **Click the Insert button in the lower-right corner.**

   Figure 5-5 shows an online image we've inserted into the document.

Your own images

Another way to move images to your document is to drag them from another location or app. In Figure 5-6, we're dragging a file from the desktop to the document.

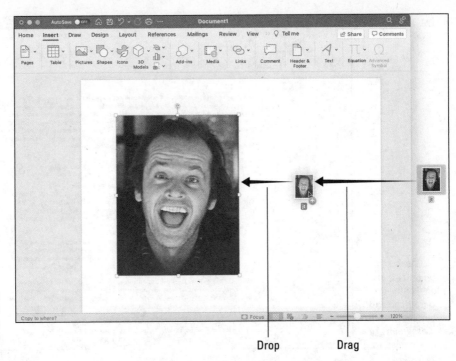

FIGURE 5-6:
Dragging an
image file from
the desktop to a
document.

Drop   Drag

TIP

This technique works also in other apps such as iPhotos or Safari — just click a photo in Photos or Safari, drag the photo to your document, and drop it where you want it.

We talk more about images later in this chapter, in the "Changing the look of images" section.

Selecting Text for Editing and Formatting

Much of what you do in Word can happen only after you've selected the text you want to do it to. In other words, when you choose a command from a menu or click a button or an icon, what you choose or click usually affects only whatever text you've selected in your document.

Selected text is highlighted in a contrasting color, as shown in Figure 5-7.

To select text, use the cursor, which you can move by using the mouse or your laptop's trackpad. Although you can use the keyboard to move the cursor around (described in a moment), the easiest way to move it is with the mouse or trackpad.

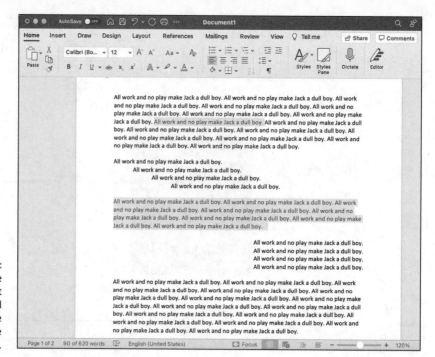

FIGURE 5-7:
A sentence in the
middle of the first
paragraph and
another entire
paragraph are
selected.

Word has a number of different cursors, but the two cursors used to select text are the I-beam (or text) cursor and the arrow cursor.

When you move the cursor over text in a document, the I-beam cursor is displayed. When you click somewhere within text, the insertion point cursor appears, as shown in Figure 5-8. Note that Figure 5-8 shows examples of three types of cursors, but only one will appear during actual use.

Click and drag across some text in a document. As you drag, the text under the I-beam cursor is highlighted. When you release the mouse button, all text between that point and the insertion point (where you first clicked) is selected.

Another way to select text is by moving the cursor into the left margin of your document. When you do that, the cursor turns into an arrow that faces up and to the right. This arrow cursor indicates that you can now select an entire line of text with a single click. Just point at the line of text you want to select, and click. Presto! That line of text is selected.

When you click in the left margin and drag down or up without releasing the mouse button, additional lines below or above where you clicked are selected. And if you press the ⌘ key before you click, you select all text in the document.

Insertion point cursor

Left margin

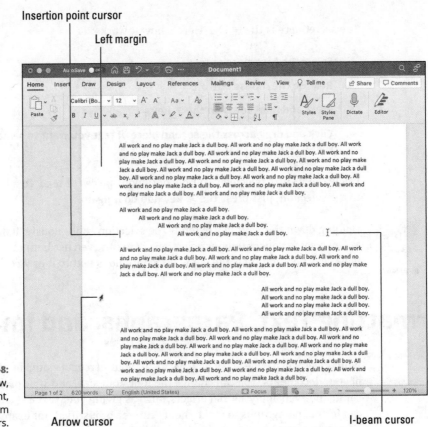

FIGURE 5-8:
The arrow,
insertion point,
and I-beam
cursors.

Arrow cursor

I-beam cursor

You can get a little fancy with this selection technique and select a larger chunk of text. Follow these steps:

1. **Click where you want the selection to start.**

2. **Press and hold down on the Shift key.**

3. **Click again somewhere else. Release the Shift key.**

   Everything between the two clicks is selected. If you click in a block of text, all text between the insertion point and your second click is selected. If you click in the left margin, every line of text between your first and second click is selected.

The selection methods we've discussed in this section select only contiguous blocks of text. What if you want to select a sentence in the middle of the first paragraph and then the entire second paragraph?

The secret here is the ⌘ key. Here's how it works:

1. **Select the first piece of text.**

2. **Release the mouse button.**

3. **Press and hold down on the ⌘ key.**

4. **Click and drag across the second piece of text you want to select. Release the ⌘ key.**

Voilà! You've just selected two noncontiguous pieces of text. To add pieces of text to the selection, just press the ⌘ key and do it again.

REMEMBER

Holding down the Shift key extends the selection contiguously; holding down the ⌘ key creates noncontiguous selections. You can even use both to create a contiguous selection and then add some noncontiguous text to it or vice versa.

Formatting Text, Paragraphs, and Images

Word gives you a wide array of ways to put your personal stamp on the appearance of your documents. You can change the font, font size, and style of text; change its color; and even apply special effects, such as giving your text a shadow effect. You can format paragraphs to make them centered or justified, for example. Word also gives you some basic tools for changing the size and appearance of images you insert into your documents.

Changing the look of the font

As mentioned, you usually have to select text or images before you can modify their attributes. To change the font your text appears in, select the text and then follow these steps:

1. **Choose Format ⇨ Font (or press ⌘+D).**

   The Font dialog appears.

2. **Click the Font pop-up menu, scroll down the list, and click a font of your choice.**

3. **In the Font Style menu, choose bold, italic, or any other attributes you want.**

4. **To make the text bigger or smaller, click the Size menu and select a size.**

5. **Click OK.**

In Figure 5-9, we chose these attributes: Chiller for the font, Bold for the font style, and 36 for the size.

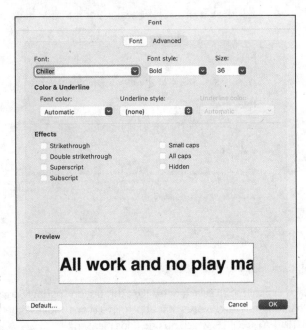

FIGURE 5-9:
Choose a font, style, and size in the Font dialog.

Figure 5-10 shows the results of clicking OK to accept these modifications.

Changing other attributes of text in the Font dialog is just as easy. In addition to choosing the font color and underline style and color, you can apply the following variety of effects to selected text:

>> **Strikethrough** places a single line through the middle of selected text, like so: ~~strikethrough~~.

>> **Double Strikethrough** places two lines through the middle of selected text so that it looks like this: ~~double strikethrough~~.

>> **Superscript** changes the characters you select to superscript, like so: ^{super}script.

>> **Subscript** changes the characters you select to subscript: $_{sub}$script.

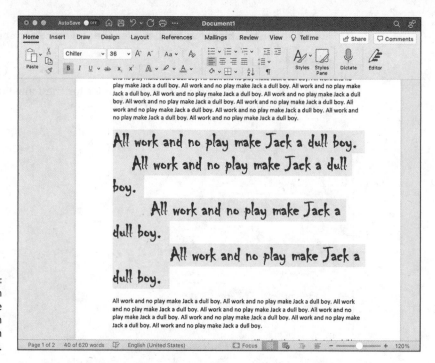

FIGURE 5-10:
A paragraph
reflecting the
choices made in
the Font dialog in
Figure 5-9.

>> **Small Caps** look like this: SMALL CAPS.

>> **All Caps** capitalizes all selected text. Use this option sparingly, especially within paragraph text. Words that appear in all caps implies that the text is SHOUTING AT PEOPLE, which no one finds pleasant.

>> **Hidden** hides the selected text onscreen and when printing. Deselect the box to make the text reappear.

Look at the Preview area near the bottom of the Font dialog (refer to Figure 5-9) to see the effect of your choices before you click the OK button.

TIP

For even more font-formatting fun, try applying text effects and experiment with shadow, outline, emboss, and engrave. Also, the Advanced tab in the Font window offers several other options (such as character spacing) to fancify your text.

Changing the look of paragraphs

Changing font attributes is just one way you can change the way text looks. Another way is to change the text's paragraph attributes. In this case, rather than changing words and letters, you change the way entire paragraphs appear.

The rules for selecting paragraphs to modify are slightly different than the rules for selecting text. To format a single paragraph, just click anywhere within that paragraph. To format multiple paragraphs, however, select them in the usual way.

Try performing the following steps both ways. In other words, first click somewhere in the first paragraph and follow the steps to format just the first paragraph. Then select the second and third paragraphs and follow the steps again to format those two paragraphs:

1. **Click anywhere in the first paragraph.**

2. **Choose Format ⇨ Paragraph (or press ⌘+Option+M).**

   The Paragraph dialog opens. If the Indents and Spacing tab isn't highlighted, click it.

3. **In the Alignment pop-up menu, choose an option, such as Centered.**

4. **Change the Left and Right Indentation values to whatever you want, such as 1".**

   You can either type the new value or use the little arrows to the right of each value to change them.

TIP

5. **Change the Spacing After value to whatever you want, such as 24 pt (points).**

6. **In the Line Spacing pop-up menu, choose a line spacing, such as Double.**

   Based on the suggested choices in these steps, the Paragraph dialog looks like Figure 5-11. (Yours, of course, reflects your own choices.)

7. **Click OK.**

Because the insertion point is in the middle of the first paragraph of the document in Figure 5-12, it's the only paragraph that reflects the choices made in the preceding steps.

The ribbon's Home tab and its formatting options also let you change font and paragraph attributes.

REMEMBER

If the ribbon is collapsed so that only its tabs appear, click the Home tab to display its contents.

So, unlike the dialog approach, when you use the ribbon's Home tab, you avoid that big, ugly dialog in front of your document and you don't have to click the OK button to see the results of your changes. Frankly, we use the Font and Paragraph dialogs only when the ribbon's Home tab doesn't offer a feature we need.

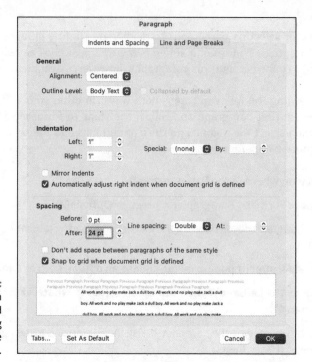

FIGURE 5-11:
The Paragraph
dialog should
look something
like this before
you click OK.

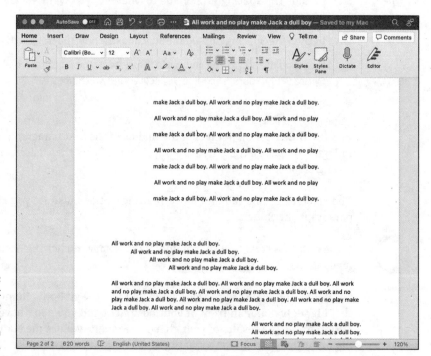

FIGURE 5-12:
Your document
reflects the
choices you made
in the Paragraph
dialog.

In Chapter 3, you discover how to put any command on the Quick Access toolbar. You can, at least in theory, put every font- or paragraph-related feature you'll ever need on the Quick Access toolbar and avoid using the dialogs.

The tabs on the ribbon are context-sensitive, so if you select an object such as a photo, shape, table, or chart in your document, new tabs such as Picture Format, Table Design, Layout, or others may appear among the default tabs.

We also like how the Font menu on the ribbon's Home tab, unlike the Font dialog, shows you previews of what fonts look like (see Figure 5-13).

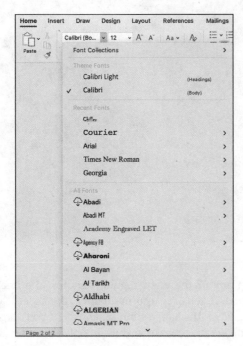

FIGURE 5-13:
The Home tab's Font menu offers previews of fonts before you apply them to your text.

If you can't find the tab or tool you need on the ribbon, ask yourself, "What is selected" or "Where is my cursor?"

Changing the look of images

Microsoft Word is, of course, a word processor, but it offers a surprising amount of control over the look of images in your documents as well.

To modify an image — clip art or photo — in your document, click the image to select it. When an image is selected, it displays handles on each corner and in the middle of each side. It also displays a rotation handle that extends from the middle handle on the top side, as shown in Figure 5-14.

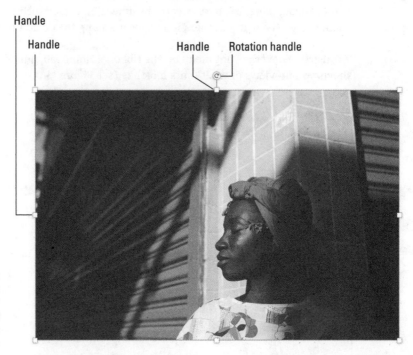

Handle

Handle

Handle   Rotation handle

If you click and drag any of the eight regular handles, the image stretches or shrinks in that direction. If you drag a corner handle, the aspect ratio remains the same and the height and width change simultaneously. If you drag a handle in the middle of a side, the image stretches or shrinks in only that direction. Give it a try.

You can make additional image modifications in a couple of ways:

>> Our favorite is to use the ribbon's Picture Format tab. To display it, click the image you want to modify; the Picture Format tab appears on the ribbon, with several great tools to help you jazz up your images. For example, you can use the Artistic Effects Options to add an icon to your image, as shown in Figure 5-15. Choose from filters such as Watercolor Sponge, Paintbrush, Blur, or Pencil Sketch.

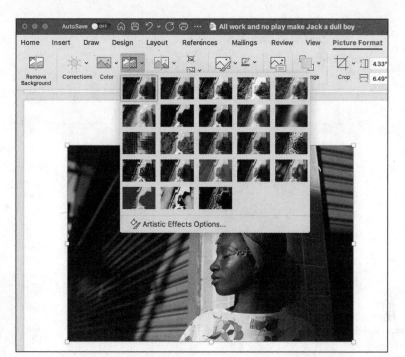

FIGURE 5-15:
Spice up your
images using
Artistic Effects in
the Picture
Format tab of the
ribbon.

» The second way is to use the Format Picture pane by either double-clicking
the image you want to modify to open the pane on the right side of the
window, or by clicking the image once to select it and then clicking the Format
Picture pane icon on the ribbon's Picture Format tab. The Format Picture pane
offers a whopping 14 different options in the Fill & Line, Effects, Layout &
Properties, and Picture tabs — Fill, Line, Shadow, Reflection, Glow, Soft Edges,
3-D Format, 3-D Rotation, Artistic Effects, Text Box, Picture Corrections, Picture
Color, Picture Transparency, and Crop.

The following steps shows you an example of choosing settings in the Format
Picture pane. With an image selected and the Format Picture pane open, do this:

1. **On the Effects tab, click the Shadow item.**

2. **Click the Presets pop-up menu and select one of the options in the Outer
   section.**

3. **Set the Angle value to 45°.**

4. **Set the Size value to 103%.**

5. **Set the Blur value to 16 pt.**

6. **Set the Distance value to 8 pt.**

7. **Set the Transparency value to 70%.**

   The Format Picture pane and image now look like Figure 5-16.

TIP

Unlike in the Font and Paragraph dialogs, where you make changes and click OK before seeing their effects, changes you make in the Format Picture pane and on the ribbon's Picture Format tab are displayed and updated immediately.

We suggest that you check out some of the settings in the other Format Picture pane tabs. (Try Reflection in the Effects tab or Picture Transparency in the Picture tab, for starters.)

REMEMBER

Not all these screens are appropriate for all pictures, so don't be alarmed if some of them don't appear to do anything to your image. For example, if you choose Text Box in the Layout & Properties tab of the Format Picture pane with an image selected, all options appear dimmed and are unavailable because they work only on text in text box objects and don't make sense for a graphical image.

When you're satisfied with your handiwork, click the gray X in the upper-right corner of the Format Picture pane to close it.

Copying Words and Images from Other Sources

You have a couple of techniques available for moving text and graphics out of another program and into a Word document: drag and drop and copy and paste. Sometimes, one works when the other one doesn't. Read on for details on both.

Dragging and dropping

Drag and drop is the simplest way to move text or images to your Word document from another app. To do so, follow these steps:

1. **Launch Word and create or open a document.**

2. **Launch your browser and surf to a website of your choosing.**

3. **On the web page, select the text, image, or text and image you want to copy to your Word document.**

4. **Click in the selected (highlighted) area and drag it to your Word document.**

    The cursor turns into the copy cursor (green circle with a plus sign), as soon as you start dragging the items, as shown in Figure 5-17.

5. **To drop the text into the Word document at the insertion point, release the mouse button.**

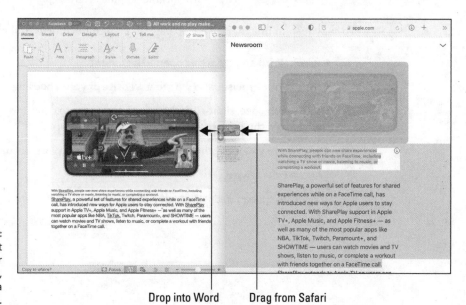

FIGURE 5-17:
Dragging text from your browser (Safari, in this case) to a Word document.

Drop into Word   Drag from Safari

Dragging and dropping only an image works almost the same way. To copy an image to your Word document, merely click the image on the web page, drag it to your Word document, and then release the mouse button. Like magic, the image appears in your Word document at the insertion point.

REMEMBER

One last thing about drag-and-drop: You can also drag image files from Finder to your Word documents (refer to Figure 5-6).

Copying and pasting

Some programs don't support drag and drop. If you try it and it doesn't work, here's an alternative way of moving text and graphics from another program to a Word document:

1. **Launch Word and create or open a document.**

2. **Launch your browser and surf to a website of your choosing.**

3. **On the web page, select the text you want to copy to your Word document.**

4. **Choose Edit⇨Copy (or press ⌘+C) in your browser to copy the text to your Mac's clipboard.**

5. **Click where you want the text to appear in your Word document.**

6. **Choose Edit⇨Paste (or press ⌘+V).**

   The text appears in the Word document at the insertion point.

To copy just an image from a web page to a Word document, follow these steps:

1. **Launch Word and create or open a document.**

2. **Launch your browser and surf to a website of your choosing.**

3. **On the web page, right-click the image you want to copy and choose Copy Image from the contextual menu, as shown in Figure 5-18.**

4. **Click where you want the image to appear in your Word document.**

5. **Choose Edit⇨Paste.**

   The image appears in the Word document at the insertion point.

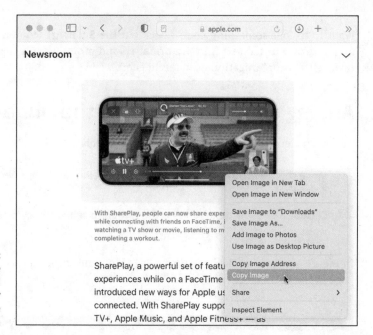

FIGURE 5-18:
Right-click the
image and
choose Copy
Image from the
contextual menu.

Working with Other Document Elements

Earlier in the chapter, we show you how to add text and graphics to a document. And by knowing how to do that, you also know how to add other elements on the Insert menu, such as movies, symbols, shapes, and text boxes. However, by using the ribbon, you can add and modify even more elements, such as headers and footers, page numbers, charts, and tables.

You can find extensive support for adding and modifying document elements on several of the ribbon tabs. The following list describes what you can do with them:

>> **References tab:** Add to your document preformatted and professionally designed elements, such as citations, tables of contents, and bibliographies.

>> **Insert tab:** Add to your documents preformatted and professionally designed tables (grids), shapes, SmartArt, icons, and 3D models.

>> **Draw tab:** Create drawings and add them to your documents.

>> **Design tab:** Apply preformatted themes, watermarks, page borders, and more to your documents.

>> **Layout tab:** Create columns, add page breaks, format indentations and spacing, align various elements on the page, and more.

TIP

Want to try out something cool? Check out the SmartArt icon on the Insert tab: Add or turn selected text into preformatted and professionally designed illustrations, such as organization or pyramid charts.

Adding elements by using the ribbon

To add an element to your document from the ribbon, follow these steps:

1. **Move the cursor to wherever you want the element to appear in your document.**

2. **Click one of the little arrows on the ribbon to select the element you want to insert.**

In Figure 5-19, we clicked the Cover Page icon and inserted the Feathered cover page in the document.

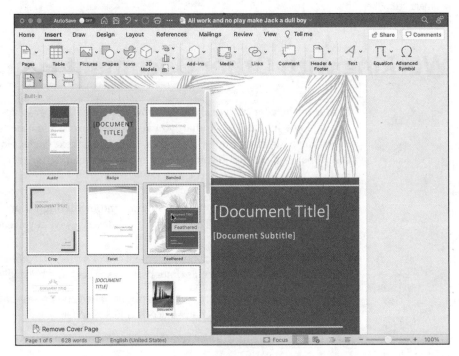

FIGURE 5-19:
The Insert tab on the ribbon, with the Cover Page option selected.

Modifying elements by using the ribbon

To format or modify an element in your document, follow these steps:

1. **Single-click an element to select it.**

2. **Select the effect (color, line thickness, glow, bevel, line color, or whatever) that you want to apply to the element.**

For example, in Figure 5-20, we're applying a reflection to the selected object (the 3D starry-eyed emoji).

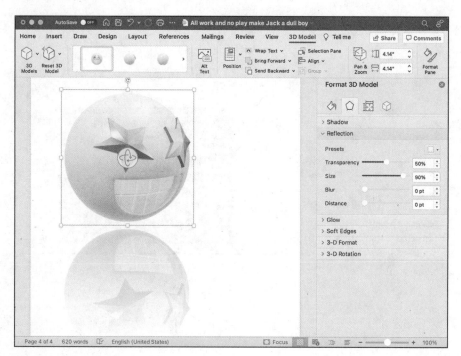

FIGURE 5-20:
Applying a reflection effect to a 3D emoji.

Removing elements

We want to tell you something about elements that you probably ought to know, and that's how to remove one from your document.

To remove elements that aren't full-page elements — such as charts, tables, and SmartArt Graphics — just select the element you want to remove and press the Delete key on your keyboard.

To remove a full-page element, such as cover pages, use its shortcut menu, which you should see near the upper-left corner of any cover page when you hover your mouse pointer over it. Click it and choose (in this case) Remove Cover Page, as shown in Figure 5-21.

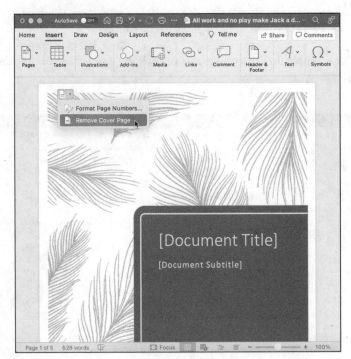

FIGURE 5-21:
Using the
shortcut menu
to remove the
cover page.

» Checking your spelling and grammar

» Correcting automatically with AutoCorrect

» Using Word's built-in and online reference tools

» Finding and replacing for faster revisions

Chapter **6**

Refining and Editing Documents with Word

Moving right along, it's now time to refine your word-processing skills and, at the same time, find out how to refine your documents, making them better in every way. As high school English teachers say, "The art of writing is rewriting." This chapter shows you how.

In this chapter, you find out how to refine and edit documents to make them better. You see techniques for experimenting with the order in which your words and images appear on the page as well as how to find and fix errors that have crept into your documents. And you find out how to use Word's built-in thesaurus to explore alternatives to words you use or overuse in your documents.

Moving Text and Images in Your Documents

In the old days, when you wrote using a typewriter or longhand with pen and paper, editing and experimenting with a document wasn't easy. After you finished a page, it was difficult to move sentences or paragraphs to see them arranged in a different order. And doing it more than once was a serious hassle.

With word processing, your document is never finished until you say it's finished. In other words, you're free to tweak and modify every element at any time. Better still, you can easily make changes to a document even after you've printed it — just make the changes and print it again.

This section shows you ways to move words, sentences, paragraphs, and images in your document. If you no longer think that quote should appear in the lead paragraph, just move it elsewhere in the document. If you wonder how that picture would look in the middle of page 3 instead of at the end of page 2, move it there and find out.

Word offers a couple of ways to move things around in your document and several features that make it easier to move them around.

Moving items easily within a document

Chapter 5 shows you how to copy, paste, drag, and drop text and images into your documents from other programs, such as the Safari web browser. Well, we've got good news for you: You can copy and paste and drag and drop text and images within your documents in the same way. The only difference is that you drag or copy within the Word document you're creating rather than from another document.

TIP

Chapter 5 discusses selecting and copying text in more detail, but here's the nitty-gritty: To move a section of text or an image by cutting and pasting, just select the item you want to move and choose Edit⇨Cut, or use its keyboard shortcut, ⌘+X. Scroll to wherever you want to paste your selection and click, and then choose Edit⇨Paste or use its keyboard shortcut, ⌘+V.

TECHNICAL STUFF

We've been asked many times by computer novices why the keyboard shortcut for the Paste command is ⌘+V instead of ⌘+P. The answer is simple: ⌘+P is for Print, so that one's taken. Also, similar commands for Copy — ⌘+C — and Cut — ⌘+X — are right next to the V key, keeping all three commands in the same easy-to-reach area.

To move an item by dragging and dropping, select it and then hold down the left mouse button (or the left side of your mouse button, if your mouse only has a single button) while dragging to the new location. If you're using a trackpad, select the item, click and hold down on it with one finger, and then use another finger (probably using your other hand) to drag it to the new location. Release the mouse button or the trackpad and — presto! — your selection is in its new home. And to copy the selection to another location without moving the original, press the Option key before you drag.

By the way, you can also use both techniques — cut and paste *and* drag and drop — to move text or images from one Office document (that is, a Word, Excel, or PowerPoint document) to another. The process is just as explained in the Tip a couple of paragraphs back, except that you click the document you want to move the text or image to before you scroll to where you want to paste your selection and click.

Using special Word features that make moving stuff easier

Dragging and dropping as well as copying and pasting are easy in a document that's only one or two pages long. But when your documents are longer than a few pages, copying, pasting, dragging, and dropping can be a drag (pun gleefully intended) because of all the scrolling you have to do. Fortunately, Word offers several features that make it easier to move text or images in long documents.

Splitting a window

One useful feature when moving text or images is to split the window. As you might expect, this feature splits the active window into two separate panes, reducing or eliminating the need to scroll long distances.

You can split the active window in one of these two ways:

>> Choose Window⇨Split to split the window into two equal parts.

>> On the ribbon's View tab, click the Split Window button.

Click and drag the resizer control (refer to Figure 6-1) and release it where you want the split to occur.

If you want the parts of the window to be different sizes, the second method is best.

FIGURE 6-1:
Split the window
to see two
different parts of
your document.

In any event, you end up with a window split into two parts, each displaying a different part of the document (refer to Figure 6-1).

Click in either part to make it the active pane. When a part of the window is active, you can change its zoom percentage and scroll up or down without affecting the other part.

To unsplit a window, choose Window⇨Remove Split. You could also click the ribbon's View tab, and then click the Remove Split button.

Opening a new window

Opening a new window for a document works along the same lines as splitting a window. To open a new window for a document, choose Window⇨New Window. In this case, rather than have one window with two parts, you have two separate windows, as shown in Figure 6-2.

The main differences between splitting a window and creating a new window are that with a new window, you can arrange the two windows any way you like on your screen, and you can have more than just two windows. To create a third (or fourth or fifth or however many you want) window, choose Window⇨New Window again (and again and again, if you like).

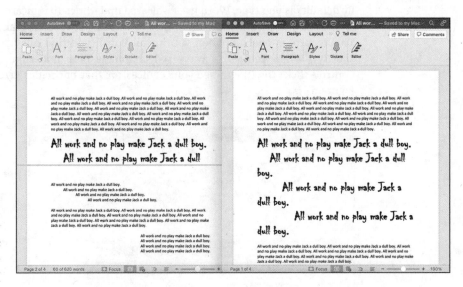

FIGURE 6-2:
Two windows,
same document.

REMEMBER

Creating a new window doesn't create a new document; it merely creates a new *view* of the current document.

Each new window is independent of the other, so scrolling or zooming (see Chapter 4) in one window has no effect on another. In fact, the only thing that *isn't* independent is editing, which is reflected immediately in the other window or windows. Further, each window behaves just like any other window. You click to activate the window you want to work with, and then you can drag and drop between them to your heart's content and click the Close button to close the window, for example.

Check It Out: Checking Your Spelling, Grammar, and Hyphenation

Word has a number of features to help you spiff up your presentation by eliminating errors and choosing just the right words. Word offers built-in spelling and grammar checkers, and it can correct mistakes automatically. It also offers an extensive hyphenation dictionary and a comprehensive thesaurus.

Read on to find out how to use these features.

Double-checking your spelling and grammar

By default, as you type, Word uses wavy red underlines to indicate words not in its dictionary and blue double underlines to indicate suspected grammatical errors. This feature is enabled when you install Word (you find out how to turn it off shortly). When you see a wavy red or double blue underline, right-click (or Control-click) the line to see your choices for that particular error, as shown in Figure 6-3.

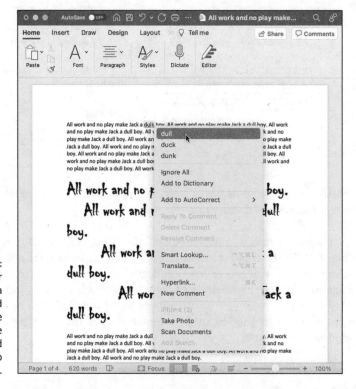

FIGURE 6-3:
Right-click (or Control-click) a wavy red underline to see choices for the misspelled word on a pop-up menu.

Figure 6-3 shows the choices Word gives you for the correct spelling of *dulk*. To replace this "word" with the correct one, just select it (*dull*, in this case) from the pop-up menu, and the misspelled word is immediately replaced with the correctly spelled one.

You can also choose Ignore All to have Word ignore all instances of *dulk* in this document. Or you can choose Add to Dictionary to add *dulk* to your personal spelling dictionary so that it isn't flagged as misspelled in documents you create later.

If you choose Add to AutoCorrect, a submenu with the same set of spelling choices (in this case, *dull, duck,* and *dunk*) appears. The difference is that if you choose *dull* from this submenu, Word adds it to your list of words that are automatically corrected. Then if you happen to type *dulk* again, Word changes it to *dull* automatically.

The process is the same for grammar errors, except that they're underlined in double blue lines instead of wavy red lines.

Having all those red and blue underlines on the page bugs some people. To turn off automatic spelling and grammar checking, follow these steps:

1. **Choose Word ⇨ Preferences, or use its keyboard shortcut, ⌘+, (comma).**

2. **Click the Spelling & Grammar icon to open the Spelling Grammar preference pane, as shown in Figure 6-4.**

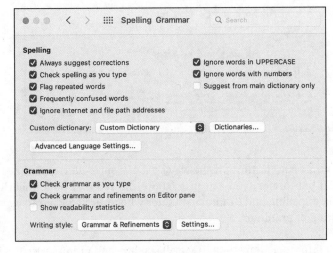

FIGURE 6-4:
The Spelling Grammar preference pane.

3. **Deselect the Check Spelling as You Type check box and then the Check Grammar as You Type check box to turn off automatic spelling and grammar checking.**

Utilizing Word's built-in editor

If you don't care to use the automatic spelling or grammar checkers, you can still check the spelling and grammar in a document by choosing Tools ⇨ Spelling and Grammar ⇨ Editor. Word inspects the entire document and displays the Editor dialog shown in Figure 6-5 when it finds possible spelling or grammar errors.

You can access Editor also by clicking its button on the Home tab of the ribbon.

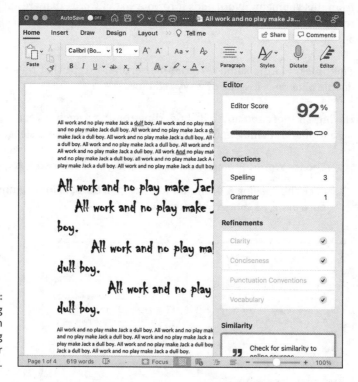

You don't *have* to turn off the wavy red or double blue underlines to use this dialog. If you prefer, you can just ignore the red and blue underlines and choose Tools⇨Spelling and Grammar⇨Editor whenever you want to check a document's spelling or grammar.

The Editor tool allows you to see all spelling and grammar errors in one spot, in a pane on the right side of the document window, without the need to hunt and peck for underlines. You also see a spelling and grammar score for your document (refer to Figure 6-5), which lets you know just how elegant or how much of a mess your document is. In the Refinements section, Editor offers suggestions for areas such as clarity and punctuation. And in the Similarity section, Editor can even check the web for sources that may be similar to what you've written.

Click an item in a section to see what suggestions Editor thinks you should consider. For example, with Editor open, we clicked the Grammar option under the Corrections section, and were alerted to the fact that we've accidentally capitalized the word *and* in a sentence; see Figure 6-6.

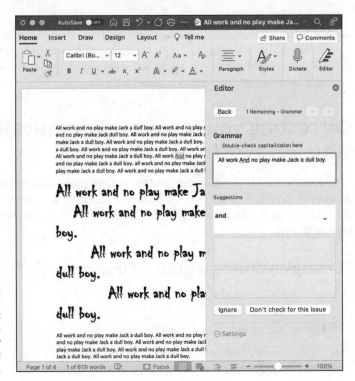

All work and no play make Ja...

FIGURE 6-6:
Editor is kind
enough to alert
us that we've
mistakenly
capitalized
a word.

In the Editor dialog, you can

>> See the sentence containing your mistake.

>> Click one of the suggestions to use it.

>> Click Ignore to have Word move along without making any corrections.

>> Click the Don't Check for This Issue button if you want Word to ignore this particular "error" from this point forward.

>> Click the Back button to return to the Editor's main window.

Note that if an area of concern has been addressed or there are no occurrences of it, a check mark will appear to the right.

WARNING

When Word says that a word isn't spelled correctly, it doesn't always mean that the word isn't spelled correctly. In other words, Word makes mistakes. One of the most common is if you receive a document from someone outside the country — say, from Great Britain. In that case, you may see a word such as *colour* underlined as a spelling mistake because Word expects it to be spelled the American way, which is *color*. Neither does Word correctly flag spelled words that are used incorrectly. For example, if you type *wierd* to refer to something as weird, Word flags the word as misspelled. But if you accidentally type *wired*, which is a word (though not the word you intended to type), Word doesn't recognize your mistake. The point is that you shouldn't rely on these tools too much and should always proof-read your work carefully. Forewarned is forearmed.

Correcting your errors automatically with AutoCorrect

The AutoCorrect feature provides another way to guard against those pesky typos that sneak in all too easily. In a nutshell, AutoCorrect watches what you type and corrects common mistakes on the fly, without bothering you with wavy under-lines or dialogs.

Turning on and configuring AutoCorrect

To enable AutoCorrect, do one of the following:

» Choose Tools ⇨ AutoCorrect Options.

» Choose Word ⇨ Preferences (or press ⌘+comma) and then click the AutoCorrect icon.

Either way, you see the AutoCorrect preference pane, as shown in Figure 6-7. If you select the Automatically Correct Spelling and Formatting as You Type check box at the top of this pane, your common mistakes are corrected automatically as you type.

AutoCorrect comes populated with dozens of useful items. For example, if you type **(c)**, Word automatically replaces it with the proper copyright symbol (©). Or if you type **(r)**, Word automatically replaces it with the proper registered trade-mark symbol (®).

You can click an entry in the list under the Replace Text as You Type option to display it in the Replace box and With box. For example, Figure 6-7 shows an AutoCorrect entry that replaces (tm) with ™ automatically. Due to this entry, whenever you type **(tm)** — the letters *t* and *m* inside parentheses — Word auto-matically replaces it with the trademark symbol.

To add your own automatic replacement pairs, just type what you want replaced in the Replace field and type what you want it replaced with in the With field.

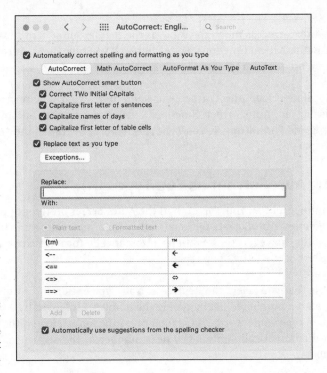

FIGURE 6-7:
Set your
options in the
AutoCorrect
preference pane.

TIP

By the way, this function is shared among all Office apps. In other words, replacement pairs you create in Word are available also in Excel, Outlook, and PowerPoint, and replacement pairs you create in Excel, Outlook, or PowerPoint are available also in Word.

TIP

The AutoCorrect feature is useful for more than just symbols. Our favorite way to use it is to save time when typing long sentences that we use over and over again or when using common phrases such as

>> vty for *very truly yours*

>> iow for *in other words*

>> imho for *in my humble opinion*

>> ssbf for *scum-sucking bottom feeder*

>> ofd for *Office For Mac For Dummies*

>> tpf for *the party of the first part*

To add your own AutoCorrect replacement pairs like these, type the abbreviation in the Replace field, type what you want the abbreviation replaced with in the With field, and then click the Add button. From then on, whenever you type that abbreviation, it's replaced with the word or phrase you typed in the With field.

Math AutoCorrect is much the same as the regular AutoCorrect except that it corrects mathematical functions. For example, if you type **\beta**, AutoCorrect replaces it with a proper beta symbol (β).

We absolutely love AutoCorrect, but some users find it annoying. If you'd like to disable all AutoCorrect functions, just deselect the Automatically Correct Spelling and Formatting as You Type check box at the top of the AutoCorrect preference pane.

Using AutoFormat as You Type

The AutoFormat as You Type tab in the AutoCorrect preference pane works a lot like the other AutoCorrect options. Rather than replace specific letters with specific words, however, these options automatically format text styles and options, regardless of the letters you type.

Suppose that you select the Replace as You Type option for Automatic Numbered Lists, start a numbered list by typing the number **1** followed by a period and a tab, and then type some words. When you press the Return key at the end of list item 1, Word automatically enters the next number in the sequence, the period, and the tab.

In other words, if you type the following line, with [Tab] indicating where the Tab key is pressed:

1. [Tab]This is the first point in the numbered list.

Word automatically types this line when you press the Return key:

2. [Tab]

Other options include replacing straight quotation marks (") with curly (smart) quotation marks ("), ordinal numbers with proper superscripts (1st with 1st), and fractions with fraction characters (1/4 with ¼).

Using AutoText

Last but not least is the AutoText tab. AutoText offers to automatically complete certain words when you type certain characters. AutoText displays an AutoComplete tip in a little gray box. If you want to use the word or phrase in the AutoComplete tip box, just press the Return key. If you don't want to use that word or phrase, just continue typing — no replacement occurs.

If you think AutoText sounds a lot like AutoCorrect, you're right. The difference is that AutoText gives you a choice of whether to correct something or not. If you press Return, the text in the AutoComplete tip replaces the word you're typing; if you don't press Return, you can keep typing and the word or phrase isn't replaced.

Hypnotic hyphenation

Word includes an extensive hyphenation dictionary, which you can use manually (the default) or automatically. To access the hyphenation tools (shown in Figure 6-8), choose Tools ⇨ Hyphenation in the menu at the top of the screen.

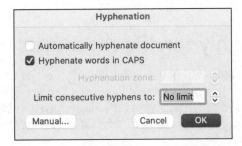

FIGURE 6-8:
The Hyphenation
dialog and its
options.

Hyphenating manually, one word at a time

To hyphenate an entire document manually, choose Tools ⇨ Hyphenation and then click the Manual button at the bottom of the Hyphenation window. To hyphenate part of a document, select the part you want to hyphenate, choose Tools ⇨ Hyphenation, and then click the Manual button at the bottom of the Hyphenation window. Either way, you see the Manual Hyphenation dialog, which shows you the proposed hyphenation for each word. Accept it by clicking Yes or reject it by clicking No.

Hyphenating a document automatically, in one fell swoop

To turn on automatic hyphenation for your document, choose Tools ⇨ Hyphenation and select the Automatically Hyphenate Document check box. Word then automatically hyphenates words that require hyphenation without displaying the dialog.

When do you hyphenate manually, and when do you let Word do the heavy lifting? Here's our recommendation: Use automatic hyphenation unless you're extremely picky about hyphens. Word usually does a decent job of hyphenating, and we agree with its hyphenation choices at least 95 percent of the time. For what it's worth, we're picky about hyphenation but almost always let Word do the dirty work for us.

Discovering the Reference Tools

Word has several useful reference tools — available at the click of a mouse — that can help you improve your writing. These tools include a thesaurus, a dictionary, an encyclopedia, a bilingual dictionary, a translation service, and a web search option.

The thoroughly terrific thesaurus

The thesaurus, which offers alternative word choices, is one of Word's most useful writing tools. It works just like a printed thesaurus, but it's even better because it's faster than leafing through pages, and it's always just a couple of clicks away when you're using any Office app. Besides, who uses a printed thesaurus anymore (we're a bit sad to ask)?

To display a list of suggested synonyms, follow these steps:

1. **Right-click or Control-click a word for which you want to find a synonym.**

2. **Choose Synonyms from the pop-up menu that appears.**

3. **Click the word you want to replace it with from the list of suggestions, as shown in Figure 6-9.**

Another way to look up synonyms is by using the thesaurus, which can be accessed by either

>> Choosing Thesaurus from the pop-up Synonyms submenu (refer to Figure 6-9)

>> Choosing Tools ⇨ Thesaurus to open the Thesaurus pane

The Thesaurus pane opens on the right side of your document, as shown in Figure 6-10.

To find synonyms for another word, type it in the search field at the top of the pane and press Enter.

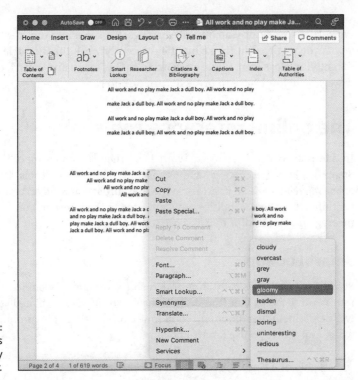

FIGURE 6-9:
The word *dull* is
being replaced by
the word *gloomy*.

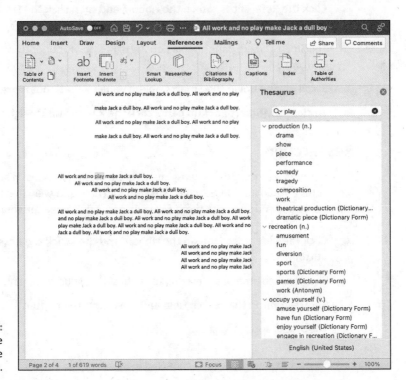

FIGURE 6-10:
Looking up the
word *play* in the
Thesaurus pane.

TIP

Word keeps track of your recent searches. To see a pop-up menu displaying all words you've typed in the search field recently, click the little triangle next to the magnifying glass icon. Choose a word from this menu and Word looks it up immediately; you don't have to press Return or Enter.

The online reference tools

In addition to the thesaurus, Word has other reference tools in its repertoire: Smart Lookup, Researcher, and Translator. These three tools are known as the *online reference tools.* In contrast to the thesaurus, you need an active internet connection to use them. If you're not connected to the internet, you'll receive an error message if you attempt to use these tools.

Smart Lookup

Smart Lookup is basically Bing, Microsoft's version of Google, if you will, built into Word. It helps you find definitions of words, locate related content on other websites (including photos), sometimes offers an audio pronunciation of the word, and more. To use Smart Lookup:

1. **Highlight a word in your document.**

2. **Click the References tab on the ribbon, and then click the Smart Lookup button.**

    The Smart Lookup pane appears on the right side of your document, as shown in Figure 6-11.

3. **Scroll up and down the Smart Lookup pane to check out more content.**

4. **To close the Smart Lookup pane, click the X in the upper right.**

Researcher

Researcher is a tool used for doing just what its name implies: researching topics. Search for a topic and Researcher will find journals and websites that discuss the topic in detail, and then list them for your perusal. To use the tool:

1. **Click the References tab on the ribbon, and then click the Researcher button.**

    The Researcher pane appears on the right side of your document.

2. **Enter a topic in the search field and press Return or Enter.**

    The results appear, as shown in Figure 6-12.

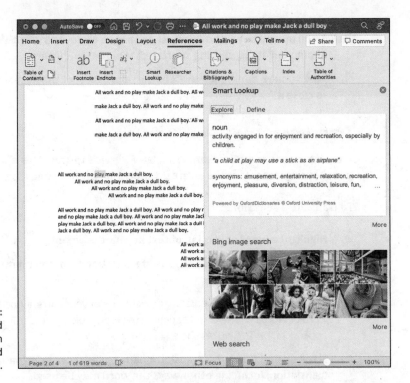

FIGURE 6-11:
Scroll to find more information on your selected word or topic.

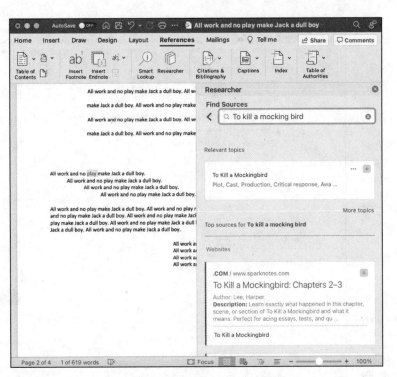

FIGURE 6-12:
Researching one of the great American novels.

3. **Scroll up and down the Researcher pane to discover a wealth of info about your topic, clicking sources that pique your interest.**

4. **When you're done, click the X in the upper right of the Researcher pane to close it.**

Translator

Translator uses the Microsoft Translator service to translate a selection of text from your document, or the entire document itself, from one language to another.

To translate a selection:

1. **Highlight a word or section of text in your document.**

2. **Choose Tools ⇨ Translate ⇨ Translate Selection from the menu at the top of the screen.**

   The Translator pane appears on the right side of your current document. The word or words you selected appear in the From field and the translation appears in the To field, as shown in Figure 6-13.

3. **Scroll up and down the Translator pane to see more information on the translation, including other ways the word may be used.**

FIGURE 6-13:
Translating the word *play* from English to Spanish.

106   PART 2 Mastering Microsoft Word

4. **If you want to select different languages, change the languages in the From and To fields.**

5. **If you want to insert the translation in place of the original selection you made in Step 1, click the Insert button.**

6. **When you're done, click the X in the upper right of the Translator pane to close it.**

To translate an entire document:

1. **Choose Tools⇨Translate⇨Translate Document from the menu at the top of the screen.**

   The Translator pane appears on the right side of your current document.

2. **In the From and To pop-up menus, select languages you want to translate from and to.**

3. **Click the Translate button to begin.**

   The process shouldn't take long unless the document is large. When the translation is finished, a Translation Complete message appears in the Translator pane of the original document, and a new document containing the translation opens on the left, as shown in Figure 6-14.

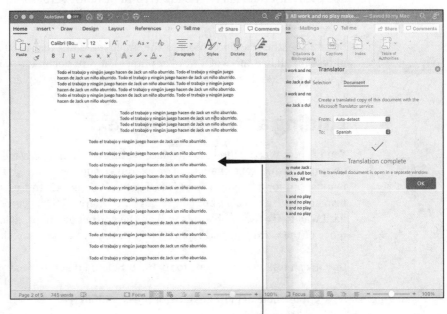

FIGURE 6-14:
A perfect translation of the document from English to Spanish.

Translated document

4. **If you want to make a new translation of the original document, click OK and repeat Steps 2 and 3.**

5. **When you're finished, click the X in the upper right of the Translator pane to close it.**

Saving Time with the Find and Replace Feature

Another feature that makes a word processor superior to a typewriter is Find and Replace, which is a real timesaver and can make your life easier. First, it lets you find a word or phrase (or all instances of a word or phrase) in your document instantly, regardless of the document's length.

TIP

We often take advantage of the Find and Replace capability when we have to stop working in the middle of a lengthy document. Before we save and quit Word, we type a sequence of characters that won't occur elsewhere in the document — usually **** or #### — where we want to continue working the next time we open the file. Then, rather than scroll through 50 or 100 pages, looking for the spot where we left off, we just choose Edit ⇨ Find, type the sequence of characters, and then click the Find Next button. Word instantly scrolls to the place where we stopped working.

But wait — there's more. Most of the time, you don't just need to find a word or phrase (or all instances of a word or phrase) in your document; you need to correct it somehow. Read on for two examples of how Find and Replace can save the day.

Finding and replacing text

You can use Word's Find and Replace feature like a magic wand for making fast, document-wide text changes. For example, suppose that you've worked on a manuscript for a long time and just finished. You decide to try using the word *fun* instead of the word *play*, but you're not sure where all the occurrences appear. The hard way to fix this problem is to read the entire document, deleting each occurrence of the word *play* and typing *fun* in its place. Can you say "boring"?

Or you can follow these steps to fix the problem all at one time:

1. **Choose Edit ⇨ Find ⇨ Replace (or press ⌘+Shift+H).**

   The Find and Replace pane appears in the sidebar on the left side of the window.

2. **Click in the first field and type** play.

3. **Click in the second field and type** fun.

   Your Find and Replace pane should now look like Figure 6-15.

4. **Click the Replace All button.**

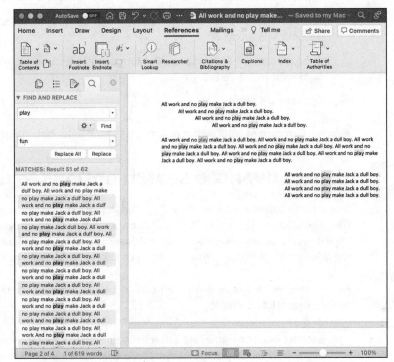

FIGURE 6-15:
You can change
as many
instances of a
word as you like
in a fraction of a
second.

Using Find and Replace to make formatting changes

You're not limited to making word replacements when you use Find and Replace. Here's another handy use: Say that you've just finished the aforementioned manuscript when your editor informs you that the publisher's in-house style sheet requires all instances of the word *work* to appear in bold, red, italic text. As things stand, it's in the same font as the rest of the manuscript — plain, with no bold, red, or italic applied to it.

Using Find and Replace, making this change is no dilemma. Here's how to fix it in a jiffy:

1. **Choose Edit➪Find➪Find (or press ⌘+F).**

   The cursor moves to the search field on the Quick Access toolbar.

2. **Type** work **in the search field.**

   You don't have to press Enter or Return; Word highlights matches in your document as you type.

3. **Choose Format➪Font, change the font color to Red, and then choose Bold Italic in the Font Style list.**

4. **Click the OK button.**

Every occurrence of *work* in the document is now bold, red, and italic.

Using advanced search options to do more

One set of features available in the Find and Replace dialog can save you even more time and effort than others. These advanced search options, shown in Figure 6-16, appear when you choose Edit➪Find➪Advanced Find and Replace and then click the downward-pointing arrow button in the lower-left corner of the window.

As you can see in Figure 6-16, you can use a number of criteria for any find or replace operation, including:

» **Match Case:** Makes the find and replace operation case-sensitive. For example, if you search for the word *rat* and replace it with the word *rodent*, any time *rat* is found in a sentence, it's replaced — properly — with *rodent*.

» **Find Whole Words Only:** Finds only whole words. For example, if you search for *do* and replace it with *perform*, words that contain the word *do*, such as *dog, doughnut,* or *domestic,* wouldn't be changed. If this option were deselected, the first two letters in each of those words would be replaced with *perform,* so they would be *performg, performughnut,* and *performmestic.*

» **Use Wildcards:** Lets you choose wildcard items, such as Any Character, from the Special menu near the bottom of the dialog.

» **Sounds Like:** Lets you search for homonyms. For example, searching for *so* would also find *sew* and *sow.*

» **Find All Word Forms:** Finds all forms of the word you search for. For example, if you search for *show* and replace it with *display,* this option also finds *showed, showing,* and *shows* and replaces them with *displayed, displaying,* and *displays,* respectively.

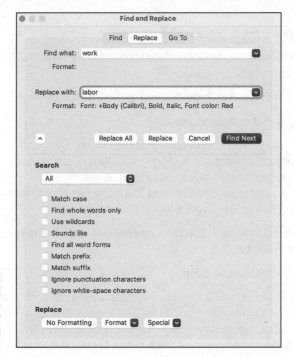

You can fine-tune your search or replace operation even further with choices from the Format and Special menus. On the Format menu, you can specify font, paragraph, highlight, style, language, and other attributes that you want to either search for or use in your replacement text. The Special menu lets you search for invisible attributes, such as tab characters, paragraph marks, column breaks, and page breaks.

You may recall the earlier example where we made all instances of the word *work* appear in bold, red, and italic text. Another way to resolve that situation is with these advanced search options. Note that, in Figure 6-16, the Replace operation finds *work* and replaces it with *labor* formatted in bold, italic, and red.

Clicking the Replace All button gives the same results as the four-step process described earlier in this chapter — all occurrences of the word *labor* would now be red, bold, and italic.

Here's how to change every occurrence of *work* to *labor* and make every occurrence of *labor* then appear in red, bold, and italic type, using the advanced search options:

1. **Choose Edit⇨Replace or use its keyboard shortcut, ⌘+Shift+H.**

2. **In the Find and Replace dialog that appears, type** work **in the Find What field.**

3. **Type** labor **in the Replace With field.**

Make sure not to click anywhere outside the Replace With field. Otherwise, Step 4 won't work.

4. **On the Format menu at the bottom of the dialog, choose Font.**

The Replace Font dialog appears.

WARNING

The way you choose font and paragraph formatting options for the Find What and Replace With fields can be a little tricky. To specify options for the Find What field, you must first click in that field. To specify options for the Replace With field, you must click in that field. The active field is outlined in blue, as the Replace With field is in Figure 6-16.

5. **Choose red in the Font Color list, choose Bold Italic in the Font Style list, and then click OK.**

6. **Click the Replace All button.**

All occurrences of *work* are replaced with *labor* in red, bold, and italic type.

TIP

The arrows to the right of the Find What and Replace With fields indicate pop-up menus that let you reuse recent search terms. If your last Find and Replace action replaced the word *Frammus* with *Ding-a-Ling*, those words would reappear in these fields, along with any other words or phrases you've searched for or replaced with since you last launched Word. These lists are cleared when you quit Word.

WARNING

Use the Replace All option with care, and review your document for unintended consequences. For example, if you forget to enable the Find Whole Words Only option in the example earlier in this chapter, where you replace *do* with *perform*, you would replace the words *dog, doughnut,* and *domestic* with *performg, performughnut,* and *performmestic.*

TIP

Sometimes, using the Find Next and Replace buttons is safer — so that you can review each replacement before you make it. It takes a little longer than using Replace All, but you'll sleep better at night knowing that all your replacements make sense.

Chapter **7**

Using Templates and Other Design Elements

In earlier chapters in this part of the book, we tell you all about creating documents in Word. The focus in those chapters is primarily on getting the words right, paying scant attention to making the words look the way you want them to look on the page.

Never fear. In this chapter, you focus on Word features that affect the appearance of your documents. More specifically, you start by exploring templates and how to customize them so that they're perfect for your needs. Then you see how to get the most out of page elements, including headers and footers, tabs, margins, and indents.

But wait — there's more! You also see how to work with columns, lists, and text boxes and discover why tables aren't just for dining.

Canned Design: Working with Word Templates

We named this section "Canned Design" because it deals with using Word templates, which, to use Word's own definition, are computer files that are used as master copies for creating other documents similar to them. Canned design isn't a bad thing, mind you. Designing good-looking documents might not be your forté, or maybe you just don't have the time to do it. Frankly, we're tickled pink if we can start a project with a template designed by a professional who, unlike us, has some sense of design.

The good news is that Word comes with dozens upon dozens of professionally designed templates that you can use for almost any occasion.

Getting started with the Document Gallery

The easiest way to start a project from a template is by using the Document gallery, which you open by choosing File ⇨ New from Template.

As described in Chapter 3, the Document gallery contains templates in more than a dozen categories — brochures, calendars, forms, flyers, labels, and more.

Sample project: Starting a custom newsletter from a template

A good way to get a feel for working with Word templates is to walk through the basics of using one. This section shows you how to create a document from a Word newsletter template and customize it as an example of the general steps involved in modifying a template so that it's just the way you want it.

Here's how to get your project started:

1. **Click New in the left pane of the Document gallery.**

   Figure 7-1 shows what the Document gallery window should look like at this point.

2. **Click the Newsletter template in the center pane (scroll down, if necessary).**

3. **Click the Create button.**

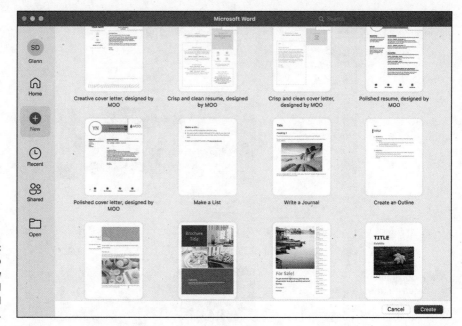

FIGURE 7-1:
Click Create to
start a new
document based
on the selected
template.

A new document based on the Newsletter template opens, as shown in Figure 7-2.

If you create a document based on the Newsletter template and it doesn't look like the one shown in Figure 7-2, make sure you're in print layout view (choose View ⇨ Print Layout), for two reasons:

>> If you're in another view, your page might not look like the page in the figures.

>> Some views (Draft and Outline, to be precise) don't display graphical elements in documents.

The bottom line: Print Layout is the only view that lets you follow along with the upcoming instructions.

You can download more templates from Microsoft by visiting https://templates.office.com. You'll find templates for just about any type of document you can imagine, and then some.

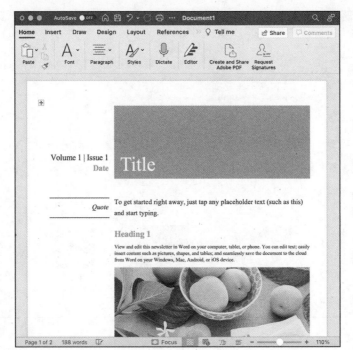

FIGURE 7-2:
A new document
based on the
Newsletter
template,
before being
customized.

Creating a customized version of a Word template

Continuing with the newsletter example from the preceding section, let's customize the newsletter. Double-click the word *Title* at the top of the page and replace it with the name of your newsletter. Then double-click the word *Date* on the left side of the page and replace it with the current month and year. When you're finished, the screen should look similar to Figure 7-3.

Saving your customized template

You can stop working on customizing your template in midstream and come back to it later. Or when you're finished, you can save it to reuse this version of the template repeatedly later. Either way, give it a descriptive name so that you can locate it easily. To do so, follow these steps:

1. **Choose File ⇨ Save As.**

2. **In the Save As field, name the template something meaningful.**

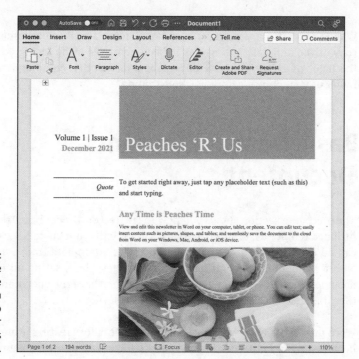

FIGURE 7-3:
The title and date of the template have been modified to reflect our newsletter's information.

3. **In the Where drop-down menu, choose Templates.**

   Be sure to save the template to the Templates folder so you can find it easily. Here's the path in case you need to browse to it or find it later:

   Home/Library/Group Containers/UBF8T346G9.Office/User Content/Templates

4. **In the File Format drop-down list, choose Word Template (.dotx).**

   The Save As sheet should look like Figure 7-4.

5. **Click Save.**

   From now on, you can open this template by selecting it in the Personal section at the top of the Document gallery window.

FIGURE 7-4:
Saving the modified template for future use.

TIP

When you create a document based on a template, Word automatically opens a copy of the template and names it Document1. To avoid losing your work, get in the habit of giving the new document a descriptive name and saving it in the folder of your choice before you start typing.

Adding Basic Design Elements to Your Document

The preceding section shows you how to create a document based on one of Word's included templates, customize it, and save it with your customizations. When you can do all that, you also know how to create a template from scratch. Just start with a blank document rather than a Word template; set up all elements of the document just the way you want them; and then save the document as a template. (See the preceding subsection for details on saving it.)

Word provides a wide variety of design elements for creating professional looking documents, no matter what your purpose. You can use these elements when you create a document from one of Word's own templates and for templates you create from scratch (that is, by starting with a blank document).

Some standard design elements you can use in your documents include the following (all of which are covered in greater detail later in this chapter and in Chapter 8):

» **Headers and footers:** These elements appear at the top and bottom of a page, respectively, and repeat on subsequent pages.

» **Images:** Images are pictures, drawings, clip art, and other elements you can use to enhance your documents so that they're not all text (and all boring).

» **Text boxes:** Use text boxes to position blocks of text anywhere on the page.

» **Columns:** Use columns to create several narrower areas, just as you see in newspapers, rather than one big block of text.

» **Tables:** Use tables to present information in a grid rather than in columns or blocks.

» **Lists:** Two kinds of lists are available, bulleted (unordered) and numbered (ordered). This book is chock-full of both types, and in fact, what you're reading right now is part of a bulleted list.

» **Styles:** You use styles to apply multiple formatting attributes to selected text quickly and easily. For example, with a single click, you can assign the selected text all the following attributes: Times New Roman font, 10-point size, indented one inch, and set flush left, with 11 points of line spacing and 5.5 points of white space after each paragraph. (We used these attributes for bulleted lists in the manuscript for this book.)

Using a letterhead as an example, the following sections show you how to add each of these elements to your new document. But first you need to create that document. To do so, choose File⇨New Document (or press ⌘+N).

Imagine that: Adding and resizing an image

Word lets you use almost any type of image (picture) as an element in your document. You can use clip art or image files from your hard drive (as you can see in a moment), or you can even drag a photograph from Photos into your Word document.

Say that you want to add a logo to your document. To do so, follow these steps:

1. **Locate the image file you want to use on your hard drive.**

2. **Drag the image file to the Word document.**

In Figure 7-5, the file Dwight.jpeg is being dragged from the desktop to the Word document.

3. **Resize the image, if necessary.**

If you find that the image is too large or too small, you can resize it by clicking and dragging its handles (the eight little white squares on the borders of the image) until it's exactly the size you want.

TIP

If you drag a corner handle, the image resizes proportionally. If you grab a handle in the middle of any side, the image resizes in only one direction — horizontally if you grab a side handle or vertically if you grab the top or bottom handle.

Moving images around documents

If you were to click the image shown in Figure 7-5 and try to drag it to another spot in your document, you'd be frustrated at best. Go ahead: Try it and you'll see that although the image can be resized, it can't be moved.

That's because images are considered *inline graphics* by default — Word treats each image as though it were a single character of text. If you drag an image into text, as we did in Figure 7-6, the image breaks up the text as shown.

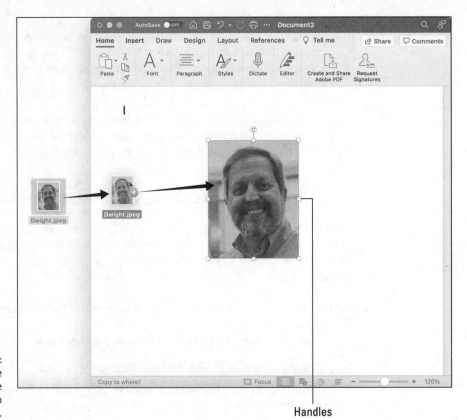

FIGURE 7-5:
Adding an image
by dragging a file
from the desktop
to the document.

Handles

WARNING

If you don't see an image you dragged into a document or you see only part of it, first make sure that you're using print layout view. If that's not it, choose Format⇨Paragraph and set the line spacing for the paragraph containing the image to Single, 1.5 Lines, or Double. If it's set to one of the other line spacing options — At Least, Exactly, or Multiple — inline graphics taller than a single line of text might be partially or totally hidden.

When you drop an image in the middle of text this way, you can't drag it anywhere on the page — all you can do is move it from place to place within the flow of text. Chances are good that you prefer the text to run around your picture. Here's how to make text run around your graphic:

1. **Click the image to select it.**

Eight handles and a rotation handle appear on the image to indicate that it's selected.

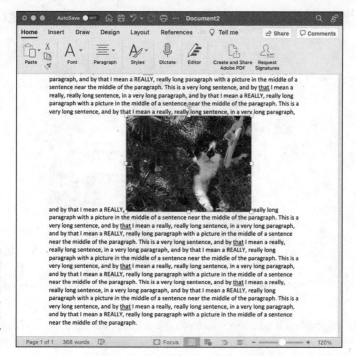

paragraph, and by that I mean a REALLY, really long paragraph with a picture in the middle of a sentence near the middle of the paragraph. This is a very long sentence, and by that I mean a really, really long sentence, in a very long paragraph, and by that I mean a REALLY, really long paragraph with a picture in the middle of a sentence near the middle of the paragraph. This is a very long sentence, and by that I mean a really, really long sentence, in a very long paragraph,

and by that I mean a REALLY,   really long paragraph with a picture in the middle of a sentence near the middle of the paragraph. This is a very long sentence, and by that I mean a really, really long sentence, in a very long paragraph, and by that I mean a REALLY, really long paragraph with a picture in the middle of a sentence near the middle of the paragraph. This is a very long sentence, and by that I mean a really, really long sentence, in a very long paragraph, and by that I mean a REALLY, really long paragraph with a picture in the middle of a sentence near the middle of the paragraph. This is a very long sentence, and by that I mean a really, really long sentence, in a very long paragraph, and by that I mean a REALLY, really long paragraph with a picture in the middle of a sentence near the middle of the paragraph. This is a very long sentence, and by that I mean a really, really long sentence, in a very long paragraph, and by that I mean a REALLY, really long paragraph with a picture in the middle of a sentence near the middle of the paragraph. This is a very long sentence, and by that I mean a really, really long sentence, in a very long paragraph, and by that I mean a REALLY, really long paragraph with a picture in the middle of a sentence near the middle of the paragraph.

FIGURE 7-6: We dropped the cat image between the comma after *REALLY* and the lowercase *really* that follows it.

2. **On the ribbon, click the Picture Format tab.**

   As soon as you select the image in Step 1, the Picture Format tab will appear on the ribbon.

3. **Click the Wrap Text button on the ribbon and choose a text wrap option, as shown in Figure 7-7.**

   The images on the page in Figure 7-7 are all wrapped Tight.

TIP

If you don't see the Wrap Text button, it might be hidden in another option because the document window isn't large enough to display it. Click the Arrange button to display hidden options and you'll find the Wrap Text button there.

Creating headers and footers

Some types of documents need the same information to appear on every page. In a letter, for example, you likely want your contact information — your name, address, phone and fax numbers, and email address — at the top or bottom of every page. That's what headers and footers are for. If you want certain text or images (or both) to appear on *every* page of a document, put them in the header or footer.

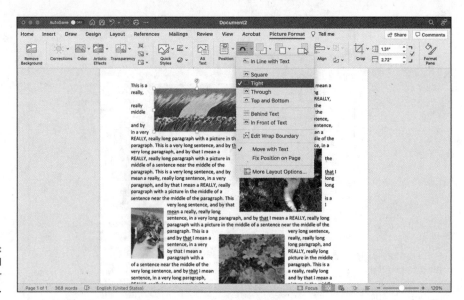

TIP

FIGURE 7-7:
Text wrapped
around four
different images.

If you have a logo image that you want to appear on only the first page of a mul-tipage letter, don't place the logo in a header. Instead, place only the contact information that you want on every page in either a header or footer. Another approach is to select the Different First Page box on the ribbon's Header & Footer tab, add the logo to the header or footer on the first page, and then add the contact to the header or footer on the second page.

To add a header or footer to a document, follow these steps:

1. **Choose View ⇨ Header & Footer.**

The view switches to print layout view, if necessary, and the header and footer areas appear, as shown in Figure 7-8.

FIGURE 7-8:
Adding contact
information in
the footer of a
letterhead
document.

2. **Click anywhere inside the header or footer and type your text.**

3. **On the ribbon, click the Header & Footer tab.**

   A bevy of header- and footer-related tools appear on the ribbon (refer to Figure 7-8). Here's a rundown of a few selected tools:

   ● *Header and Footer drop-down menus:* These menus have a variety of ready-made headers and footers, as shown in Figure 7-9.

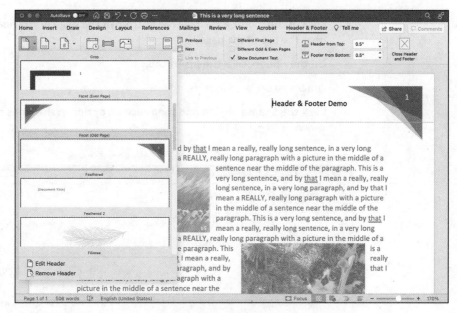

FIGURE 7-9:
Use the Header &
Footer tab on
the ribbon to
use its tools.

   ● *Different First Page:* Create a different header and footer (or no header and footer) on the first page of your document. This option is ideal when your document has a title page.

   ● *Different Odd and Even Pages:* Create different headers and footers for odd- and even-numbered pages. This option is useful if you're creating a book-style document with odd and even (right and left) pages side by side and you want different information on each one, such as the book title in the left header and the chapter title in the right one.

   ● *Show Document Text:* Select or deselect to show or hide the text between the header and footer, respectively.

   ● *Header from Top and Footer from Bottom:* Move the header and the footer down or up. The default is 0.5 inches: The header begins half an inch from the top of the page, and the footer ends half an inch from the bottom of the page.

4. **To exit the header or footer when finished, double-click anywhere outside the header or footer, or if you're viewing the Header & Footer tab on the ribbon, click the Close Header and Footer button on the right side.**

Adding lines to your header or footer

A *line* is a design element that can add simple elegance or visual clarity to your header or footer material. To insert a line, follow these steps:

1. **Click in the footer area near the bottom of the page or the header area near the top of the page.**

2. **On the ribbon, click the Insert tab.**

   The Media browser appears.

3. **Click the Shapes button and then click an option in the Lines section shown in Figure 7-10.**

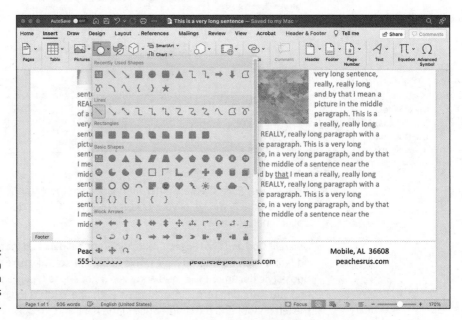

TIP

FIGURE 7-10:
Select a shape in the Lines section of the Shapes menu.

4. **To draw your line, click and drag in the header or the footer.**

   If you have a picture in a supported graphics file format — such as JPEG, GIF, TIFF, or PNG — you can drag the file from Finder to the document (refer to Figure 7-5).

5. **Click the line to select it.**

   The line displays handles when it's selected.

6. **Drag the line to move it to the desired location.**

Now type your contact information. The steps that follow and the next section (on tabs) are for formatting your contact information, as shown in the footer of Figure 7-8. You might have to adjust where you put your tabs and returns if you want to format your contact information differently:

1. **Type your full name or company name and then press Tab.**

2. **Type your street address and then press Tab.**

3. **Type your city, state, and zip code, and then press Return.**

4. **Type your phone number and then press Tab.**

5. **Type your email address and then press Tab.**

6. **Type your website (or fax number or social media site or whatever).**

Don't worry if the text doesn't align correctly. We show you how to fix that problem in the next section.

Arranging text with some help from tabs

Word tabs let you line up text consistently across the page. When you press the Tab key, an invisible tab character is inserted in your text before the next visible character you type.

Click the Show All Nonprinting Characters button on the Home tab on the ribbon (shown in Figure 7-11), and each of the tabs you type appears on the screen as a little blue arrow (also shown in Figure 7-11).

Word creates two tabs automatically in every header and footer. The location of each tab appears on the ruler at the top of the document window.

Fortunately, for the example, the default tabs are right where we want 'em. If they're not right where you want them, find out more about setting tabs in the following section.

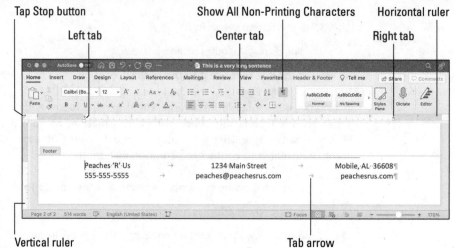

Tap Stop button · Left tab · Show All Non-Printing Characters · Center tab · Horizontal ruler · Right tab · Vertical ruler · Tab arrow

FIGURE 7-11:
It's sometimes helpful to be able to see the nonprinting characters that populate your document.

Setting Tabs, Margins, and Other Types of Indents

Tabs, margins, and indents all have to do with the way text lines up relative to the page and the text above it, below it, or both. Tabs let you determine where on a line text begins, is centered, and ends. Margins govern how much white space appears at the top, bottom, left, and right of your page. And indents determine how far from the margin your text begins and ends. In this section, you work with all three.

Setting tabs

When you open a new, blank document, Word creates tab stops every half-inch by default. You can change them, though, by dragging them wherever you need them.

To set a tab stop, follow these steps:

1. **Select the text you want the tab stops to affect.**

   If you want the tabs to affect the entire document, choose Edit⇨Select All.

   TIP

   If you don't see a ruler at the top of the document, choose View⇨Ruler. You'll then see a horizontal ruler across the top of the window and a vertical ruler on its left side.

2. **Click the Tab Stop button (refer to Figure 7-11) to select the type of tab stop you want to create.**

Keep clicking until you see the option you want. Your options are

- *Left:* Aligns text on its left edge
- *Centered:* Aligns text on its center point
- *Right:* Aligns text on its right edge
- *Decimal:* Aligns numbers on their decimal points
- *Bar:* Draws a vertical line down the page at the location you select on the ruler

3. **Click in the ruler where you want the tab stop(s) to appear.**

   If you haven't selected any text, pressing Tab moves text to the right of the cursor to the tab stop. If text with a tab in it is selected, every selected line aligns with that tab stop.

Ignore the lines and triangles at the left and right ends of the rulers for now. You find out about them shortly, when you explore margins and indents.

Setting tabs using the Tabs dialog

Rather than use the ruler to set tab stops, you might find it easier to set and modify tabs by using the Tabs dialog, which you open by choosing Format ⇨ Tabs.

TIP

Before you open the Tabs dialog, make sure you select the text you want to work with, whether it's in the main body of your document or in the header or footer.

The Tabs dialog displays any tab stops in the selected text. In Figure 7-12, the Tabs dialog displays the settings for the footer text shown in Figure 7-11. If no tab stops were set, the Tab Stops field would be empty, as would the area below it where you see tab stops at 3.25 and 6.5 inches.

To set a tab stop using this dialog:

1. **In the Tab Stops field, type the position you want.**

2. **Choose an Alignment option.**

3. **Choose a Leader type.**

   If you don't want a leader, choose None.

TIP

   A *leader* is a series of characters that appear to the left of a tab stop. Your options are None, Dots, Dashes, or Line, as shown in Figure 7-13.

4. **When you've set all your options, click the + button below the Tap Stops list.**

5. **Click the OK button.**

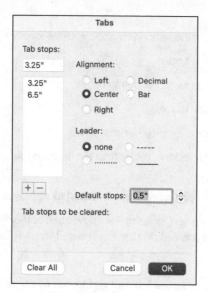

FIGURE 7-12:
Use the Tabs
dialog to create
and modify
tab stops in
selected text.

```
None        →        1¶
Dots .........→.......2¶
Dashes ----→----3¶
Line_____   →      4¶
```

FIGURE 7-13:
Leader types:
none, dots,
dashes, and a
thin line.

Clearing tab stops

To clear (delete) a single tab in the selected text, select the tab in the area on the left of the Tabs dialog (where it says 3.25 and 6.5 in Figure 7-12) and then click the – button under that area.

To clear all tabs in the selected text, just click the Clear All button. However, when you click the – or Clear All button, the tab stops aren't cleared instantly. Instead, they're listed below the words *Tab Stops to Be Cleared* at the bottom of the Tabs dialog. The tab stops aren't deleted until you click the OK button, so you can still change your mind at this point by clicking the Cancel button.

You can use other techniques to accomplish the same results, like this:

>> If you click a tab stop and drag it off the horizontal ruler, it disappears as soon as you release the mouse button. To clear one or two tab stops, this method is faster than the – button.

>> You know that you can open the Tabs dialog by choosing Format⇨Tabs. What you may not know is that double-clicking anywhere on the horizontal ruler opens the Tabs dialog too, but with an added twist:

- If you double-click on the lower-half of the horizontal ruler where there's no tab stop, two things happen simultaneously: A new tab stop appears at that spot on the horizontal ruler, and the Tabs dialog appears with the newly created tab stop listed along with any others that may already exist.

- If you double-click an existing tab stop on the horizontal ruler, the Tabs dialog opens, but a new tab stop isn't created.

>> You can adjust all your tabs visually by selecting the text and dragging the tab stop markers left or right. As you move them, the selected text moves left or right in real time. We find this method much easier than working with inches and fractions in the Tabs dialog.

When you create or modify tabs using the Tabs dialog, you don't see the results until you click OK.

REMEMBER

Making your margins

To specify margins for a document, choose Format⇨Document. For a standard-letter-size document, Word sets the margins, as shown in the Document dialog in Figure 7-14, by default.

The shaded margin indicators in the rulers reflect the document's margins specified in the Document dialog.

You can adjust margins without even opening the Document dialog. To do so, click at the edges of the margins on the horizontal ruler or on the vertical ruler and drag them to wherever you want the margin. Or you can use the Margins section of the Layout tab on the ribbon to change the values for the left, right, top, or bottom margin.

TIP

Either way, any changes you make via the ruler or the Margins section of the Layout tab on the ribbon appear in the Document dialog the next time you open it.

One last thing: All these tab and margin options (and the indent options in the following section) affect the current document only. If you want to change any of these attributes for all new documents, open the Normal template and make the changes to it (as described in Chapter 8).

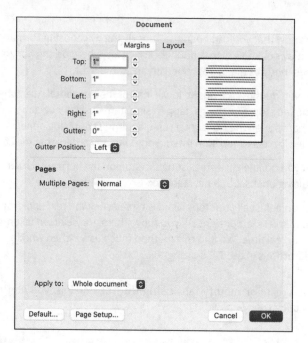

FIGURE 7-14:
The Word default
margins for a
standard
8½-x-11-inch
page.

Working with indents

The margins you specify pertain to the entire document. But sometimes you want certain paragraphs to have margins that are different than the rest of the document. To do so, follow these steps:

1. **Choose Format⇨Paragraph.**

   The Paragraph dialog appears.

2. **Click the Indents and Spacing tab.**

   The Indents and Spacing tab is displayed.

3. **Change the values for the left and right indents.**

   The left value in Figure 7-15 is set to .75 inch, and the right value is set to 1.5.

Another way to specify indents for selected text is with the indent markers on the horizontal ruler, as shown in Figure 7-16:

» **Left indent marker:** Drag this marker to specify where the left edge of a paragraph should appear.

» **First-line indent marker:** Drag this marker to specify where the first line of a selected paragraph should appear. If the marker is set to the right of the left indent marker, you create a standard indent, as you see at the start of a paragraph. If the marker is set to the left of the left indent marker, you create a hanging indent, with the first line of the paragraph extending into the left margin and all subsequent lines in the paragraph lined up with the left indent marker.

» **Right indent marker:** Drag this marker to specify where the right edge of a paragraph should appear.

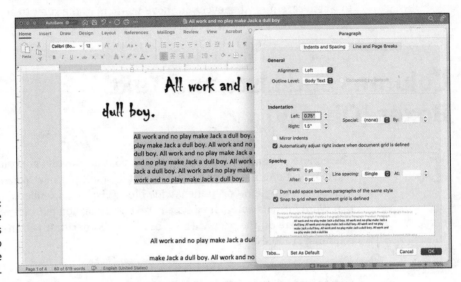

Left indent marker

First line indent marker

Right indent marker

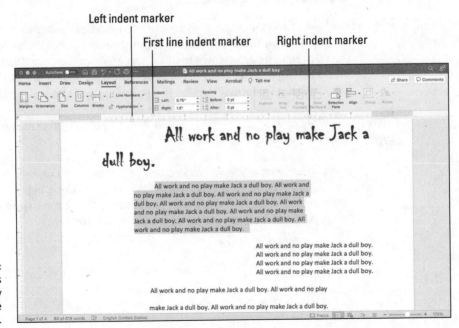

FIGURE 7-16:
Using markers to specify indents for the selected text.

The best way to see how to use these markers is to select some text in your document and drag each one around while watching its effect on the selected text.

WARNING

Indent markers can be tricky to drag. Sometimes, you accidentally click the left indent marker when you want to move the first-line indent marker and vice versa. Other times, you accidentally drag the margin indicator (the blue areas at the left and right ends of the ruler) instead of an indent marker. The point is that you need to watch carefully whenever you move markers in the ruler to ensure that you're getting the results you expected.

Columns and Lists and Text Boxes (Oh, My)

Three more options for formatting text in your documents are columns, lists, and text boxes. Columns let you display text in multiple newspaper-like columns, instead of a single 6- or 7-inch-wide block; lists are numbered or bulleted lists that Word formats automatically; and text boxes let you put independent blocks of text anywhere on the page without having to bother first with margins, indents, columns, or tables.

Column creation

The easiest way to create a document with multiple columns is to click the Columns button on the Layout tab of the ribbon and select the number of columns you want from its drop-down menu. Choose Two or Three and your text reformats itself into two or three columns of equal width, as shown in Figure 7-17. Or select Left or Right to reformat the text in two columns of unequal width.

TIP

If you're not in print layout view, you're switched to it after making your selection from the Columns drop-down menu.

If you select part of the document before you use the Columns button, only that part is displayed as columns. If you don't select any text before you use the Columns button, the entire document is displayed as columns. (And it's a darn good thing, considering that you see no columns in draft view.)

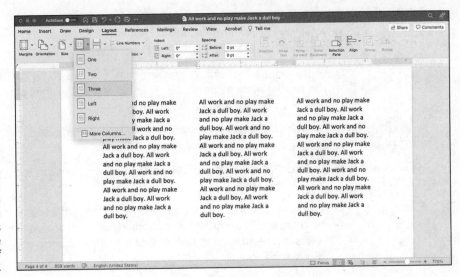

FIGURE 7-17:
Creating a
cool-looking
document with
columns like
these is easy with
the Columns
button on the
Layout tab of
the ribbon.

TIP

For finer control over the number and spacing of columns, or to have Word place a vertical line between them, choose Format⇨Columns to open the Columns dialog, shown in Figure 7-18. Its options follow:

>> Preset buttons for one, two, or three equal-width columns, Left (two columns with a wider left column), and Right (two columns with a wider right column).

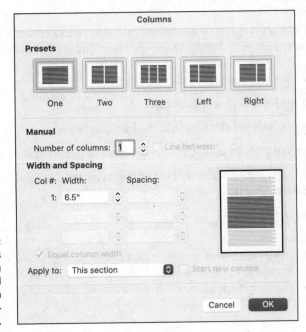

FIGURE 7-18:
The Columns
dialog gives you
greater control
over columns in
one easy-to-
access place.

>> A field for specifying the number of columns (which can be any number between 1 and 12).

>> Width and spacing fields for however many columns you've specified. Width controls the width of the column; spacing controls the amount of space between it and the column to its right.

Changing the values for any column's width or spacing changes the width or spacing values for all other columns. Be careful.

>> An Equal Column Width check box, which makes the width and spacing of all columns the same.

>> A pop-up menu that lets you choose to apply the dialog's current settings to the entire document or from the insertion point forward (so that everything before the insertion point stays the same and the columns appear only below the insertion point).

Lists made easy (and pretty)

Throughout this book, you see lots of numbered and bulleted lists. Numbered lists are typically used for presenting information that requires a chronological order, such as how-to steps; bulleted lists organize a set of separate but related concepts for high impact and easy mental digestion. If you need a numbered or bulleted list in your document, Word can help you format it nicely with little effort on your part.

If you've already typed the entries in your list and want to give them bullets, here's how (the same essential steps work for numbers instead of bullets):

1. Select the text you want to turn into a list.
2. Click the Home tab on the ribbon.
3. Click the Bulleted List button in the Paragraphs section.
4. (Optional) Click an Indent button to indent or unindent your list.
5. (Optional) Choose a different bullet character from the Bullets button's drop-down menu.

Figure 7-19 shows all these steps in action.

You can turn your text into a numbered list just as easily by clicking the Numbered List button instead of the Bulleted List button in Step 3 and by choosing a different numbering style from the button's drop-down menu in Step 5.

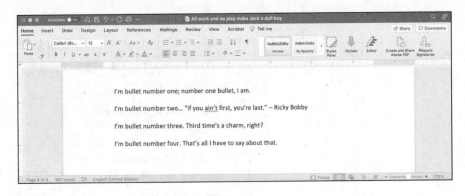

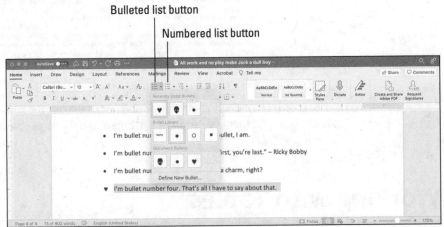

Bulleted list button

Numbered list button

FIGURE 7-19:
Before (top) and
after (bottom)
turning the
text into a
bulleted list.

Text anywhere with text boxes

Sometimes, you want to stick a chunk of text somewhere on a page without having to mess with margins, indents, columns, or tables. That's where text boxes come in. To place a text box in your document, choose Insert ⇨ Text Box ⇨ Text Box, or go to the Insert tab on the ribbon, click the Text Box button, and select Text Box from the options. The cursor turns into a special text-box-placement cursor.

Click and drag in the document where you want the text box to appear. Now type some text and format it as usual with the Home tab on the ribbon.

To control the way text in your document interacts with your text box — known as *wrapping* — click the Layout tab on the ribbon, click the Wrap Text button, and then select an option from the list, as shown in Figure 7-20.

WARNING

The items in the Arrange section of the ribbon's Layout tab — Position, Wrap Text, Bring Forward, and Send Backward, for examples — appear dimmed and are unavailable if the text box isn't selected (that is, showing its handles).

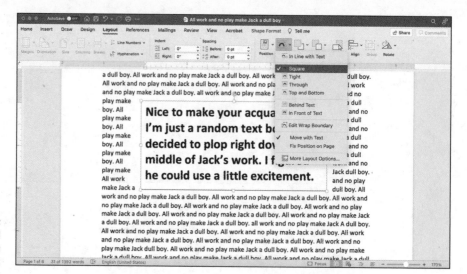

FIGURE 7-20:
A text box and
the Layout tab on
the ribbon.

TIP

The best way to find out about the options available on the ribbon's Layout tab is to click them and then try different settings and options as you watch their effects on your text box.

Working with Tables

Sometimes, the best way to present information is in the form of a table. Tables allow you to organize and analyze ideas or data that would be tedious to slog through and hard to comprehend in regular paragraph form. In Word, you can easily create tables — sometimes called *grids* — anywhere in your documents. In this section, you find out how to create and format tables.

Although tables are important enough to have an entire ribbon tab of their own, we have only so much space to devote to them here. That's the bad news. The good news is that much of what you find out about tables in the Excel chapters can be applied to tables you create in Word. So, be sure to check out Part 4 (Chapters 13 through 16) to find out more about Excel tables.

Whatever you do, go ahead and dive into creating and using tables in Word.

Creating a table

Word offers several different ways to make a table. Perhaps the easiest way is to click Insert tab on the ribbon, click the Table button, and drag down and to the right, as shown in Figure 7-21. The table appears in your document at the insertion point.

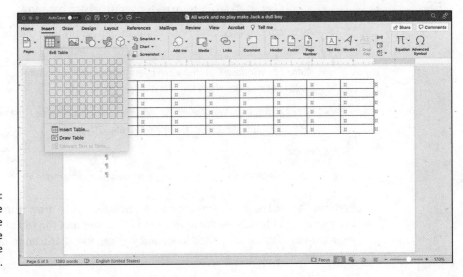

FIGURE 7-21:
Click the Table button on the Insert tab on the ribbon to create a table.

Another way to create a table is by using the Insert Table dialog. To do so, follow these steps:

1. **From the main menu at the top of your screen, choose Table⇨Insert⇨Table.**

The Insert Table dialog appears, as seen in Figure 7-22.

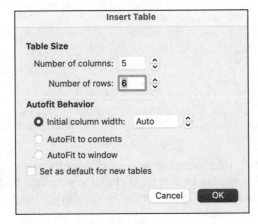

FIGURE 7-22:
The Insert Table dialog offers more options for creating a table.

2. **Specify the number of rows and columns you want.**

3. **(Optional) Set any of the following options:**

   - *Initial Column Width:* Determine the width of each column.

   - *AutoFit to Contents:* Columns expand automatically to fit the content you type.

   - *AutoFit to Window:* Columns are evenly sized and distributed across the width of the page from the left margin to the right.

   - *Set as Default for New Tables:* Select this check box to use the current Insert Table dialog settings for all future tables.

4. **Click OK.**

   The table appears in your document at the insertion point.

Perhaps the coolest way to create a table, however, is to draw it in your document by choosing Table⇨Draw Table from the main menu at the top of the screen. The cursor turns into a little pencil icon, and you can use that icon to draw the cells of your table, as shown in Figure 7-23.

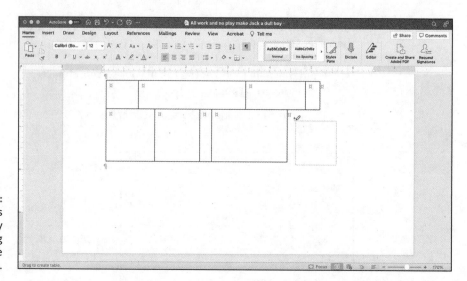

FIGURE 7-23:
Drawing a table is a fun but possibly more challenging way to create a table.

This method is useful for creating cells of different sizes, as we're doing in Figure 7-23, but it can also be a little tricky. If you're in a hurry or you know exactly what you want, you should probably use one of the first two methods described in this section instead.

TIP

On the other hand, choosing Table ⇨ Draw Table lets you draw new lines on tables you've created using one of the other techniques, so you can add columns or rows by drawing them. Using Draw Table this way gives you the best of both worlds.

Formatting a table

After you've created a table, you may want to change some of its aspects. Read on for a look at some things you can do to refine your table's appearance.

Dragging boundary lines isn't a drag

Lines in a table are called *boundary lines*. You can drag any boundary line anywhere you like at any time to resize a row or column. When you hover the cursor over a boundary line, it turns into a resizing cursor:

>> **Horizontal:** Click and drag with this cursor to resize the adjacent row.

>> **Vertical:** Click and drag with this cursor to resize the adjacent column.

To resize an entire table, hover the cursor over its lower-right corner. When a handle appears (it looks like a tiny white box), click and drag to resize the whole table.

After you resize some rows and columns this way, you may discover that you would prefer to have some or all of the rows or columns be the same height or width. No problem: Just select the rows or columns you want to affect and then choose Table ⇨ AutoFit and Distribute. Then choose Distribute Rows Evenly from the submenu to make the selected rows equal in height, or choose Distribute Columns Evenly to make the selected columns equal in width.

Using the ribbon's table tabs

The Table Design tab and the Layout tab for tables on the ribbon offer myriad useful options for sprucing up your tables. Start by selecting a table, cell, row, or column in a table and then click the Borders button on the Table Design tab. In Figure 7-24 we've selected All, so every cell has lines on all four sides.

The buttons on the table tabs that have a little arrow to the right of them (that is, AutoFit, Border Styles, Shading, Borders, Pen Color, and others) have menus associated with them.

Table Styles button

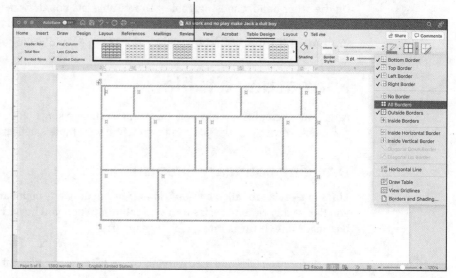

FIGURE 7-24:
The Borders
drop-down menu
gives you full
control over
every line in
your table.

The Table Styles button (labeled in Figure 7-24) is a little wacky (and much longer than other buttons), as described in this list:

>> It has *two* little arrows, one on its right and the other on its left (which might not appear until you've clicked through to the right), neither of which represents a drop-down menu.

>> Those particular arrows display the next and previous styles on the ribbon.

>> A third arrow *does* represent a drop-down menu, but it's below the Table Styles button.

Before we proceed, take another look at the Table Styles button in Figure 7-24. You don't see a little arrow below the Table Styles button, do you? That's because it appears only if the cursor is hovering over the Table Styles button, as it is in Figure 7-25.

Table Styles let you try a number of different "looks" for your table quickly and easily.

TIP

If you make your document window as wide as possible, you see more table styles on the ribbon than if your window is narrow.

We wish we had the space to show you how to use all the tools shown in Figure 7-25, but we don't. So, once again, we urge you to select some cells and spend time clicking every one of the tools.

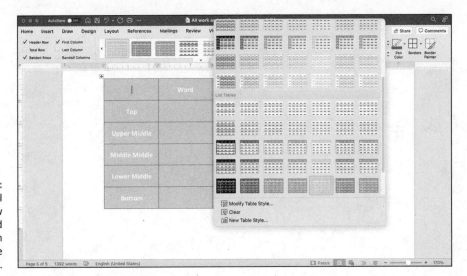

FIGURE 7-25:
The bashful
arrow below
Table Styles and
the myriad design
choices you see
when you click it.

Uncovering the (sometimes) hidden tools of the Layout tab for tables

Some, but not all, of the tools on the ribbon's Layout tab for tables (it's labeled *Layout* and is immediately to the right of the Table Design tab) are also available on Word's Table menu. Like the Table Styles arrow, the slightly shy Layout tab for tables comes out only when all or part of a table is selected, so you can easily overlook it.

That would be unfortunate. As you see in Figure 7-26, the Layout tab for tables includes a variety of timesaving tools. Because these tools are available also in Excel, you find out about them in Part 4.

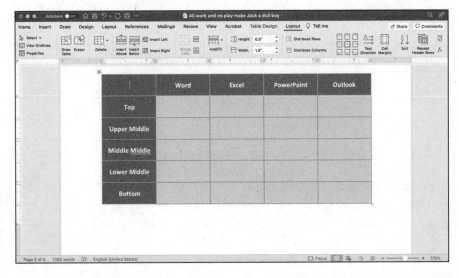

FIGURE 7-26:
The ribbon's
Layout tab for
tables appears
only if all or part
of a table is
selected.

Chapter **8**

This and That: Advanced and Collaboration Features

I n this, the final chapter in this part on Word, we show you some of its more advanced features and its collaboration features. By *advanced features*, we mean that they're mostly features you don't *have* to use. But if you choose to use them, these features can make Word easier to use and help you get more done in less time. And by *collaboration features*, we mean tools for people who work on documents with others, such as writers and editors, or co-authors in different geographic locations.

In this chapter, you find out about assigning styles to text elements. If you master only one feature in this chapter, this is the one to choose. Styles let you easily create documents with consistent formatting throughout. You'll never have to look back in your document to try to figure out which font you used for subheads or what size the body text is. Instead, using Word styles, all it takes are a few clicks to format the text the same as all other similar text. Styles make all your chapter titles look the same, your figure captions match, and your bullet lists look alike throughout a document.

You also discover how to customize some of your most frequently used elements, such as the ribbon and the Quick Access toolbar. We show you how to automatically generate a table of contents, an index, and other types of tables. Then you discover Word's excellent features for collaborating with others in composing and polishing your documents. Finally, we show you how easily you can use Word to address and print envelopes, create labels, and save documents as web pages (though the latter isn't one of Word's best features).

Going in Style: Defining Styles for Easy Formatting

Word styles let you apply formatting to selected text quickly and easily. For example, you might want every chapter title in your novel to appear in 36-point Helvetica font, bold, italic, centered, with 72 points of space above it and 72 points of space below it. Remembering all those characteristics, not to mention choosing and applying them every time you start a new chapter, would be quite a hassle.

Letting you skip all that hassle is what styles are for. Just create a style for chapter titles and you can format them exactly the way you like with one click.

The easy way: Defining a style by example

The easy way to define a style is to format a paragraph exactly the way you want the style to appear. When you're satisfied with the way the paragraph looks, select it (be sure to select everything that you want to include in the new style, including any intentional spaces or blank lines), click the Home tab on the ribbon (if it's not already selected), click the Styles Pane button to open the Styles pane on the right side of the window, and then click the New Style button. The Create New Style from Formatting dialog appears, as shown in Figure 8-1.

TIP

Another way to access the Create New Style from Formatting dialog is to choose Format ⇨ Style and click the New button in the Style dialog that opens.

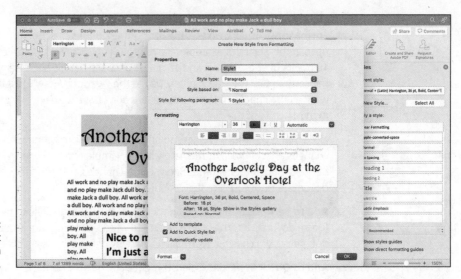

FIGURE 8-1:
The selected text
is formatted as a
chapter title.

The following list describes the items in the Create New Style from Formatting dialog:

>> **Name:** Type a name for your newly created style. We named this style Jack's Chapter Titles.

>> **Style Type:** Your choices are Paragraph, Character, Linked (paragraph and character), Table, and List. Choose whichever is appropriate for the style you're creating. (In this section's example, it's Paragraph.)

>> **Style Based On:** You don't have to worry about this option when you create a new style by example, as we're doing here. We tell you more about it in the next section.

>> **Style for Following Paragraph:** If you're creating a paragraph that follows a chapter title, for example, you might want it to be styled as body text with the Normal style. You select Normal from this menu and then, whenever you type Return after a paragraph formatted in the Chapter Title style, the next paragraph you type is automatically formatted as Normal.

TIP

The Style for Following Paragraph feature is powerful and useful. If you don't make a selection from this menu, the next paragraph looks the same as the current one. In other words, it's formatted with the Chapter Title style instead of Normal (body text). If you know that a certain paragraph style is always followed by a different paragraph style (such as a Chapter Title, which is always followed by Normal), specifying it on this menu saves you time and effort later.

>> **Formatting:** As you can see, the formatting options describe the style being used in this section's example: Harrington font, 36 points, bold, centered, with 18 points of space above and 18 points of space below. Because we formatted the sample text ("Another Lovely Day at the Overlook Hotel") just the way we want all the chapter titles to appear, we don't have to make any adjustments in this section of the dialog.

TIP

Note that if you make changes to any item in the Formatting section, those changes are reflected immediately in the sample text shown in the white box below the Formatting items. Sadly, these changes aren't reflected in the document until you click the OK button.

>> **Add to Template:** Select this check box if you want the style to be available in future documents. The style is added to whichever template is used by this document, which is the Normal template by default.

>> **Add to Quick Style List:** Select this check box if you want the newly created style to appear in the Quick Style list.

TIP

The Quick Style list, on the ribbon's Home tab, is a convenient way to apply styles. But because it has a bashful disclosure arrow, like the Table Styles button in Chapter 7, we feel obliged to call it to your attention, which we do (quite nicely, we might add) in Figure 8-2.

To recap, the disclosure arrow that summons the Quick Styles list appears only when the cursor hovers over the Quick Styles button.

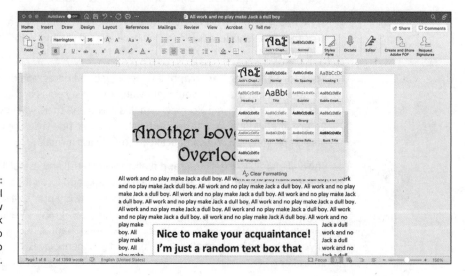

FIGURE 8-2:
Click the bashful disclosure arrow to use the Quick Styles list to apply a style to selected text.

>> **Automatically Update:** Select this check box if you want the Chapter Title style to update itself automatically if you change it. For example, if you select this check box and later decide that you want your chapter titles to appear in the Courier font instead of Helvetica, when you change the font of any paragraph with the Chapter Title style, the style is changed so that all paragraphs assigned the Chapter Title style appear in Courier instead of in Helvetica.

So now you know the easy way to define a style: Create a paragraph with the attributes you want for the style, select the paragraph, click the Styles Pane button on the Home tab of the ribbon, click the New Style button in the Styles pane, do your thing in the Create New Style from Formatting dialog, and click OK.

Now, to assign your style to a paragraph, place the insertion point anywhere in the appropriate paragraph and choose the style name from the list of styles in the Styles pane or the aforementioned Quick Style list on the ribbon's Home tab.

The harder way: Defining a style by dialog

The harder way to define a style is by choosing Format ⇨ Style, clicking the New button in the Style window, and then making selections in the Create New Style from Formatting dialog. You start from scratch and define the style by clicking and choosing its attributes.

WARNING

If you want to format an existing paragraph of text, do it the easy way, as described in the earlier section "The easy way: Defining a style by example." But if you decide to try the harder way, be sure to place the insertion point in an empty paragraph before you begin or else you'll format the paragraph it's in with your new style. (If you want to format a paragraph of existing text, it's easier to format it first and then define the style the easier way, by example.)

This is where the Style Based On item in the Create New Style from Formatting dialog can come in handy. For example, you might want to create a subhead style that's similar to, but not exactly the same as, the Chapter Title style. If you choose Chapter Title from the Style Based On menu, the New Style dialog populates itself with the formatting from the Chapter Title style. You can then modify it as you like.

Customizing Interface Elements

In contrast to some apps, the programs in the Office suite are extremely customizable. You're free to modify the included ribbon tabs and menus by adding or deleting items. You can also create your own ribbon tabs from scratch and even add or change keyboard shortcuts for most commands.

Customizing ribbon tabs and menus

As described in Chapter 3, you can add or delete commands from any ribbon tab or menu. To get started, follow these steps:

1. **Choose Word ⇨ Preferences to open the Word Preferences dialog.**

2. **Click the Ribbon & Toolbar button.**

3. **Select the Ribbon tab near the top of the dialog.**

   As shown in Figure 8-3, the dialog is divided into two sections: Choose Commands From and Customize the Ribbon.

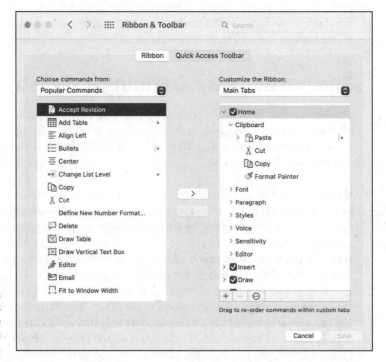

FIGURE 8-3:
Add commands to or remove them from ribbon tabs with ease.

4. **Select an option in the Choose Commands From pop-up menu, scroll through the list of available commands, and then click to select the one you want.**

5. **Select an option in the Customize the Ribbon pop-up menu, and then select the tab to which you want to add the command you chose in Step 4.**

6. **Click > in the middle of the dialog to add the selected command to the selected ribbon tab.**

To remove a command from a tab, simply select it under the Customize the Ribbon list and click < in the middle of the dialog to send it back to the commands list on the left.

7. **To save your changes, click the Save button in the lower right.**

You should now find your new command listed on the ribbon tab you chose for it to appear under.

Note in Figure 8-3 that the main tabs in the tabs list may also include tab groups, which are basically subcategories within the tab. For example, in Figure 8-3, we expanded the Home tab so you can see the Clipboard, Font, Paragraph, and other tab groups listed below it. Simply click > next to a tab group to expand its contents. You can place commands within tab groups by selecting the tab group in Step 5 instead of the main tab itself.

What if you'd like to move a command to a different location in a tab or tab group, or move it to another tab or tab group altogether? Good ol' tried and true drag-and-drop, at your service! Just click the command you want to move, drag it to the new location where you want it to reside, and then drop it right in.

Display or hide ribbon tabs and tab groups by selecting or deselecting, respectively, the check box to the left of their names.

Create ribbon tabs and tab groups

A cool trick is to create your own ribbon tabs and tab groups to suit your specific needs, as opposed to working within the confines of the predefined tabs. You can make tabs and tab groups that help you work efficiently on certain types of projects, or that contain your favorite commands in one easy-to-reach spot. Customize to your heart's content.

To do so:

1. **Choose Word ⇨ Preferences to open the Word Preferences dialog.**

2. **Click the Ribbon & Toolbar button.**

3. **Select the Ribbon tab near the top of the dialog.**

4. **Click the + button at the bottom of the tabs list on the right, as shown in Figure 8-4, and choose New Tab from the menu that appears.**

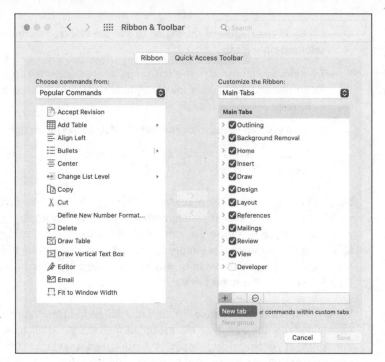

FIGURE 8-4:
Create your own
ribbon tab by
clicking the +
button.

5. Select the New Tab entry that now appears in the tabs list.

6. Click the Options button (three dots) at the bottom of the tabs list and select Rename from the menu, as shown in Figure 8-5.

7. In the Display Name field, enter the desired name and then click the Save button.

8. To add new tab groups to your new tabs in the same manner, repeat Steps 4-6 but choose New Tab Group instead of New Tab in Step 4.

TIP

Changes you make to menus, toolbars, and keyboard shortcuts (which we get to in a moment) are saved in the Normal document template by default, which is automatically applied to new documents you create.

Customizing the Quick Access toolbar

The Quick Access toolbar is a holding place for tools you need quick access to in any document. While the toolbar may sound somewhat like the ribbon, the ribbon is something you can show or hide, or you may use a different set of ribbon tabs in certain types of documents. The tools in the Quick Access Toolbar, however, are the same in every window.

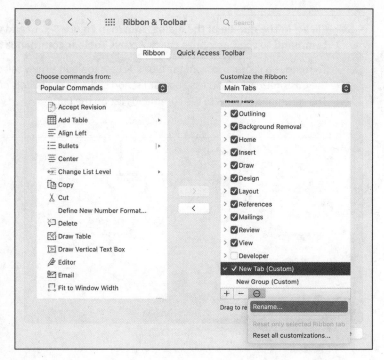

FIGURE 8-5:
It's important to
rename your tabs
and tab groups
so you can easily
tell them apart.

You can find the Quick Access toolbar, shown in Figure 8-6, at the top of every Word document window, just above the ribbon and to the immediate right of the red, yellow, and green buttons on the left side of every Mac window.

FIGURE 8-6:
The Quick Access
toolbar gives you
quick access to
common tools.

As with the other items we've discussed thus far, the Quick Access toolbar is customizable, too. Follow these steps to make modifications:

1. **Choose Word ⇨ Preferences to open the Word Preferences dialog.**

2. **Click the Ribbon & Toolbar button.**

3. **Select the Quick Access Toolbar tab near the top of the dialog.**

4. **Select an option in the Choose Commands From pop-up menu, scroll through the list of available commands, and then click to select the one you want.**

5. **Click > in the middle of the dialog, shown in Figure 8-7, to add the selected command to the Customize Quick Access Toolbar commands list.**

TIP

To remove a command from the Quick Access toolbar, simply select it under the Customize Quick Access Toolbar list and click < in the middle of the dialog. The command returns to the commands list on the left.

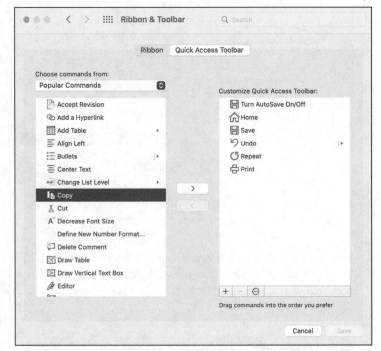

FIGURE 8-7:
Customize the
Quick Access
toolbar easily in
Preferences.

6. **Drag and drop commands in the order you would prefer them to appear in the Quick Access Toolbar, if you like.**

7. **Click the Save button in the lower right to save your changes.**

Any changes you made appear in the Quick Access toolbar.

Customizing keyboard shortcuts

Sometimes, Word doesn't have a keyboard shortcut for a task you perform regularly, or maybe you prefer to use a combination of keypresses that's different from the ones Word has. No problem: You can simply add or change the keyboard shortcut for any command:

1. **Choose Tools⇨Customize Keyboard to open the Customize Keyboard dialog, shown in Figure 8-8.**

Customize Keyboard

Specify a Command

Categories:

Commands:

| File |
| Edit |
| View |
| Insert |
| Format |
| Tools |
| Table |

Q Search

FormFieldOptions
GotoTableOfContents
InsertAddress
InsertAnnotation
InsertAnnotationCoAuth
InsertAnnotationInsert

Specify a Keyboard Shortcut

Current keys:

Remove

Press new keyboard shortcut:

Command+Option+I

Assign

Currently assigned to: [unassigned]

Description:

Inserts an address from your Personal Address Book

Save changes in: Normal.dotm   Reset All...   OK

FIGURE 8-8:
Assigning the keyboard shortcut ⌘+Option+I to the InsertAddress command.

2. **Select a command to assign a keyboard shortcut to.**

   To do so, you can either search for a command using the search field or select a category and scroll through the list of commands it contains.

3. **In the Press New Keyboard Shortcut box, enter the key combination you want for that command by actually pressing the keys on your keyboard.**

   As you press the keys, the box populates with the new shortcut.

4. **To assign the shortcut to the command, click the Assign button.**

5. **When you're finished, click OK.**

TIP

If the shortcut you're trying to assign is already in use by another command, you see which command it's assigned to just below the shortcut. If you still prefer to use the shortcut with this new command, go ahead and click the Assign button anyway.

You don't want to use a keyboard shortcut that's already in use by macOS, such as ⌘+Option+D for Hide/Show Dock or ⌘+Shift+Q for Log Out. Check the Keyboard Shortcuts pane in the macOS Keyboard System Preferences pane to avoid conflicts.

Creating a Table of Contents Automatically

Word can automatically create a table of contents (TOC) from a document. All that's required is to use styles consistently throughout your document. For example, you might choose to have four levels of headings (one that serves as the heading for a main topic and lower-level headings that divide your text into subtopics). To make all four heading levels appear in your table of contents, you assign a heading style to each one throughout the document. For example, the various headings that appear in the document shown in Figure 8-9 are styled as Heading 1, Heading 2, and Heading 3 (not pictured). If we tell Word to generate a table of contents, these styles will correspond to the heading and subheading levels that appear in it.

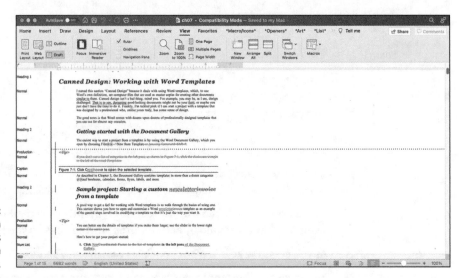

FIGURE 8-9:
Draft view of a document with its style names on the left.

REMEMBER

To assign a style to a paragraph, place the insertion point anywhere in the paragraph and choose the style name from the list of styles on the Home tab's Styles pane.

TIP

If you want to see the names of the styles listed to the left of any text formatted in that style (refer to Figure 8-9), choose View ➪ Draft. If you don't see them in draft view, open the Word Preferences dialog (choose Word ➪ Preferences), click the View icon, and type **1.5** in the Style Area Width field near the bottom of the pane.

This action tells Word to show those styles in a column that's 1.5 inches wide, which is what you see in Figure 8-9. The Styles Area remains visible in draft view until you either change this setting or click the line between the Styles Area and the body of the document and drag it to the left until the Styles Area disappears.

To generate a table of contents, follow these steps:

1. **Click at the beginning of the document so that the insertion point is placed before the document text begins.**

   You do this so that the table of contents will be inserted before the document text starts.

2. **Choose Insert ⇨ Index and Tables.**

   The Index and Tables dialog appears.

3. **Click the Table of Contents tab and then click the Options button.**

   The Table of Contents Options dialog appears.

4. **Assign the appropriate Table of Contents level to each of the styles you want included in your table of contents, as shown in Figure 8-10.**

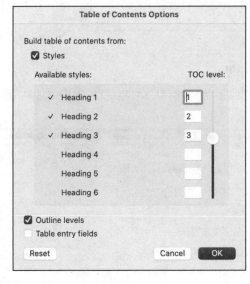

FIGURE 8-10:
Assigning three styles to a table of contents (on the left) with the TOC level assigned to each one (on the right).

5. **Click the OK button.**

   The Table of Contents Options dialog closes and the Index and Tables dialog reappears.

6. Select a format for your table of contents.

The Formal format is selected in Figure 8-11.

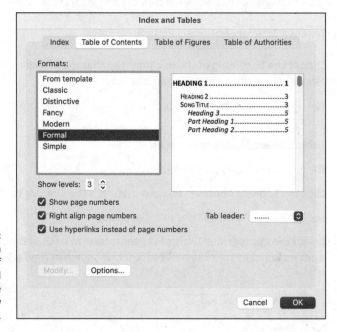

Index and Tables

Index   Table of Contents   Table of Figures   Table of Authorities

Formats:

From template
Classic
Distinctive
Fancy
Modern
Formal
Simple

HEADING 1 1

HEADING 2 3
SONG TITLE 3
Heading 3 5
Part Heading 1...........5
Part Heading 2...........5

Show levels: 3

☑ Show page numbers
☑ Right align page numbers
☑ Use hyperlinks instead of page numbers

Tab leader: ....

Modify...   Options...

Cancel   OK

FIGURE 8-11:
Word builds a formal table of contents that will look just like the preview shown here.

7. Click the OK button.

Word instantly builds the table of contents, as shown in Figure 8-12.

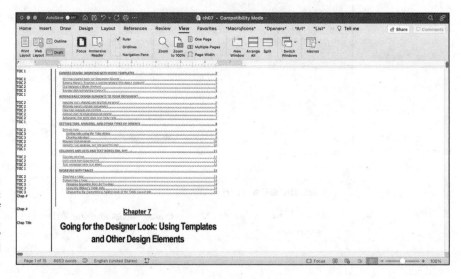

FIGURE 8-12:
A table of contents, automatically generated in Word.

Consider how much time and effort it would take to assemble that table of contents manually!

Think about the table of contents as you compose a document and assign styles to headings and subheadings. If you plan the table of contents properly from the start, creating it is a snap.

As you may have noticed, Word can also help you create these elements:

>> **Table of figures:** If you've assigned the same style to all figure captions in the document, you can automatically compile a table of figures (illustrations) in the same way you create a table of contents.

>> **Table of authorities:** Ditto for creating a table of authorities.

>> **Index:** You use this item to compile an index for a document.

Click the appropriate tab in the Index and Tables dialog to access these features.

Using Collaboration Features

Between the two of us, we've written more than 120 books and composed every one of them in Microsoft Word. The reason isn't that our publishers are Bill Gates devotees, but rather because Word offers excellent features for collaborating with other people.

Here's how it works: We turn in a chapter to our editor as a Word file. The editor makes changes and adds comments and then sends the chapter back to us. When we reopen the document, all the editor's changes and comments are highlighted on the screen so that it's clear what text has changed since we submitted the file.

Figure 8-13 shows a Word document with an editor's changes and comments marked up. Changes appear in color.

Looking at the figure, here's how to interpret those changes and comments made in the file by another Word user:

>> The black vertical bar on the far left side denotes a line with changes. When someone changes a single character in a line, you see a black bar next to that line to alert you to the change.

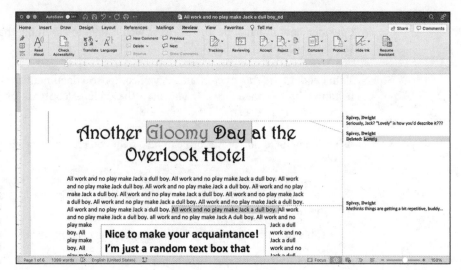

>> Deletions and comments appear in the markup area to the right of the text. For example, the original chapter title was changed from "Another Lovely Day at the Overlook Hotel" to the more appropriate and accurate "Another Gloomy Day at the Overlook Hotel," and you can see the deletion in the Comment box on the right. You can also see the other comments inserted by the other user.

Turning on the Track Changes feature

To make collaboration magic happen in *your* documents, follow these steps:

1. **Choose Tools ⇨ Track Changes ⇨ Highlight Changes.**

2. **In the Highlight Changes dialog that appears (see Figure 8-14), select the Track Changes while Editing check box.**

   The Highlight Changes dialog has three additional check boxes. Select them if you want to keep track of moved text or see changes in color on your screen or when you print:

   - Track Moves while Tracking Changes

   - Highlight Changes on Screen

   - Highlight Changes in Printed Documents

FIGURE 8-14:
These options
help you
determine how to
view changes
made to your
document.

3. **(Optional) Click the Options button to open the Track Changes preference pane, shown in Figure 8-15, and change the colors used and the types of changes to be flagged.**

4. **When you're done, click OK to close the Highlight Changes dialog.**

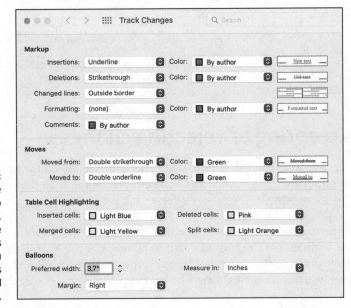

FIGURE 8-15:
Customize the
colors used to
indicate changes,
especially if the
default colors
don't help you
discern changes
quickly and
clearly.

To see comments in the markup area to the right of the document (refer to Figure 8-13), you need to be in print layout or full screen view. You still see the changes in the document in draft view, but you don't see the markups or the additional information they offer (Deleted or Comment, for example, and the name of the reviser, date, and time).

TIP

You can, however, see much of the same information if you hover the cursor over the changed content. Hold the cursor still for a second or two and a tooltip appears with information about that change.

Never fear: On the ribbon, click the Reviewing button to display the Reviewing pane, shown on the far left side of Figure 8-16. Unlike seeing the markups, you can see the Review pane in any of Word's views.

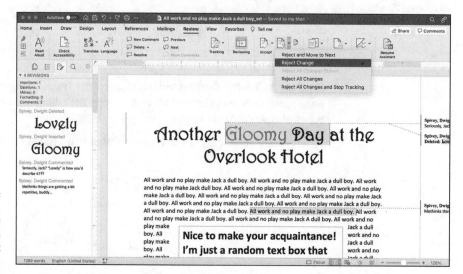

Accepting or rejecting changes

The reviewing topic is so important that an entire tab on the ribbon is dedicated to nothing but. When you need more editing oomph than the Highlight Changes dialog can provide, the ribbon's Review tab is there for you.

To review the changes in a document, first click the Review tab and then click at the beginning of the text you want to review. Use the Next or Previous button to move to the next or previous change, respectively, which is highlighted onscreen. Then use the Accept and Reject buttons to accept or reject that change.

Note that clicking the Accept or Reject button accepts or rejects (respectively) the current change, but both buttons also have menus containing time-saving options (refer to Figure 8-16).

Here's a quick rundown of some of the other buttons on the Review tab:

>> **Comments section:** *Comments* are notes from one author or reviewer to the others. If you select text before you create a new comment, the text it refers to is highlighted in pink (by default). If you don't select any text, the comment is placed at the insertion point.

To see a comment, hover the cursor over the highlighted text and the comment appears in a pop-up, as shown in Figure 8-17, in the Review pane, or in the markup area to the right of the document.

Review pane   Pop-up   Comments section

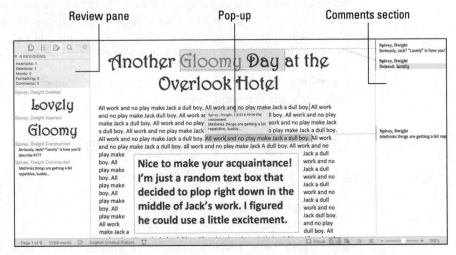

FIGURE 8-17: This comment is displayed three ways: as a pop-up, in the Review pane, and in the markup area.

>> **Tracking section:** Turn revision tracking on and off and control what appears on the screen while you work.

- *Track Changes switch:* Click to turn revision tracking on or off.

- *Display menu:* You have four options for viewing the document: Simple Markup, All Markup, No Markup, and Original.

  We frequently open a second document window (choose Window⇨New Window) and view Final text in one window and Final Showing Markup text in the other. Give it a try!

- *Markup Options menu:* Select the types of edits you want to see (comments, insertions and deletions, or formatting) as well as which reviewer's comments are shown (if the document has more than one reviewer).

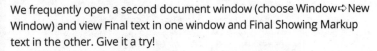
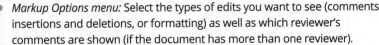

TIP

TIP

If you prefer other options instead of using the Next and Previous buttons, right-click (or Control–click) the changed text and choose either Accept Change or Reject Change from the contextual menu.

Addressing Envelopes and Creating Labels

Two types of documents that can be tricky to create and print are envelopes and labels. Sometimes, you need to be able to just whip out a printed envelope to a single recipient, though doing this with a computer can seem like a formidable task. (These are the times when you wish you had a typewriter sitting around.) Or you need to prepare a mailing for a bunch of recipients and the last thing you feel like doing is spending hours trying to set up address labels.

Fortunately, Word includes special tools that let you easily create addresses for both single envelopes and labels.

Creating and printing an envelope

To create an envelope, just follow these steps:

1. **Open a new, blank document by choosing File⇨New Blank Document or by pressing ⌘+N.**

2. **Choose Tools⇨Envelopes to open the Envelope dialog, shown in Figure 8-18.**

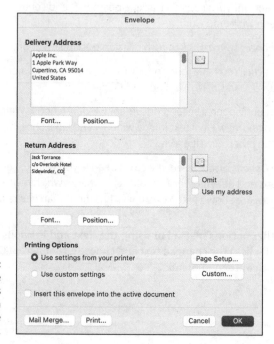

FIGURE 8-18:
The Envelope dialog makes making an envelope nice and easy.

3. **In the Delivery Address field, type the name and address of your recipient.**

If the address of the person you're sending this envelope to has been entered in Microsoft Outlook (see Part 5 for more about Outlook), you can click the little address book next to the Delivery Address field and choose that person's name. You can also allow Word access to your Apple Contacts when prompted.

The Position button next to both addresses opens a dialog in which you can position that address on the envelope. Use the dialog to reposition either address higher or lower or to the left or right.

4. **In the Return Address field, type your own address.**

If you've entered your personal information in the Word Preferences User Information pane and want to use it as your return address, select the Use My Address check box.

TIP

Use the Font button next to either field to change the font.

To print your envelope now, click the Print button. Otherwise, click the OK button, and a preview of your envelope will appear, as shown in Figure 8-19.

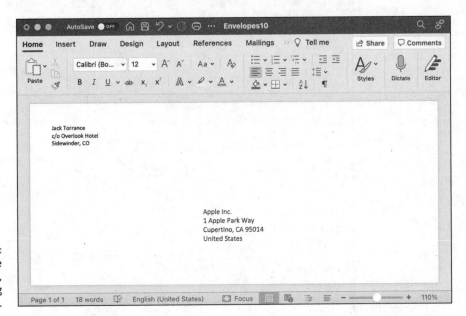

FIGURE 8-19:
An envelope document, awaiting editing or printing.

The document shown in Figure 8-19 is editable, so if you want to change its font or any of its information, just select the appropriate text and go for it.

If either address doesn't appear where you expect it when you print, use the Position button next to either field in the Envelope dialog to adjust the position of that item. If you can't get it to print properly that way, click the Custom button in the Envelope dialog to choose alternative envelope sizes or feed methods that may work better with your printer.

Creating labels

Making labels is as easy as making an envelope, and the process works much the same way. To create labels, follow these steps:

1. **Open a new, blank document by choosing File⇨New Blank Document or by pressing ⌘+N.**

2. **Choose Tools⇨Labels to open the Labels dialog, shown in Figure 8-20.**

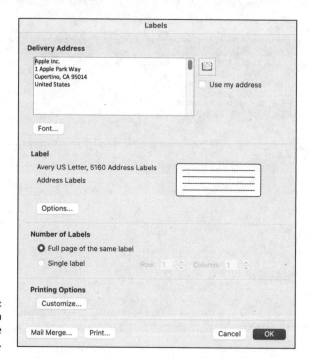

FIGURE 8-20:
Making labels is a
breeze with the
Labels dialog.

3. **In the Address field, type the name and address.**

If you've used Microsoft Outlook to enter the address, click the little address book next to the Address field, choose the person's name in the Office Address Book dialog that appears, and then click the Insert button. You can also use addresses of contacts in your Apple Contacts app.

4. **In the Label section, click the Options button.**

The Label Options dialog appears, as shown in Figure 8-21.

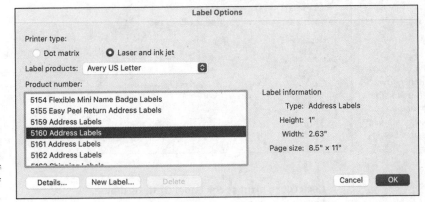

FIGURE 8-21:
Word knows how to create hundreds of different types of labels.

5. **Select the type of label you want to print. Or, if you don't find a label you want:**

a. *Click the New Label button to open the Label Details dialog, shown in Figure 8-22.*

b. *Name your new label and fill in all the fields to set it up.*

c. *Click OK to save the label and return to the Label Options dialog.*

TIP

Although the Labels dialog (refer to Figure 8-20) offers only one field for the contents of your labels, and that field is named Delivery Address, rest assured that you can create many other types of labels by using the Label Options dialog (refer to Figure 8-21). In fact, Word enables you to use hundreds of different labels by Avery and several other manufacturers. (Click the Label Products pop-up menu to see more manufacturers.) You can create name badge, file folder, ID card, and many other types of labels with a single click. But, regardless of the kind of label you're making, you still type the information in a field named Delivery Address in the Labels dialog.

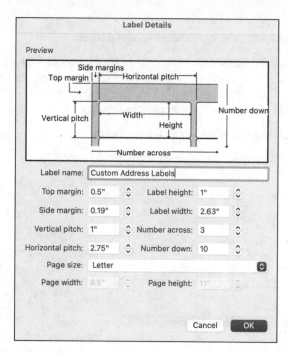

Label Details

Preview

Label name: Custom Address Labels

Top margin:	0.5"	Label height:	1"
Side margin:	0.19"	Label width:	2.63"
Vertical pitch:	1"	Number across:	3
Horizontal pitch:	2.75"	Number down:	10
Page size:	Letter		
Page width:	8.5"	Page height:	11"

Cancel   OK

FIGURE 8-22:
If Word doesn't
know how to
create the label
you want, you can
teach it how in
the Label Details
dialog.

6. **Click OK to dismiss the Label Options dialog.**

7. **In the Number of Labels section of the Labels dialog, choose to print either a full page of the same label or a single label at the specified position.**

   Refer to Figure 8-20, which shows the Full Page of the Same Label option selected. If you want to print a single label, select the Single Label option and enter the row and column number where you want the single label printed.

8. **To print your labels immediately, click the Print button in the Labels dialog.**

   Or click the OK button to see your labels onscreen, as shown in Figure 8-23.

The document shown in Figure 8-23 is editable, so if you want to change the font or any information in a label, just select the appropriate text and go for it.

And that's how you create a sheet of labels.

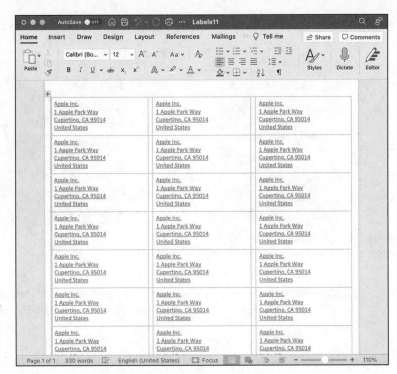

Creating Web Pages

Word lets you save any document as a web page. This feature was unreliable in previous versions of Word, but now it may be the fastest, easiest way to get Word files onto web pages!

TIP

We say that the Save as Web Page option in Word has improved, but it's still not the best choice for anything but the simplest of web pages. For "real" websites, any other tool — Dreamweaver, Wix, or WordPress, to name a few — is probably a better bet.

For what it's worth, most web page development apps, including Dreamweaver, can import Word documents, and all of them support copy-and-paste. Unless your web page is simple and your site is small, we think you'll get better results with another program.

That said, if you want to save a document as a web page in Word, just choose File ➪ Save as Web Page. A Save sheet appears, and you can save the document as an .htm file that any web browser can open. Figure 8-24 shows a Word document displayed alongside its web page version, which we opened using Safari.

FIGURE 8-24:
The original
document (left)
and its web page
preview (right).

If you need a quick page or two, give this command a try. And if you have tried it in the past and been disappointed, you might be surprised by how much better it is now.

3

Powerful Presentations with Microsoft PowerPoint

Discover how to dazzle your audience and impress them with your presentation prowess.

Use themes and layouts and take advantage of slide masters to reduce your labor and ensure continuity.

Add transitions, animations, and other effects to your slide shows.

Share presentations with other people in the most professional manner possible via print or digital documents and, of course, live.

Chapter **9**

Getting to Know Microsoft PowerPoint

P*owerPoint* is the Office app you use to create presentations, also known as slide shows. We'd be surprised if you haven't seen someone using PowerPoint to deliver a message to a group at some point in your life. Heck, kids have been using PowerPoint for presentations at school for years.

A PowerPoint *presentation* is a series of slides that contain text, graphics, video, sound, or a combination of any of these elements. You can display everything on a slide all at one time or introduce individual items on a slide one at a time. You can also animate the transition from one slide to the next. Used judiciously, PowerPoint creates attractive, appealing, and dramatic slide shows that you can use to sell, convince, persuade, inform, entertain, and more. Put another way, when you have a point to make, PowerPoint helps you make it memorable.

You can share a PowerPoint presentation with other people in many ways. You can

» Project a presentation onto a large screen for a large audience.

» Show a presentation on a TV or an external monitor connected to your Mac.

» Broadcast a presentation wirelessly to a streaming device, such as an Apple TV or a wireless projector.

>> Display a presentation on your laptop or desktop computer screen for a smaller audience.

>> Save a presentation as a video file, a Photos album, or a PDF document you can share with other people.

>> Share a presentation with others via websites such as SlideShare (www.slideshare.net/) or authorGEN (www.authorgen.com) or save it as a video file and upload it to YouTube (www.youtube.com).

>> Print the presentation so that you can provide it to others as a hard copy (sans any audio or video you've added, of course).

Furthermore, all PowerPoint files you create on the Mac work fine in PowerPoint for Windows, and vice versa.

In this chapter, we introduce you to the latest Microsoft PowerPoint for Mac and get you comfortable with its interface elements and how they work. You explore PowerPoint menus, the ribbon, toolbars, and palettes; check out the various views; find out how to navigate the program; and understand how to get a presentation started by organizing your thoughts in an outline.

Creating PowerPoint presentations isn't hard, but creating good ones takes some thought and planning. Don't worry: If you read the entire chapter, you'll know what you need to create a decent slide show — and how to avoid goofing up. So, without further ado, go ahead and start working with PowerPoint.

Viewing Slides with Various Views

You can view your work in PowerPoint in seven ways: normal, slide sorter, slide show, notes page, outline (discussed at the end of this chapter), reading, and presenter views. The program also has three master views — slide, handout, and notes — which we cover in Chapter 10.

You can choose any view from the View menu, or you can click the icons on the right side of the status bar of every document window to easily switch to any of the four primary views (normal, slide sorter, reading, and slide show), as shown in Figure 9-1. (That's pretty good thinking on Microsoft's part because these four views are the ones you use most often.)

The following sections take a closer look at each view.

Normal view

Normal view, shown in Figure 9-2, is your workhorse view and the one where you'll probably spend the most time.

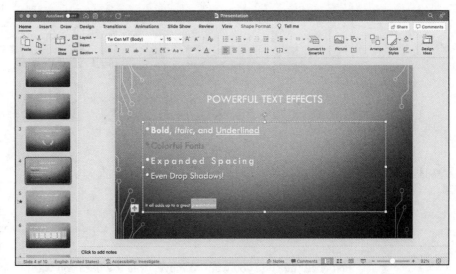

In normal view, you edit and format the text on your slides and arrange objects — text boxes, graphics, or both — on your slide. Note that in Figure 9-2, Slide 4 is selected in the left pane, which is known as the Slides pane. So Slide 4 is what you see and work on in the right pane. To edit a different slide, you just click it in the left pane and it appears in the right pane, ready for editing.

To make the Slides pane wider or narrower, first click the bar separating the left and right panes (refer to Figure 9-2). Then drag to the right to make the pane wider or drag to the left to make it narrower.

Also note that, in contrast to Word, which lets you type text directly into a document, all text on a PowerPoint slide is contained in text boxes. In Figure 9-2, for example, the text box in the slide is selected, so we can use its handles to enlarge, shrink, or rotate it. Also, the last word of text in the text box is selected, so we can apply font and paragraph formatting to the word.

We tell you much more about normal view in later pages and chapters, so we're leaving it at that for now.

Slide sorter view

Slide sorter view, shown in Figure 9-3, is just what its name implies — the view used to rearrange the order of your slides.

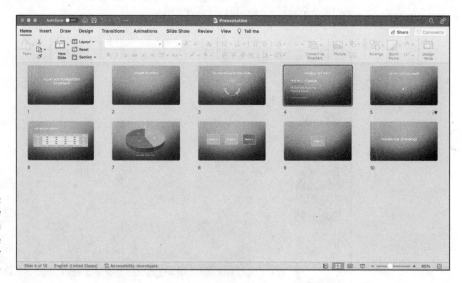

FIGURE 9-3:
Slide sorter view lets you rearrange the order of your slides.

Just click the slide you want to move, drag it where you want it, and drop it there. It couldn't be easier.

TIP

If you hold down the Option key, dragging a slide (rather than moving it) creates a duplicate of it. This is standard operating procedure in the Mac world when you're duplicating something.

You can also drag and drop slides in the left pane of normal view to reorder them. But reordering your slides is much easier when you can see all of them at the same time, as you can in slide sorter view.

Slide show view

Slide show is the view you use to present your slide show to others. When you switch to this view, PowerPoint hides everything else — the menu bar, document windows, toolbars, palettes, and other elements — and your active slide takes over the entire screen, as shown in Figure 9-4.

FIGURE 9-4:
Slide show view: a
full-screen
rendition of your
slides.

You can find out in Chapter 12 much more about the features you can use in your slide shows. For now, we want to tell you just one more thing — how to get *out* of slide show view.

You can do so in three ways:

>> Press the Esc key on your keyboard.

>> Click the options icon (a circle containing an ellipsis) in the lower-left corner and then select End Show at the bottom of the menu, as shown in Figure 9-5.

>> Right-click anywhere on the slide and then choose End Show from the pop-up menu.

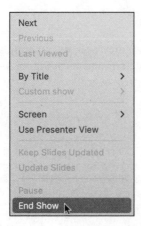

FIGURE 9-5:
Use this menu to
get out of slide
show view.

Notes page view

You can add notes to any slide, if you want. Notes page view displays your slide above a large area where you can type those notes, as shown in Figure 9-6. Heck — fling caution completely to the wind and drag graphics there, too!

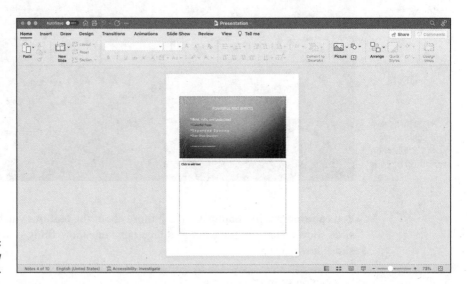

FIGURE 9-6:
Notes page view
= slide + notes.

TIP

You can also add notes in normal view, but the notes area is much, much smaller. To clarify, it's a very tiny area below the active slide. If your notes are longer than a few sentences, notes page view is a better bet.

The formatting and look of the notes pages is determined by the notes master, which we describe in Chapter 10. We also tell you more about working with notes in Chapter 11.

Presenter view

Presenter view, which is what the presenter sees on a secondary screen while slides are displayed on the primary screen, is shown in Figure 9-7. This view has a set of tools that provide additional control over your slide shows.

You can find out in Chapter 12 how to use these tools to deliver better presentations.

FIGURE 9-7:
Presenter view
makes presenting
your slides easier
than using slide
show view.

Reading view

Reading view, shown in Figure 9-8, is basically a simple way to read through your slide show without being in presenter or slide show view. A resizable full-screen window opens when you enter reading view; simply click each slide to continue to the next.

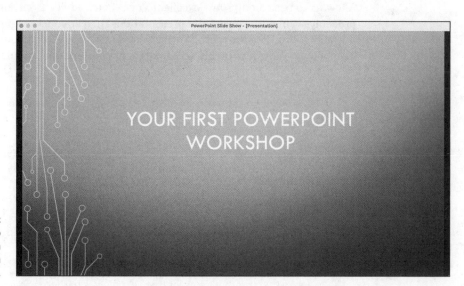

FIGURE 9-8:
Just click a slide to
progress through
your slide show in
reading view.

You can exit reading view in a couple of ways:

>> Press the Esc key on your keyboard.

>> Click all the way through each slide until the reading view window closes and you're returned to the view of your slides you were using before entering reading view.

If you click the red dot in the upper-left of the reading view window, PowerPoint thinks you want to close the entire presentation. If you don't want to exit the presentation, click the Cancel button when prompted to save any changes.

Planning Your Presentation: A Few Tips for Making Your Slide Shows Better

The rest of the PowerPoint chapters focus on designing slides and slide shows and delivering presentations. In this section, we offer some food for thought before you start creating presentations.

Use the 10/20/30 rule

Allow us to pass along some excellent PowerPoint advice from someone who has probably seen more PowerPoint presentations than anyone we know. We are talking about Guy Kawasaki, the former Apple evangelist and founder of Garage Technology Ventures. In his opinion, every presentation should adhere to the 10/20/30 rule:

A PowerPoint presentation should have 10 slides, last no more than 20 minutes, and contain no font smaller than 30 points.

Check out Guy's website at www.guykawasaki.com, and also give a listen to his fascinating podcast, *Guy Kawasaki's Remarkable People*, on Apple's Podcasts app.

Guy's three suggestions make a lot of sense:

>> Use the fewest number of slides possible to convey your message.

>> Take as little time as you can to make your points.

>> Be aware that text that's smaller than 30 points is hard to read from a distance and may not get your ideas across.

We suggest that you give the 10/20/30 rule some thought as you create your Power Point presentations. It certainly isn't the *only* school of thought: Some people believe that slides should have no bullets, for example, and others believe that presentations should have no slides. And, you'll surely want to (or need to) violate one or all of these rules.

Start with an outline

PowerPoint provides an outline mode that you can use to develop the first draft of your presentation, and we recommend that you use this mode. If you just dive in and start creating slides, you're liable to spend too much time making them look pretty and not enough time thinking about the message you're trying to deliver.

By using an outline, you can focus on organizing your thoughts and continue to refine text in the outline until you're satisfied that it gets your points across clearly. After you're happy with the outline, you can start turning it into slides. But until the prose is perfect (or close to it), we suggest that you don't even think about slides.

To create an outline, you can either start a new PowerPoint document by choosing File ⇨ New Presentation or open a presentation you've already created. Next, select Outline view from the View menu.

Outline view, shown in Figure 9-9, displays the text content of your slides in outline format in the left sidebar. This view doesn't show any graphics, freeing you up to see only the text they contain for better reading and organization.

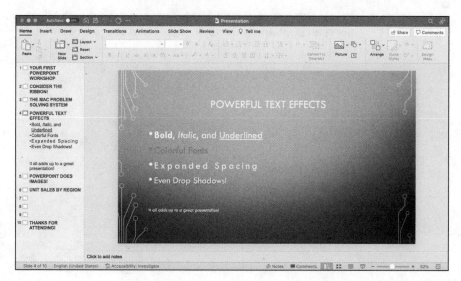

FIGURE 9-9:
Outline view displays an outline of your slides on the left side.

Just click to the right of the first slide icon (where we typed *Your First PowerPoint Workshop* in Figure 9-9) and start typing. Press Return at the end of each topic. To make a topic subordinate to the item above it, press the Tab key. To elevate the topic, press Shift+Tab.

Or, if you're more comfortable using the mouse than the keyboard, move the cursor over the box to the left of any slide title, topic, or subtopic. After the cursor is properly positioned over the box, it changes into the move cursor, which looks like a crosshair with arrows pointing up, down, left, and right. When the cursor changes, click and drag to the left or right to indent or unindent, respectively, or drag up or down to move the item to a different location in the outline.

TIP

Note that whatever text you type in the outline in the left pane automatically appears on the slide in the right pane. We suggest that you pay no attention to the slide for now. Just type the words and arrange them into slide titles, topics, and subtopics. Keep working on your outline until you feel that it tells the story you're trying to tell in the fewest possible slides and words.

Finally, you can import slides from an outline you've already created in Word. (Note that the Word document must be saved in Rich Text Format, or RTF.) After you decide on the place in the PowerPoint Outline pane where the imported material should start, click the slide at the spot where the slides should be imported. In the menu at the top of the screen, choose Insert ⇨ Slides From ⇨ Outline, and then select the outline file on your computer. Just remember to format the headline for each slide with the Heading 1 style and to format bullet points with Heading 2 through 9 styles before you save the Word document. Text that isn't styled with one of the Heading styles won't appear in PowerPoint.

Now you can start thinking about what you want your slides to look like, which, not coincidentally, is the topic we cover in the rest of Part 3.

Chapter **10**

Creating Slide Shows

I f you've read Chapter 9, you may have taken our recommendation to heart and, before you begin creating slides, given some thought to what you want your presentation to accomplish. In this chapter, we show you how to create a slide show. You start by choosing an appropriate theme, and then you explore slide layouts and the concept behind slide masters. You also find out how to make the text in your slides look great. You can add pizzazz to your slides by including SmartArt, charts, images, sounds, movies, and more. Finally, we tell you why everything on a slide should align with everything on every other slide, and then we show you how to make it so.

The goal of this chapter (and the PowerPoint chapters, for that matter) is to help you ensure consistency in every slide show you create. Themes, layouts, and slide masters are all tools that help you be consistent. You almost always want every slide to have the title and bullet points in the same place, the same font for titles, and the same color scheme.

We say *almost* because these rules have occasional exceptions. But for most slide shows, these rules apply most of the time.

TIP

If you insist on using a different font or color scheme on certain slides, or on changing the position of an object (title, text, or image) from its usual place on a presentation's other slides, make sure that you have a good reason to do so. Consistency makes your presentation look more professional, and inconsistency makes it look amateurish.

Getting Started

You can start creating your presentation with a blank slate by choosing File ⇨ New Presentation. Or, if you took our advice at the end of Chapter 9 and decided to create an outline, start with that file instead of a new presentation. Next, make sure that you're in normal view by either clicking the normal icon on the right side of the status bar, pressing ⌘+1, or choosing View ⇨ Normal from the menu.

TIP

As you work your way through the sections in this chapter, remember that you can always go back later and change anything you do. So don't sweat finding the absolutely perfect theme or slide layout right away. Just find something you can live with for now, and if you later decide that you don't want it, you can easily change it.

Giving Your Presentation a Visual Theme

According to Microsoft, a *theme* is a "predefined set of colors, fonts, and visual effects that you apply to your slides for a unified, professional look." PowerPoint includes a variety of themes you can either use as is or modify to suit your tastes. Furthermore, you can use these themes also in Word and Excel to give all your documents a unified look and feel. In this section, we show you how to do both.

Using a theme as is

To apply a theme to your presentation, select one or more slides in it and then click the Design tab on the ribbon. Move the cursor over any thumbnail in the Themes strip and the theme's name appears. Click a thumbnail and the theme is applied to all slides selected in the left pane, as shown in Figure 10-1.

TIP

To select multiple noncontiguous slides (such as Slides 1 and 4 in Figure 10-1) in the left pane, click the first slide to select it and then hold down the ⌘ key and click another slide. As long as you keep holding down ⌘, every slide you click is added to the selection. Or, to select contiguous slides (such as Slides 1, 2, 3, and 4 in Figure 10-1), click Slide 1, hold down the Shift key, and then click Slide 4. All slides between 1 and 4 (inclusive) are selected.

Note that if your slide show has a lot of slides, selecting slides this way is somewhat easier in slide sorter view.

Go ahead and click a few thumbnails to see how the theme looks when applied to your slide or slides. To see more thumbnails, click the arrow on the right side of the Themes strip. Every time you click it, you see another group of themes. To move backward through the strip, click the arrow that appears at the left side of the Themes strip.

You can see all available themes, as well as access others you may have stored on your computer, by hovering your cursor over the Themes strip and then clicking the hidden arrow below the strip, as shown in Figure 10-2. (You may recall running into shy arrows like this one in the chapters about Word.)

The number of thumbnails in each group is determined by the width of your window. If you make the window wider, you see more thumbnails in each group. (We always expand the PowerPoint window to fill the entire screen, but laptop owners with smaller screens may be wondering why they see fewer thumbnails than are shown in Figure 10-2.)

Customizing a theme's colors or fonts

Maybe you like a theme but aren't crazy about its colors or fonts. No problem: You can modify one or both of those attributes. To modify any theme, follow these steps:

1. **Click the Design tab on the ribbon.**

2. **Click the down arrow under the Variants strip (you'll need to hover your cursor over the strip to see it), hover your cursor over the Colors option in the list, and choose a color set, as shown in Figure 10-3.**

3. **(Optional) Create a custom color set as follows:**

   a. *Click the Customize Colors option at the bottom of the Colors pop-up menu.*

   b. *Click a color box that you want to change to select it, and then select a new color from the Colors palette.* PowerPoint updates the preview to show you the change.

   c. *Click in the Name box to specify a descriptive title for your new theme color set, and then click the Save button, as shown in Figure 10-4.*

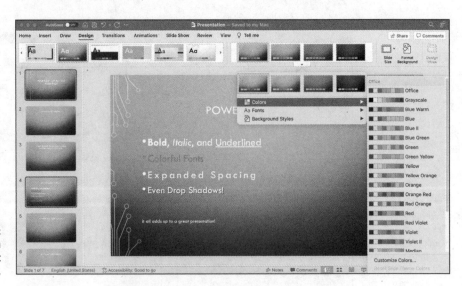

FIGURE 10-3:
Choosing a different color set for a theme.

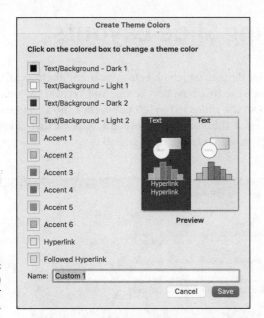

FIGURE 10-4:
Create your own
color palette for
your slides.

4. **Click the down arrow under the Variants strip (again, you'll need to hover your cursor over the strip to see it), hover your cursor over the Fonts option in the list, and choose a font set.**

   Note that every choice you make is immediately displayed in your slides.

5. **When you're satisfied with your choices of colors and fonts, click the arrow under the Themes strip and then click the Save Current Theme option.**

   A Save dialog appears.

6. **Type a name for your custom theme in the Save As field and then click Save.**

To use your custom theme later, click the Design tab and then click the custom theme in the Theme strip to apply it to your slides.

TIP

When you create a custom theme this way, it's available also in Word and Excel. To use the theme in one of those programs, click the Design tab and then click the Themes button. Click the custom theme to apply it to your Word or Excel document.

Using Laborsaving Slide Layouts

The layout of a slide defines which objects appear and their locations on the slide. Slide objects include the title box, text boxes, and vertical title and text boxes. To apply a layout, select the slides in the left pane, click the Layout icon on the Home tab, and then click a thumbnail. PowerPoint applies that layout to all slides selected in the left pane, as shown in Figure 10-5.

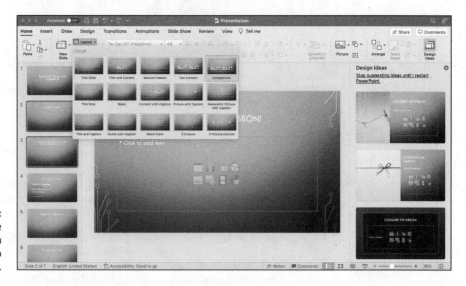

FIGURE 10-5:
Applying the
Comparison
layout to the two
selected slides.

REMEMBER

To select noncontiguous slides, click the first slide and then hold down the ⌘ key and click whichever other slides you want; to select contiguous slides, click the first slide, hold down Shift, and click the slides you want.

To summarize: Slide layouts define which objects (such as a title, text, picture, or footer) appear on slides that use that layout and where on the slide those objects appear. That's all well and good if you're happy with the layouts available from the Home tab. But what if you want to change something about one or more of these layouts, such as the title font or the footer, or add a logo to every slide in your presentation? That's where slide masters come into play.

Mastering slide masters

Slide masters ensure consistency between slides, regardless of their layout. To modify a slide master, you must first switch to slide master view by choosing View ➪ Master ➪ Slide Master or by holding down the Shift key and clicking the normal view icon on the right side of the status bar. From the keyboard, you can also press ⌘+Option+1.

In slide master view, the first slide in the Slides pane is the global slide master. Changes you make to *this* slide master affect all individual slide layout masters, which appear below it, as shown in Figure 10-6.

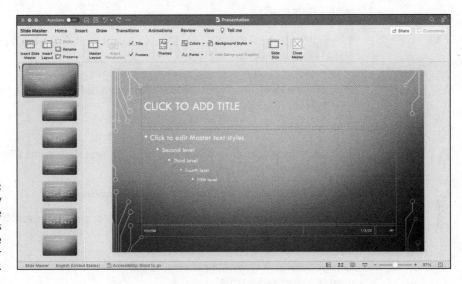

FIGURE 10-6:
You can modify
the global slide
master (as
shown) and the
slide master for
each slide layout.

TIP

Note that opening slide master view also causes the Slide Master tab to appear on the ribbon. You can use the Slide Master tab to quickly make changes.

For example, if you change the font of the Master title style on this slide to 48-point Helvetica Bold, the title of every slide layout would be in 48-point Helvetica Bold, regardless of which layout you choose. In other words, if a slide layout includes a title (not all layouts do), that title appears in 48-point Helvetica Bold because it's the font used in the first (global) slide master.

Here's another example: If you have an object — such as your company logo — that you want to appear on every slide, regardless of the slide's layout, add the logo to the global slide master.

Bottom line: If you want an object (such as your logo) to appear on every slide, or you want all objects of a particular type (such as title or text) to be formatted a certain way (such as 48-point Helvetica Bold) on every slide, you add the object or apply the formatting to the object on the global slide master.

Below the global slide master, you find the layout slide masters, each representing a different slide layout. The slide layout determines the location of objects such as titles, text boxes, and images as well as their fonts, backgrounds, color themes, effects, and animations.

If you want an object (such as your logo) to appear only on slides that use a particular layout, or if you want all objects of a particular type (such as title or text) to be formatted a certain way (such as 48-point Helvetica Bold) only on slides that use a particular layout, add the object or apply the formatting to the appropriate layout slide master.

To modify all slides, regardless of their layout, follow these steps to modify the global slide master:

1. **Choose View ⇨ Master ⇨ Slide Master from the menu at the top of the screen.**

   Slide master view appears.

2. **Click the global slide master, which is the first slide in the Slides pane on the left (refer to Figure 10-6).**

3. **Make changes to the global slide master on the right.**

   In other words, add an object (such as a logo) or change the font formatting of the Master title style or Master text style.

The changes you make appear on all layout slide masters (below the global slide master in the Slides pane).

TIP

If you were to click a layout slide master or several layout masters (by clicking the first master and then holding down the ⌘ key and clicking the others you want) at this point, your changes would be applied to only those layouts rather than to all layouts.

So imagine, if you will, that you make the following changes in Step 3:

>> Change the Master title font to Garamond.

>> Change the Master title color from white to red.

>> Change the Master text font to Arial Rounded MT.

>> Move up the title slightly to add some space between it and the text below it.

>> Add a logo by dragging an image file from Finder to the slide and then positioning the image in the lower-right corner.

When you're satisfied with your tweaks, choose View ⇨ Normal to exit slide master mode. You can then click any slide in the left pane to examine your work.

From now on, every slide will use the fonts, font colors, and logo image that you chose in Step 3, and as shown in Figure 10-7.

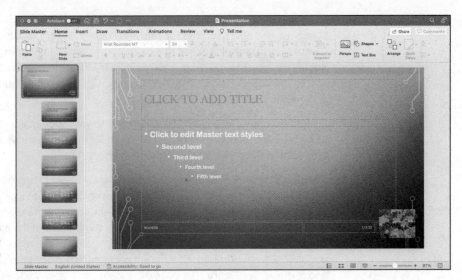

You should know about a few other concepts while working with slide masters:

» **Headers and footers:** To view the header or footer, choose View ➪ Header and Footer. The Header and Footer dialog appears, with check boxes that let you add a fixed or an automatically updated date, automatic slide numbering, and any text that you want to appear on every slide, such as copyright or confidential information. Click the Apply to All button when you're finished.

You can enable the headers or footers for individual slides and slide layouts, as well as on every slide. To have header or footer information appear on only certain slides, choose View ➪ Normal or View ➪ Slide Sorter before you choose View ➪ Header and Footer. Then select the slides you want to apply the header and footer to and click the Apply button (rather than the Apply to All button). The header and footer information then appear on only the selected slides. Or, to have the headers and footers appear on every slide, enable them on the global slide master.

WARNING

The Apply button isn't available in the Header and Footer dialog when you're viewing a slide master — you can choose only Apply to All. Apply is available only when you're using a view that allows you to select individual slides (namely, normal or slide sorter view), which makes sense if you think about it. Why? Because if you enable headers and footers for the global slide master or layout masters, they automatically appear on all slides (global master) or all slides with a particular layout (layout master).

» **Slide Master tab (on the ribbon):** When you're using slide master view, you might notice two items on the ribbon's Slide Master tab — Master Layout and Insert Placeholders.

Master Layout offers settings for Title and Footers. Simply click the Master Layout button and click either Title or Footers to enable (check mark) or disable (no check mark) them. You could instead select or deselect the Titles and Footers check boxes to the right of the Insert Placeholder button to achieve the same goal.

Insert Placeholder let you add layout objects to your slide master layouts by using the options Content, Content (Vertical), Text, Text (Vertical), Picture, Chart, Table, SmartArt, Media, and Online Image.

» **Slide backgrounds:** While in slide master view, you can change the background for any or all slides by clicking the Background Styles icon on the Slide Master tab. If you don't care for any of the default backgrounds displayed there, click the Format Background button at the bottom of the gallery to open the Format Background pane on the right side of the window, which lets you choose from hundreds of different background colors, gradients, pictures, and textures. See Figure 10-8. (While in slide master view, you can jump directly to the Format Background dialog by choosing Format ➪ Slide Background.)

» **Handout and Notes Masters:** There are separate masters for handouts and notes, which are discussed in more detail in Chapter 11.

Choose View ➪ Master ➪ Handout Master or View ➪ Master ➪ Notes Master to edit the handout or notes masters.

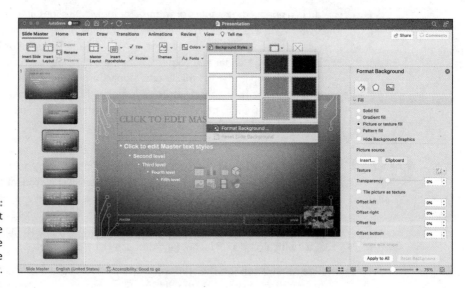

FIGURE 10-8:
The Format Background pane opens on the right side of the window.

Working with title and text objects

Boring presentations are a dime a dozen. Want to make yours capture and hold your audience's attention? This section walks you through various ways to dress up the text on your slides for a stronger effect, to make it easier to read, or to just make it prettier.

TIP

Everything you can do with your text on slide masters can be done also on individual slides.

To get started, open a PowerPoint presentation you've been working on or create one and then choose View ⇨ Master ⇨ Slide Master.

You can work with the features described in the following sections, whether or not you choose a theme for your presentation. For the examples we provide, we continue to use the modified Circuit theme and layouts that we use previously in this chapter.

The shadow knows: Creating a drop shadow effect

We're big fans of adding a drop shadow effect to text to give it a three-dimensional feeling and improve its legibility. Here are the steps to add a shadow to the Master title for a presentation so that it applies to every slide's title:

1. **Click any edge of the Master Title Style object so that it is selected and displays eight handles.**

2. **Select the text within the Master Title Style object.**

3. **Click the Shape Format tab on the ribbon.**

4. **Click the Text Effects icon in the Text Styles group (as shown in Figure 10-9) and choose Shadow from the pop-up menu.**

5. **Click a thumbnail to add a shadow effect to the title.**

   The shadow reflects the changes you make immediately, so play with them until the shadow effect looks good to you. Figure 10-9 shows the choices on the Shadow pop-up menu.

To remove the shadow effect, choose No Shadow at the top of the pop-up menu. You can also click Shadow Options to display the Shadow settings in the Format Shape dialog, where you can specify exact values for the color, angle, size, blur, distance, and transparency of your shadow effect.

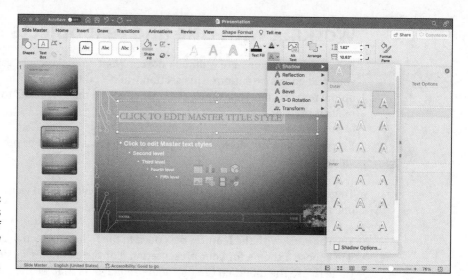

When you project your slides onto a big screen in a large room, the shadow makes the text easier to read even though the effect is subtle.

Getting your point across with bulleted or numbered lists

Chapter 9 talks briefly about bullets and lists, so let's get a closer look at them here.

Each theme comes with preset options for bulleted lists. As with almost everything about a theme, you don't have to accept the default options that come with a given theme. For example, although a plain old bullet character (a round dot) may do the trick, other characters might be more appropriate. Follow these steps to change the default bullet style to another bullet style:

1. **Click any edge of the Master Text Styles object so that it displays eight handles.**

2. **Select a text level (or select the entire block of text to change all levels).**

3. **Choose Format ⇨ Bullets and Numbering to display the Bullets and Numbering dialog.**

4. **Click the Bullets tab and choose the character you prefer.**

   Figure 10-10 shows the Master Text Styles object before and after changing the bullet character it uses in the Bullets and Numbering dialog.

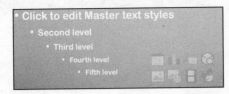

You can also change the color, size, and indentation of bullets on the ribbon's Home tab.

Or, rather than create a bulleted list, you can create a list that numbers its items automatically. To do so, click any edge of the Master Text Styles object so that it displays eight handles, and then select the entire bit of text. Choose Format ➪ Bullets and Numbering. Click the Numbering tab on the Bullets and Numbering dialog and you'll notice that it lets you choose from several different kinds of standard numbering (1, 2, 3), roman numerals (I, II, III), and letters (a, b, c).

TIP

One more thing: Although everything you may have seen to this point in this chapter has been in the context of slide masters, you can add and customize each of these features on individual slides as well. If you want to make a change or add something to every slide, make the change or addition to a slide master; if you want to make a change or add something to a specific slide or slides, make sure that you're working in normal view and not in a master view.

Working with PowerPoint Objects

In this section, you find out how to create and work with various types of media objects, such as SmartArt graphics, charts, still images, and movies.

In PowerPoint, every item on a slide is an *object*. The previous section, for example, deals with the Master Slide Title, which is in its own little box. That box is an *object*, in PowerPoint lingo. Master text styles are in a box; that box is also an object. Every element in the header or footer that's in its own little box is an object. And every SmartArt graphic, still image, chart, graph, and movie you add to any slide or slide master is an object.

When you create a new, blank slide, you can see that it has eight icons (called *content placeholders*) in the middle of the text box, as shown in Figure 10-11. These are shortcuts to add media objects, which we describe shortly. Note that some slide types (such as title slide, section header, and blank) do not have a content icon.

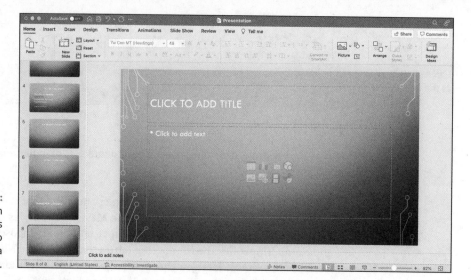

FIGURE 10-11:
The icons on
most new slides
are shortcuts to
add media
objects.

The top row of icons consists of shortcuts to creating a table, a chart, SmartArt graphics, and 3D models (from left to right). In the bottom row, they're shortcuts to add an image from a file on your hard drive, an image file from online, a movie from a file on your hard drive, and an icon from online.

WARNING

Just because you *can* add them doesn't mean that you *should*. Before you add any type of media or graphical element to a slide, ask yourself whether it improves your presentation or helps get your point across. If it doesn't, don't bother. You can waste a lot of time messing around with this stuff, only to conclude that it's tacky or doesn't add any substance to your presentation.

So think before you invest time in creating media objects for your slides. Keep this advice in mind as you read later sections on adding tables, charts, SmartArt, and other media objects to presentations.

Formatting tables

Sometimes, information is best presented in a grid made up of rows and columns, otherwise known as a table. PowerPoint has excellent tools for creating a table. To add a table to a slide, choose Insert ➪ Table, enter the number of rows and columns you'd like to start with, and then click Insert. The Table Design and Layout tabs appear on the ribbon; choose an appropriate table style from the thumbnails in the Table Styles strip in the Table Design tab.

Voilà! You now have an attractive table on your slide, as shown in Figure 10-12.

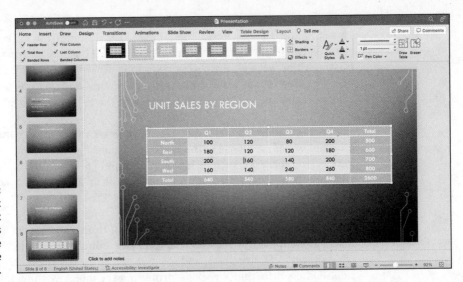

FIGURE 10-12:
This table of six rows and six columns reflects choices on the ribbon's Table Design tab.

For the table shown in Figure 10-12, we typed some values in the cells and then selected the options we wanted from the Table Options group on the far left side of the Tables Design tab. These options are Header Row, Total Row, Banded Rows, First Column, Last Column, and Banded Columns.

Here's what the options mean:

» **Header Row:** The header row is the first row and contains the labels for columns (Q1, Q2, Q3, Q4, and Total in Figure 10-12).

» **Total Row:** The total row is the last row and contains the totals for the columns (640, 540, 580, 840, and 2,600 in Figure 10-12).

» **Banded Rows:** The Banded Rows option shades alternating rows differently to provide contrast and make it easier to discern individual rows from their neighbors. In Figure 10-12, for example, the East and West rows are slightly lighter than the North and South rows.

» **First Column:** The first column is the first column (of course) and contains labels for the rows (North, East, South, West, and Total in Figure 10-12).

» **Last Column:** The last column is the last column (clever, no?) and contains the totals for the rows (500, 600, 700, 800, and 2,600 in Figure 10-12).

» **Banded Columns:** The Banded Columns option shades alternating columns differently to provide contrast and make it easier to discern each individual column from its neighbors. This option isn't enabled in Figure 10-12.

Choosing the Header Row, Total Row, First Column, or Last Column option changes two qualities about the row or column. First, the values appear in a contrasting color. Second, the row or column is separated from the other values by a line. The idea is that these options make the first and last row and first and last column stand out and appear different from the rest of the data.

After you create a table and add data to it, you can click other thumbnails to try different styles or choose Format ⇨ Font to make changes to individual attributes in selected table text, such as font size and font color. From the Table Design tab, you can change border color and shading fill or add effects to the table frame itself.

The ready-made table styles save you a lot of time. After we clicked Insert in the Insert Table dialog, it took us less than five minutes to create the nice-looking table shown in Figure 10-12, and most of that time was spent entering data. Considering how little time we spent formatting the table, we think it looks darn nice.

Creating a chart

Sometimes, a graphical representation of numerical data conveys information better than a grid full of numbers. If so, a chart may be just the ticket. To add a chart to a slide, follow these steps:

1. **Click the Insert tab on the ribbon.**

2. **Choose a chart type by clicking the Chart icon.**

   Click the appropriate type of chart for the data this chart will represent. Your choices are Column, Bar, Line, Area, Pie, Treemap, Sunburst, Histogram, Pareto, Box and Whisker, X Y (Scatter), Waterfall, Funnel, Stock, Surface, Radar, and Filled Map.

3. **Choose a chart style by clicking its thumbnail.**

   Each chart type has several styles. When you click a thumbnail, Microsoft Excel automatically opens with sample chart data for that chart type and style, ready for you to edit.

Here are the steps to create a simple chart:

1. **Select the data in the first two columns of the table shown earlier, in Figure 10-12.**

2. **Choose Edit ⇨ Copy to copy the data to the clipboard.**

3. **Switch to Microsoft Excel, which opened automatically when you clicked the thumbnail in Step 3 of the preceding set of instructions.**

4. **Click in the first cell of the sample data (North, in Figure 10-12).**

5. **Choose Edit ⇨ Paste to paste the data into Excel.**

    It replaces the sample chart data, and the result should look something like Figure 10-13.

	A	B
1		Q1
2	North	100
3	East	180
4	South	200
5	West	160

FIGURE 10-13:
We pasted this data into Excel to generate a chart.

When we switched back to PowerPoint, a pie chart depicting first-quarter sales by region had been created automatically. We clicked the chart to select it and clicked the Chart Design tab on the ribbon, clicked the Add Chart Element button on the left, and then clicked Data Labels to add data labels, as shown in Figure 10-14.

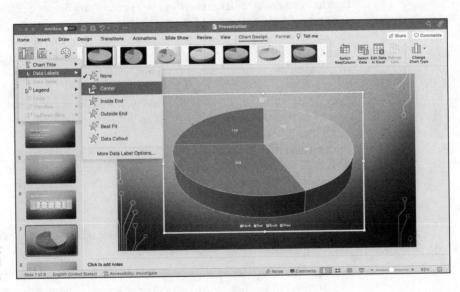

FIGURE 10-14:
Click the Chart Design tab to add data labels.

Next, we clicked the white frame surrounding the pie chart to select it, and then clicked the Home tab on the ribbon, where we made the data label font larger. Figure 10-15 is the final result.

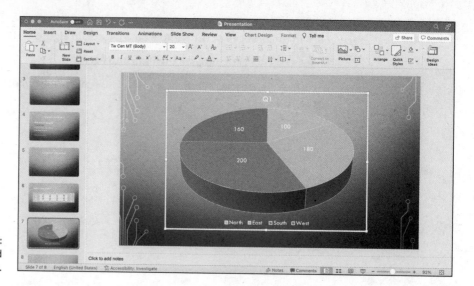

FIGURE 10-15:
The finished
chart.

WARNING

Be careful where you double-click items in slides. One of several slightly different panes could open, depending on which part of the chart you double-click. For example, double-click an individual pie slice to display Format Data Point, double-click the pie to see Format Data Series, double-click a data label (assuming that you enabled data labels in the Format Data Series or Data Point pane) to see Format Data Labels, and double-click the box surrounding the chart to see Format Chart Area. In this example, double-clicking the middle of the pie would open the Format Data Series pane, whereas double-clicking an individual pie slice would open the Format Data Point pane.

The point is to make sure that the pane you want is the one that opens when you double-click. Otherwise, your results might not be what you expect.

You can also use the icons on the Chart Design and Format tabs to modify many aspects of your chart. When a chart or any component of a chart, such as labels, pie slices, or the legend, is selected, the Chart Design and Format tabs offer several options you'll use often:

>> **Chart element styles:** Choose different color schemes for your chart and its background.

>> **Current selection:** After you select the target from the list box, click the Format tab and use its myriad options to enable or disable options specific to that item, including number formats, data labels, and a legend, or change the title of the chart.

>> **Text styles:** Also in the Format tab, the icons in this group make it easy to customize the color, fill pattern, and effects for the text in your chart.

You can see these options in Figure 10-16.

FIGURE 10-16:
The Format tab is available when you're working with a chart.

TIP

Because we don't have the space to cover every chart option on the Chart Design and Format tabs and their subtabs, we encourage you to select different parts of your charts and check out the options. Also, double-click (or right-click) different parts of your charts to open and explore the options you find in the various Format dialogs.

One more thing: If you created a chart in Excel before you started working on a slide show, you can use the chart in your presentation by selecting it in Excel, choosing Edit ➪ Copy to copy it to the clipboard, and then switching to your PowerPoint presentation and choosing Edit ➪ Paste to paste it onto the current slide.

Get smart: Use SmartArt

Sometimes, you need to convey information that is more meaningful as an illustration than as bullet points, such as an organizational chart, flow chart, a matrix, a pyramid chart, or a process chart. The PowerPoint feature SmartArt Graphics helps you create these types of graphics quickly and easily. You can start with information from a bulleted list or create a blank graphic and add text to it later. Either way, you end up with a slide that's more interesting and probably more informative than plain text.

Figure 10-17 shows a slide before and after applying a SmartArt graphic.

With almost no effort on your part, you can change a boring all-text slide into a dynamic graphical slide.

To use SmartArt graphics in a slide, start by selecting existing text — or not. If you select text before you take the next step, that text appears in your graphic. That's how we did it in Figure 10-17. If you don't select some text before the next step, you create an empty SmartArt graphic with no text in it yet.

The next step: From the ribbon's Insert tab, click the Convert to SmartArt button, and then click a style icon to specify the arrangement of the elements in the graphic. In Figure 10-17, we chose the Basic Process style from the pop-up thumbnail display; in Figure 10-18, we clicked Cycle and then chose the Text Cycle style.

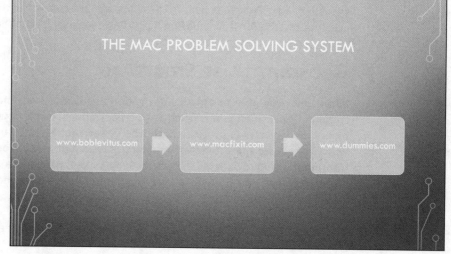

FIGURE 10-17:
The original all-text slide (top) is boring; the SmartArt rendition of the same information (bottom) is dynamic and exciting.

Click a SmartArt object to select it and a frame surrounds it (refer to Figure 10-18). The little dots in the corners and the middle of each side are handles; click and drag them to resize the entire graphic.

If you click the little arrow icon hanging off the upper-left corner of the frame, you also see a text pane with a bulleted list of the items that appear in the Smart-Art graphic (refer to Figure 10-18). When you select one of them, the corresponding item in the graphic is also selected. Or you can select an item in the graphic by clicking it in the graphic. When items are selected, you can resize them by dragging their handles, or you can apply formatting from the Format tab.

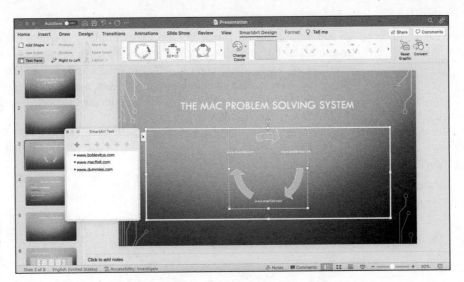

FIGURE 10-18:
A SmartArt
graphic with the
Text Cycle style
applied to it.

You can also change the color, style, or shape of SmartArt, using the icons in the SmartArt Design tab and in the SmartArt Format tab.

Finally, if you click a SmartArt graphic on a slide, you can change it to any other SmartArt graphic by clicking a different SmartArt graphic thumbnail from the thumbnail strip on the SmartArt Design tab. If you don't like it, choose Edit ⇨ Undo (the shortcut is ⌘+Z) and try a different one.

TIP

We encourage you to check out all the icons on the SmartArt Design and Format tabs. Using SmartArt instead of text on some slides makes your presentation stand out and gives it more visual appeal than if it were just plain ol' text.

More media: Adding images, movies, or sounds

Adding media to your presentation is easy: Just drag an image file, a movie file, or a sound file from Finder onto the slide you want it to appear on.

But wait — there's more! Alternatively, you can click the content placeholder icon for the type of media file you want to add to the slide. (As mentioned earlier in this chapter, the media file icons are in the bottom row of icons in the middle of most slides.) PowerPoint displays an Open File dialog for photos, clip art, or movies.

Now suppose that you want to select a photo from your Photos library, a Garage-Band jingle, or an iMovie project that you're working on? No problem: Microsoft provides the Pictures, Video, and Audio icons on the ribbon's Insert tab. To select an audio file from the Music library, for example, you would click the Audio icon on the Insert tab and choose Audio Browser. Figure 10-19 shows the snazzy window that appears, where you can listen to tracks and choose just the right audio. (Note that you can also switch to photos, movies, and clip art from the icons at the top of the Media browser window.) After you locate the perfect media, drag it from the Media browser window to the slide.

FIGURE 10-19: Adding a sound file to a slide.

No matter what type of media you're adding, a subtab appears on the ribbon that provides you with formatting options specific to images, audio, or movies. In the audio file example, we need to specify whether we want the sound file to start automatically when the slide appears or only after we click the file. Click the Playback tab (if you don't see it, be sure to select the audio file in your slide), and then click the Start pop-up menu to make the call. Because we chose Automatically, the audio file is heard when this slide comes on the screen during a presentation. (If you prefer to trigger the sound or movie manually, click the Start pop-up menu and choose When Clicked On.)

Staying with the Playback tab (shown in Figure 10-20), you can also specify whether the audio should loop and whether the audio icon (which looks like a speaker) should be visible or hidden during your presentation.

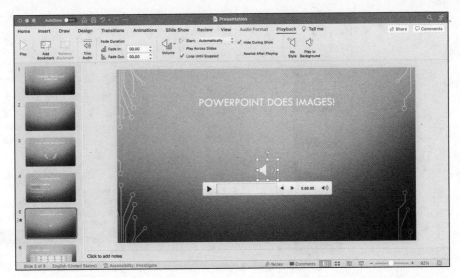

FIGURE 10-20:
You can set
media-specific
options from the
Playback subtab.

Which method of adding media to a slide should you use? It's all up to you — if you know exactly what to add, just drag the file directly from the Finder window. However, if you need to sample your media libraries before making a selection, the Media browser window is the perfect option.

Regardless of how you add the media file, we encourage you to explore the Format tab for that type of media. You'll find a number of helpful options that PowerPoint provides for customizing the media's appearance and function.

Using Quick Styles and Effects

Here's a trick for making objects look better on slides. Use the Quick Styles icon on the Home tab. The Quick Styles pop-up menu appears in the Format group and is shown in all its glory in Figure 10-21.

You have a thumbnail menu of Quick Styles to choose from. To use them on any object (or multiple objects) on a slide, select the object(s) and then click an effect button to apply it to the selected object(s).

There are other effects that you can apply to elements in your slides by using the ribbon's Format tab.

TIP

Don't forget the Undo command (choose Edit⇨ Undo or press ⌘+Z) if you decide that you don't care for an effect after you've applied it.

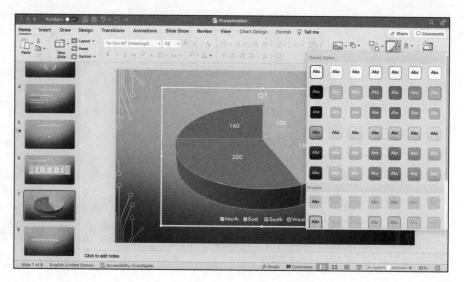

FIGURE 10-21:
Quick Styles are
just what their
name implies.

A picture is worth a zillion words here, so take a gander at Figure 10-22, which shows a bunch of objects on a slide before and after applying effects.

Following is a description of the styles and effects we used for each object:

>> **Quick Styles Demo (slide title):** We selected a thumbnail from the Quick Styles menu on the Home tab.

>> **Sample Text 1a:** On the Shape Format tab (which appears in the ribbon when text or a shape is selected), we chose the Reflection submenu, and then the Full Reflection and Touching options.

>> **Sample Text 1b:** On the Shape Format tab, we chose the Shadow submenu, and then the Outside and Top right options.

>> **Sample Text 2:** On the Shape Format tab, we chose the 3-D Rotation submenu, and then the Isometric Left Down option.

>> **Image:** On the Picture Format tab, we chose the Bevel submenu, and then the Art Deco and 3-D Rotation option and the Perspective Contrasting Left option.

Quick Styles are quick, easy to use, and all you need to spiff up a slide most of the time. In the unlikely event that you can't find a style or an effect that's perfect for your needs, apply one that's close and then right-click the object and click Format Text, Format Picture, or Format Shape. Figure 10-23 shows the Format Picture task pane.

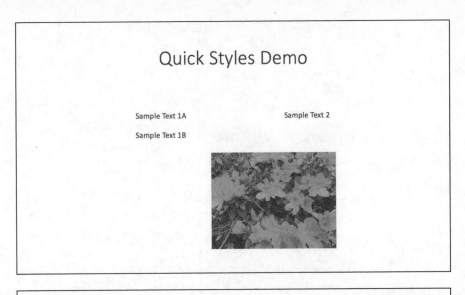

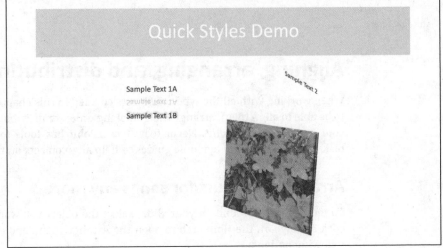

FIGURE 10-22:
Before (top) and
after (bottom)
applying Quick
Styles and other
effects.

If you can't make your picture look exactly the way you want by using the Format task pane, it probably isn't possible in PowerPoint.

We recommend that you spend some time clicking objects to select them and then looking at the formatting options available on the Format tab.

TIP

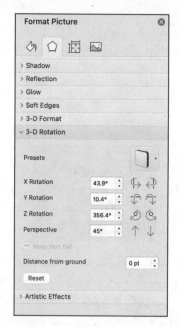

FIGURE 10-23:
The Format
Picture task pane.

Aligning, arranging, and distributing objects

When working with all the types of objects covered in this chapter, you may want to be able to align them, arrange their stacking order, or distribute them evenly on your slides at some point. Never fear: PowerPoint has tools for doing all three tasks. Plus, it has nifty dynamic guides to help align objects on the fly.

Arranging isn't just for songs any more

To move objects around on your slide, select the object you want to move. Next, click Arrange on the Home tab to open the Arrange menu and choose one of the following options:

>> **Bring to Front:** Brings the selected object to the front of all other objects on the slide

>> **Send to Back:** The opposite of Bring to Front; sends the selected object *behind* all other objects on the slide

>> **Bring Forward:** Brings the selected object forward one layer

>> **Send Backward:** Sends the selected object back one layer

For example, suppose that Object C is behind two other objects, but you want it to appear in front of them. No problem: Just select Object C and then, with the Arrange menu open, choose Bring to Front, as shown in Figure 10-24.

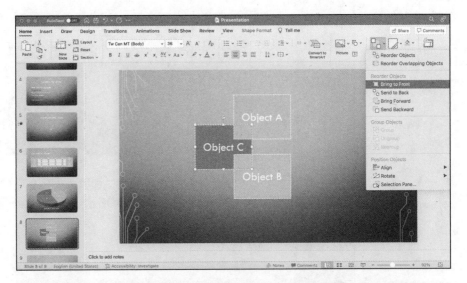

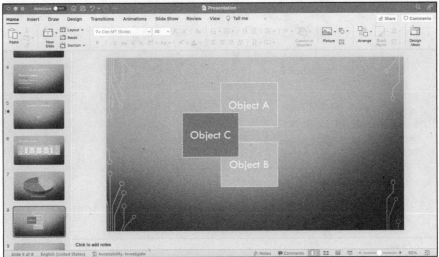

FIGURE 10-24:
Object C before
(top) and after
(bottom) being
brought to the
front.

Presto! Object C is now in front of both the other objects.

Figure 10-25 shows what happens if you choose Bring Forward instead of Bring to Front. Object C is now in front of Object B but behind Object A, as shown in the figure.

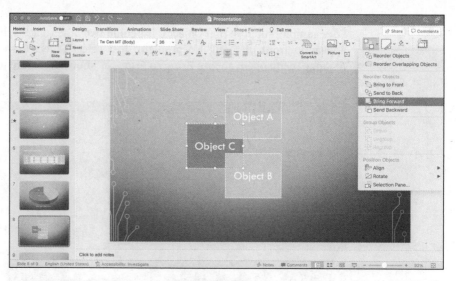

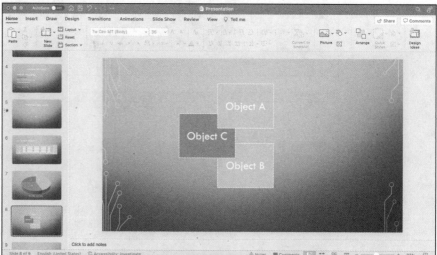

And that's that. Those four commands on the Arrange menu are the key to arranging the stacking order of objects on a slide.

Alignment isn't just for car wheels any more

Suppose that you don't care about the stacking order but you want the bottoms of three objects to align. Again, no problem. Select the three objects (hold down the Shift key as you click them) and then click Arrange. Now choose Align Bottom from the Align submenu to produce the results you see in Figure 10-26.

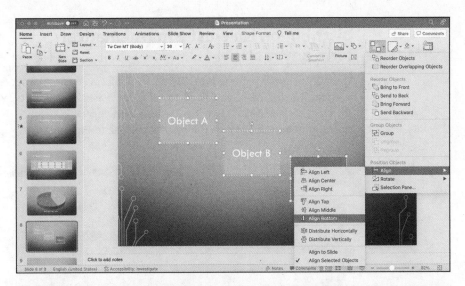

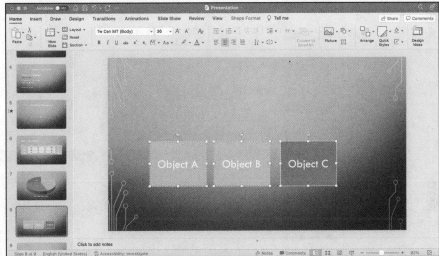

FIGURE 10-26:
Three objects before (top) and after (bottom) having their bottoms aligned.

The other items on the Align menu do exactly what you expect them to do: The first six align selected objects on their left, center (horizontally), right, top, middle (vertically), or bottom. If you choose Align Selected Objects, the objects are lined up in the same approximate location on the slide; if you choose Align to Slide, they're aligned with the slide's left, center, right, top, middle, or bottom rather than with each other.

Distribution isn't just a mathematical term any more

You may at some point want to distribute objects so that the space between them is equal. In this case, you need to select at least three objects. With the objects selected, revisit the Arrange icon — and then choose Distribute Horizontally from the Align menu to produce the results you see in Figure 10-27.

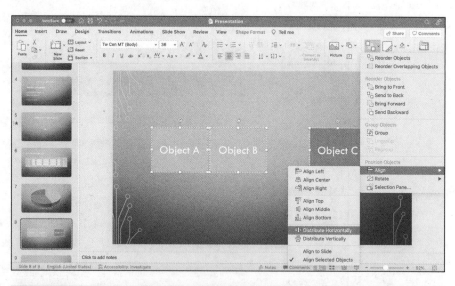

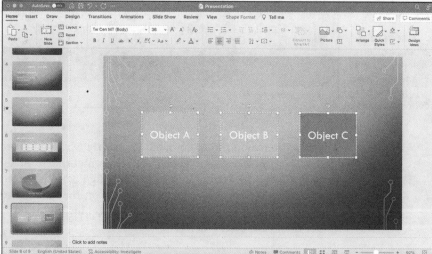

FIGURE 10-27: Objects A, B, and C before (top) and after (bottom) being distributed horizontally.

When you distribute objects, they're spread between the leftmost point on the leftmost object and the rightmost point on the rightmost object — or the topmost and bottommost, if you distribute vertically. Note that Objects A and C have not moved. They define the outer limits. Object B is the only element that has moved, so there's now an equal amount of space between it and Objects A and C.

Aligning objects with dynamic guides

One feature that you might find handy is PowerPoint dynamic guides. They're turned on by default, but to make sure that they're active, choose View ➪ Guides and ensure that the Dynamic Guides item has a check mark next to it. This command is a toggle, so if it already has a check mark, you're good to go; if it doesn't already have a check mark, select it and the check mark appears.

Dynamic guides are alignment tools that appear only when you need them; hence the *dynamic* part of their name. When you drag an object or objects on a slide, the dynamic guides try to determine what other objects on the slide you might want to align them with. For example, in Figure 10-28, Object B is being dragged from the middle of the slide toward the right corner. The dynamic guides are the lines indicating that if Object B is dropped now, its top, middle, and bottom are aligned with Object A.

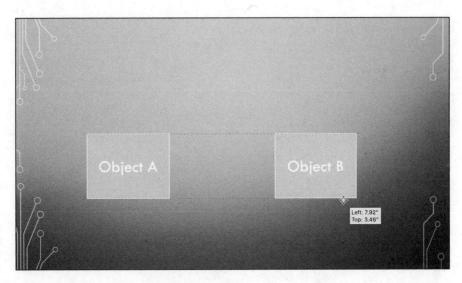

FIGURE 10-28: Using dynamic guides to align objects.

If the slide has only one object, the dynamic guides attempt to align it with the middle of the slide, as shown in Figure 10-29.

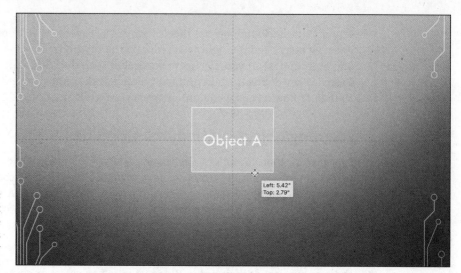

FIGURE 10-29:
The dynamic
guides indicate
that the object is
now dead-center
on the slide.

Chapter **11**

Making Your Slide Shows Sing

I n this chapter, you find out how to put the finishing touches on your slide show by adding transitions between slides and animation effects to objects on slides. Then we show you what should probably be the last thing you do before you take your show on the road (or the stage or wherever): printing handouts and exporting your presentation to share with others digitally.

By the time you're at the point of adding transitions or animations, your slides should have all the content your presentation needs. The content may still need to be tweaked, but for the most part, the words should be on the slides and the slides should be in the proper order.

Before you dig into this chapter, we suggest that you review your presentation one more time and make sure that all the points you need to cover are covered, that the slides are in the order you want, and that everything looks consistent.

Using Transitions to Create a Polished-Looking Presentation

Transitions are animations that appear between slides when you advance from one slide to the next during your presentation. Examples include a slide dissolving into the next slide, a slide pushing the previous slide offscreen, and stripes or checkerboard patterns that reveal the next slide. PowerPoint includes more than 30 different transitions, ranging from subtle and classy to garish and ugly. It's up to you to use transitions judiciously.

TIP

You should generally try to use the same transition throughout your presentation, to not only give your presentation consistency but also make it look more professional. If you use a bunch of different transitions or (gasp) a different transition for every slide change, you're essentially screaming "I'm a presentation newbie" to your audience.

The exception to this rule is that many presentations have one slide that deserves to have attention called to it. Sometimes, it makes sense to use a different transition to introduce that special slide. But, most of the time, you look more professional if you use only one transition throughout your presentation.

TIP

If a slide in your presentation is followed immediately by a similar slide, a transition may be helpful in alerting your audience that you're covering new material.

You can also decide to use no transitions between slides. If you don't use a transition, when you click to advance to the next slide, the next slide replaces the current slide instantly with no animation.

Applying transitions

You can apply transitions to slides in normal view (choose View ⇨ Normal) or slide sorter view (choose View ⇨ Slide Sorter).

Either way, the first thing you need to do is select the slides that you want to enhance with the transition. To select multiple slides, you click the first slide and then hold down either the Shift key (to select contiguous slides) or the ⌘ key (to select noncontiguous slides).

TIP

After you click any slide, you can select the rest of the slides in the presentation at one time by choosing Edit ⇨ Select All or by pressing ⌘+A. If you're using normal view and objects on your slide are selected, instead of all the slides in the left pane, click a slide in the left pane before you choose Edit ⇨ Select All (or before you press ⌘+A).

As mentioned, we strongly recommend that you use the same transition on all your slides, so we encourage you to select them all before you continue.

With some or all of your slides selected, click the Transitions tab on the ribbon.

REMEMBER

Applying a transition to a slide directly affects the slide before it. For example, if you apply a fade to slide 5, slide 4 will fade out during the transition while slide 5 fades in.

Click a thumbnail and the theme is applied to all slides that are selected, as shown in Figure 11-1. When you click a thumbnail, you see a thumbnail-size preview of the transition on each of the selected slides. And slides that have transitions applied to them display a little star icon to their left.

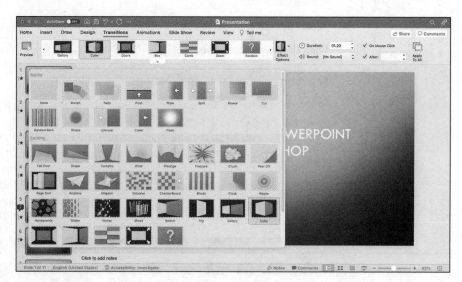

FIGURE 11-1: We've applied the Cube transition to all slides in our presentation.

TIP

Transitions work much the same as themes and layouts. Click a thumbnail to apply the transition (or theme or layout) to the selected slides.

To see how your transition will look to your audience, click the Preview button all the way to the left on the Transitions tab on the ribbon.

If you didn't apply this transition to all your slides, do so now, or at least apply another transition to the remaining slides.

TIP

Again, you don't absolutely have to have a transition between slides. But we think that almost any transition looks better than no transition. If you don't believe us, remove the transition (by clicking the None thumbnail) and then click the Preview button again.

That's pretty much it for applying transitions. Select some slides, click a thumbnail, and you're done.

Transition options

After you've applied transitions to slides, you have several options, which are, not surprisingly, also found on the Transitions tab.

To apply transition options, follow these steps:

1. **Choose View ➪ Normal or choose View ➪ Slide Sorter.**

   If the presentation has a lot of slides, it's probably easier to apply these options in slide sorter view.

2. **Select the slides to which you want apply the options.**

3. **Click the Transitions tab.**

4. **Select one or more transition options:**

   - *Effect Options:* This pop-up menu lets you choose or change a transition effect. If you chose a transition from the thumbnail strip for the selected slides, the entries on the Effect Options menu are specific to that transition — for example, in Figure 11-2, these menu items correspond to the direction in which the Cube transition, which we selected earlier, should rotate. If you haven't yet assigned a transition to the selected slides, the Effect Options menu is disabled.

FIGURE 11-2:
Selecting an
Effect option.

- *Duration:* Use this text box to choose the speed of the transition. The higher the number, the slower the transition.

- *Sound:* Choose a sound from the pop-up menu. The sound plays when you advance to the slide. Or select the Loop Until Next Sound item (at the end of the Sound pop-up menu) if you want the sound to repeat until you advance to the next slide.

   The sound you choose doesn't play when you select it from this menu. You have to click the Preview button in the Transitions tab to hear it. That's lame.

- *Advance Slide:* You usually want to advance to the next slide by clicking the mouse or trackpad, so the On Mouse Click check box is selected by default. But if you want a presentation to play automatically, select the After option and specify the number of seconds each slide should stay on the screen.

- *Apply to All:* Click to apply all the settings you've made in the Transitions tab to each of your slides in the presentation.

5. **When you're finished, click Apply to All to apply the options to all slides in this presentation.**

To see how your transitions will look to your audience with the options applied, click the Preview button on the left side of the Transitions tab.

Using Custom Animation

One cool PowerPoint feature is its capability to animate any object on any slide. Used judiciously, animation can help the audience focus on the point you're making and prevent people from reading ahead while you speak. Overused, however, animation can get really annoying really fast.

TIP

As with transitions, you usually should judiciously use the same animation effects throughout your presentation. Using the same animation effect gives your presentation consistency and makes it look more professional. If you use a bunch of different animation effects or (even worse) a different animation on every slide, your presentation will end up chaotic and hard to follow. So try to keep it simple and classy.

Animating text or graphics

To apply an animation effect to any object (text box, image, movie, or SmartArt graphic, for examples), select the object and then click the Animations tab on the ribbon. Next, select an effect from one of the three Effects strips on the Animations tab — namely, Entrance Effects, Emphasis Effects, and Exit Effects.

These three types of effects do what you expect them to, based on their names:

>> Entrance effects animate the way the object first appears on (enters) the slide.

>> Emphasis effects animate what an object does after it appears.

>> Exit effects animate the way the object disappears from (exits) the slide.

For this demonstration, we pulled down the Entrance Effects menu and selected the Fly In entrance effect so that it was applied to the bulleted text.

When effects are applied to elements in the slide, a numbered box appears next to those elements. Click the numbered box next to an element with an effect applied to it. Or in the case of text in an entire text box (as in this example), click the text box. The Automations task pane opens on the right side of the slide.

PowerPoint calls the text box surrounding these bullet points Content Placeholder 2 and automatically creates a subitem for each bullet point in the text box, which you can see in the Automations task pane in Figure 11-3.

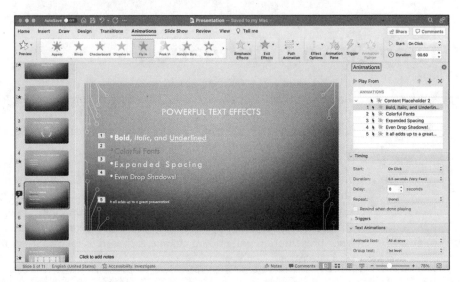

FIGURE 11-3:
The Automations task pane appears to the right of your active slide.

After you've applied an effect, you can use the settings in the Animations pane to fine-tune the animation:

>> **Timing section of the Animations pane:**

● *Start:* This pop-up menu appears in the Animations pane (and also on the far right of the Animations tab). In Figure 11-3, On Click is selected, so the subitems appear one at a time when you click. This option means that you have to click once to make each subitem appear. The two other options on this menu are With Previous and After Previous. Both options trigger the animation as soon as the slide appears and require no clicking. With Previous animates all subitems simultaneously, so all subitems would appear at one time. After Previous animates the subitems sequentially, so you see the first, and then the second, and then the third, and so on.

● *Duration:* This pop-up menu determines how quickly the animation effect plays (in seconds).

● *Delay:* This field lets you specify a delay (0 is selected in Figure 11-3) before the animation begins.

● *Repeat*: This pop-up menu lets you repeat the animation as many as ten times, until the next click, or until the end of the slide, or not repeat the animation.

● *Rewind When Done Playing:* This check box plays the animation backward after it finishes playing.

>> **Triggers section of the Animations pane:** Options in this section let you designate when individual effects should begin in the slide.

>> **Text Animations section of the Animations pane:**

● *Animate Text*: This pop-up menu lets you choose to animate text all at one time, by the word, or by the letter. You can also choose to animate text in reverse order.

● *Group Text:* This pop-up menu determines how subitems are to be grouped.

>> **Effects Options section of the Animations pane:**

● *Sound:* This pop-up menu lets you select a sound and have it play when this animation starts.

● *After Animation:* This item determines the color (if any) that each subitem changes to after its animation concludes. Other choices include Don't Dim (no change), Hide after Animation, and Hide On Next Mouse Click.

● *Smooth Start/End:* These check boxes make animations look more natural by accelerating and decelerating them at the start or end, rather than playing them at the same speed all the way through.

The Effect Options button on the ribbon's Animations tab lets you decide where on the slide an animation effect begins. The options available depend on which effect is being utilized. For the example in Figure 11-4, options are From Top, From Bottom (selected in Figure 11-4), From Left, From Right, From Top-Left, From Top-Right, From Bottom-Left, and From Bottom-Right.

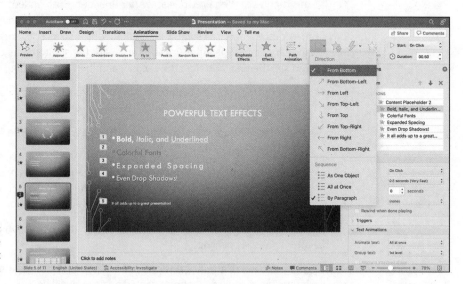

FIGURE 11-4:
Tweaking the
Entrance effect
options.

Note that some animations, such as Appear and Fade, don't require a starting point because the animation occurs with the item already in place. The Direction items don't appear on the Effect Options menu when you choose animations that don't require direction.

We clicked the Preview button to the left on the ribbon's Animations tab to preview our animation, and it looked good to us.

And so, based on the settings we made, here's how the slide appeared onscreen in slide show mode: The bullet points appear one at a time when we click, they fly in from the bottom of the slide, and they move very fast. No sound is associated with this animation. The animation starts and ends smoothly, starts without delay, and doesn't repeat or rewind. The bullet points fly in all at one time (not one word or one letter at a time). Finally, the Group text menu determines how many bullet point levels fly in at one time, but because this slide has only one level of bullet points, this setting is irrelevant.

Unfortunately, when you preview an animation by clicking the Preview button on the ribbon's Animations tab, the slide's animation plays from start to finish automatically — you don't have to click. To make sure that the bullets respond to your clicks as expected, you have to look at them in an actual slide show: Choose View⇨Slide Show and click, click, click.

In this case, everything worked as expected; every time we clicked, a bullet point flew in from the bottom of the screen.

You add emphasis and exit effects the same way you add entrance effects: Select the object you want to animate and then choose an appropriate effect from the appropriate drop-down menu.

TIP

You see the first few effects in each category from the strip controls on the Animations tab. But *dozens* of entrance, emphasis, and exit effects are available. To see more, click the arrow to the right of the strip or hover your mouse over the strip and click the down arrow that appears to display the entire menu, as shown in Figure 11-5.

FIGURE 11-5:
You can display all effects in a category by clicking the down arrow.

Last but not least, you can change the order in which individual bullets appear on the screen when you animate a bulleted list. Using the bulleted list in Figure 11-5 as an example, when we selected the text object that contains the bullet items and applied an animation effect to it with all paragraphs selected on the Group Text pop-up menu in the Animations pane, only one item appeared in the Animation Order list, as shown in Figure 11-6, on the left.

But when we chose 1st Level in the Group Text pop-up menu, PowerPoint automatically created subitems below Content Placeholder 2 — one for each first-level bullet point — as shown on the right in Figure 11-6.

FIGURE 11-6:
Animate the
bullets all at once
(left) or one at a
time (right).

Each of the subitems corresponds to one of the bullet points on the slide.

TIP

To determine which subitem is associated with which bullet point, click its name in the Animation Order list and choose Play From above the list, as shown in Figure 11-7. The subitem is associated with the bullet item that animates.

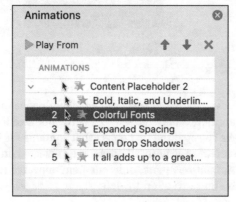

FIGURE 11-7:
Select an item
and click the up
or down arrow to
change its order
in the list.

To change the order in which the bullets appear on the slide, merely select the item in the list that represents the bullet whose order you want to change and then use the up- or down-arrow above the list to move it higher or lower in the list.

Animating a chart or SmartArt graphic

Animating a chart or SmartArt graphic works much the same as animating a text object, but with one little twist. By default, when you select a chart or SmartArt graphic and apply an animation effect to it, the entire object is animated all at one time. But you have the option of having each element in the chart or SmartArt graphic animated individually.

Here's how it works with a chart: When you select a chart on a slide and apply an entrance, emphasis, or exit effect, the last panel in the Animations pane changes from Text Animations to Chart Animations. It contains the Group Graphic pop-up menu, which offers options specific to the type of chart being used.

Figure 11-8 shows the Boomerang entrance animation for a pie chart with By Category selected on the Group Graphic pop-up menu.

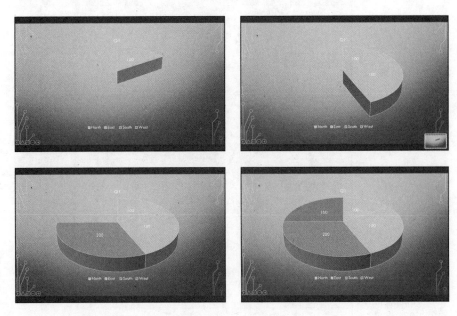

FIGURE 11-8: One pie slice appears each time we click.

Had we selected the As One Object option instead, all four slices of the pie chart would have appeared at one time.

Again, when you preview your animation by clicking the Preview button on the Animations tab, the slide's animation plays from start to finish automatically without your having to click. Therefore, to make sure that the pie slices (or whatever) respond to your clicks as expected, you have to look at them in an actual slide show. So choose View ➪ Slide Show and click your heart out. (Well, maybe don't be quite that dramatic or you might get some quizzical looks from other folks in the vicinity.)

Creating Interactivity with Action Buttons

Action buttons let you add interactivity button and navigation buttons to your slide shows. You can add them to an individual slide or to your slide master, if you want them to appear on all slides.

You choose a button design from the Action Buttons submenu (Insert ➪ Action Buttons), as shown in Figure 11-9.

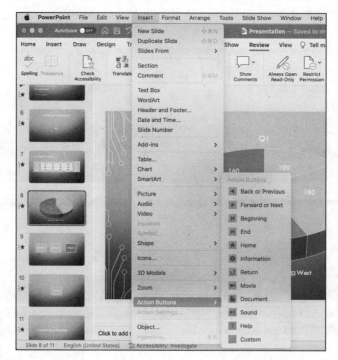

FIGURE 11-9:
The Action
Buttons menu.

To select and place an action button, follow these steps:

1. **With a slide open, choose Insert⇨Action Buttons⇨button name (where button name is the name of the button you want to place).**

   The cursor turns into a crosshair to indicate that you can now click and drag to create the button.

2. **Click and drag on your slide or slide master to place the button.**

   TIP

   Because a button is just another object on your slide or slide master, you can move it and resize it. Click it once to select it; drag one of its handles to enlarge or shrink it.

When you add an action button to a slide or slide master, the Action Settings dialog appears, as shown in Figure 11-10. There are two tabs, but the options they contain are identical. The first one, Mouse Click, specifies what happens when you click the button with the mouse or trackpad; the second, Mouse Over, specifies what happens when you hover the cursor over the button.

FIGURE 11-10:
From the Action Settings dialog, specify what your button does when it's clicked.

You usually choose an action from the Hyperlink To pop-up menu, which contains options to hyperlink to Next Slide, Previous Slide, First Slide, Last Slide, and others.

Why would you want to place an action button on a slide or on all your slides? Well, you might want to be able to jump to a specific slide during your presentation. Or you might want to show a web page at a certain point in your slide show. It would also be a handy feature for others with whom you might be sharing this presentation; the action buttons would give them a mechanism for moving from slide to slide.

Share and Share Alike

Handouts can serve as an effective way to bolster your presentation's effect on your audience. You may also want to share your presentation with your audience electronically, as a PDF or movie or another digital file. In this section, you can explore some of the options you have for sharing your finished slide shows with other people.

Printing hard copy

PowerPoint gives you numerous options for printing presentations. You can print them as slides, handouts, notes, or outlines. You can print in color, grayscale, or black-and-white. You can even print all or just part of your presentation. All these options become available when you choose File⇨Print or press ⌘+P to open the Print dialog.

TECHNICAL STUFF

What you see in the Print dialog may differ from the figures in this chapter. For one thing, we use macOS Monterey. If you're using a different version of macOS, your Print dialog may look slightly different. The other variable is the type of printer you have connected to your Mac. Your printer may have different features and capabilities that affect the way your Print dialog looks. So, if something you see in your Print dialog looks slightly different from what you see in this book, don't worry about it.

Printing slides

When it comes to printing your presentation, one option you have is to print only what appears on the screen during your presentation, one slide per page. Other options include printing multiple slides on each page, only certain slides or pages, or pages with handouts or notes included.

To print one slide per page, follow these steps:

1. **Choose File ⇨ Print or press ⌘+P to open the Print dialog, shown in Figure 11-11.**

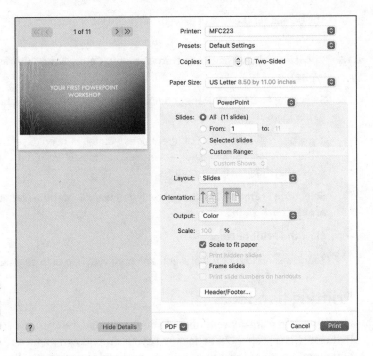

Printer: MFC223

Presets: Default Settings

Copies: 1   ☐ Two-Sided

Paper Size: US Letter 8.50 by 11.00 inches

PowerPoint

Slides: ● All (11 slides)
         ○ From: 1   to: 11
         ○ Selected slides
         ○ Custom Range:
            Custom Shows

Layout: Slides

Orientation:

Output: Color

Scale: 100 %

☑ Scale to fit paper
☐ Print hidden slides
☐ Frame slides
☐ Print slide numbers on handouts

Header/Footer...

?   Hide Details   PDF ▾   Cancel   Print

FIGURE 11-11: The Print dialog, ready to print all eleven slides in this presentation.

TIP

You might need to click the Show Details button to see all the settings in your Print dialog.

2. **In the Copies field, specify the number of copies of each slide you want to print. (The default is 1, but you can change it, if you want.)**

   The Collated check box matters only when you're printing multiple copies. When you print two or more copies of, say, a 12-page document, selecting this box causes your presentation to print each copy in its entirety before beginning to print the next copy. (That is, you print pages 1 to 12 and then print pages 1 to 12 again.) If this box is deselected, all copies of each page are printed together. (That is, if you specify two copies, your document prints as follows: page 1, page 1, page 2, page 2, page 3, page 3, and so on.)

3. **To print some (but not all) of your slides, do one of the following:**

   • *To print a range of contiguous slides* (such as Slides 6 to 9 or Slides 2 to 11), select the From radio button and specify the starting and ending slide numbers in the From and To fields.

- *To print noncontiguous slides* (such as Slides 1, 2, 5, 6, 8, and 11), select the slides you want to print before you choose File ⇨ Print. Then select the Selected Slides radio button in the Print dialog.

   The default for the Layout drop-down menu is Slides, so you don't have to change it.

4. **Choose an option from the Output menu (Color, Grayscale, or Black & White).**

5. **Select the Scale to Fit Paper check box to print your slide as big as the paper in your printer allows.**

   If you often swap paper of different sizes, you might need to set the page size in the File ⇨ Page Setup dialog — before you choose File ⇨ Print — to match the paper that's loaded in your printer.

6. **Select the Frame Slides check box if you want a hairline frame drawn around each slide.**

7. **Click the Print button.**

   Your chosen slides or full presentation print with one slide per page.

Printing handouts

If you want to print more than one slide on a page, refer to the steps for printing in the previous section, but click the Layout drop-down menu and choose a Handouts item. Your choices are 2, 3, 4, 6, or 9 slides per page. After you make your selection, the preview area displays a thumbnail of your page.

TIP

We like the three-to-a-page layout a lot because it's the only one that includes space for the recipient to jot notes.

Printing notes

If you like to add notes to your slides, as we do (see Chapter 10 for more details about the Notes feature), you might be glad to know that you can print slides and notes together. Here are two reasons to consider adding notes to your slides:

>> You can refer to them on your screen during the presentation. (We like that.)

>> Because you should keep your bullet points short on your slides, notes make your handouts more useful to your audience.

To print a handout showing a slide and notes, choose Notes from the Layout dropdown menu in the Print dialog. Only one format is available — one slide and its notes per page — but that's probably what we'd choose, even if we had other options.

Printing an outline

In Chapter 9, we wax poetic about what a good idea it is to start your presentation by creating an outline. If you decide to put together an outline, you can print it by choosing Outline from the Layout drop-down menu in the Print dialog.

This technique isn't fancy, but if you want to see only your words, thereby avoiding being distracted by your graphics or wasting paper, printing your slide show as an outline is the way to go. Figure 11-12 shows a basic outline in the Print dialog.

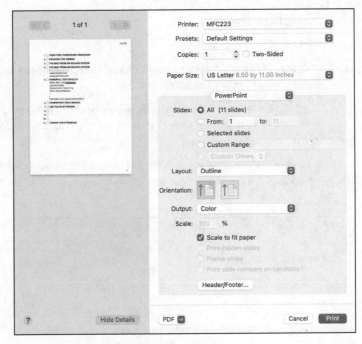

FIGURE 11-12:
Printing an outline gives you just your words with no frills.

Exporting (saving) your presentations as files

Perhaps you consider ink on paper to be too "old school" and prefer to offer your presentation as an electronic file that can be emailed, downloaded, copied to a thumb drive, shared on a network or via the cloud, or even accessed as web pages. Well, we have good news: PowerPoint offers a number of digital export options so that you can save your presentation as a digital file in a variety of formats. These formats include movies, picture files, or PDF files. You can also save your presentation to your Microsoft OneDrive or a SharePoint library.

Read on to see how it all works.

Exporting a presentation as a movie

Sometimes, you can't be there to present a slide show but you want to share it, anyway. If you know for sure that the recipients have a copy of PowerPoint and know how to use it, you *could* send them the actual PowerPoint file. But this strategy assumes that they have the same version of PowerPoint as yours, have the same fonts installed, and won't screw up your slide show before they get a chance to view it.

The answer is to export the presentation as a movie file. Here's how:

1. **Choose File ⇨ Export.**

The Export As dialog appears.

2. **Click the File Format pop-up menu near the bottom of the Export As dialog, and select MP4 or MOV.**

Whether you select MP4 or MOV is up to you, but MP4 is more compatible with slightly more devices than MOV (which is the native QuickTime video format Macs have used forever).

The movie options appear below the File Format menu, as shown in Figure 11-13. The options are the same regardless of whether you select MP4 or MOV.

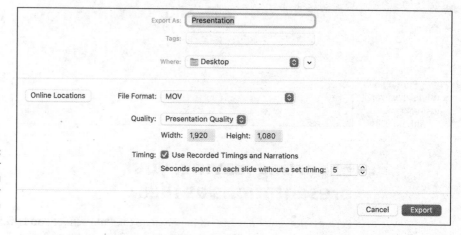

FIGURE 11-13:
These are your options when you save your presentation as a movie.

3. **Do the following:**

   a. From the Quality pop-up menu, choose an optimization. Your options are Presentation Quality (best), Internet Quality (better), and Low Quality (good, but not *too* good).

b. *If you want to include the timing between slides and any narrations, select the Use Recorded Timings and Narrations option in the Timing section.*

c. *If you don't have timings recorded in your presentation and you want to set a default timing for the exported movie, use the up and down arrows to the right of the Seconds Spent on Each Slide without a Set Timing option.*

4. **Click the Export button to begin the process of exporting your movie file.**

Any narrated audio in your presentation will be in the exported movie file, but no other embedded media files will play.

Exporting slides as individual picture files

Another option is to export the slides as individual picture files. Then you can import them into Photos, iMovie, or an editor such as Photoshop Elements, where you can create slide shows and movies, respectively, with more control over the way things look. For example, in Photos, you can use the Ken Burns effect, which simulates movement by panning and zooming on still images. And you can choose music from your Music library and use a different song every time you show the slide show. In iMovie, you can create titles, add transitions between slides, and include multiple soundtracks, and then export a movie.

To save slides as individual picture files, follow these steps:

1. **Choose File ⇨ Export.**

   The Export As dialog appears.

2. **In the File Format pop-up menu, choose a file format for your picture files, as shown in Figure 11-14.**

   Note that only five items on this menu — JPEG, PNG, GIF, BMP, and TIFF — are graphics file formats. If you intend to modify your slides using a graphics editor such as Photoshop, you should use one of these formats. Because the TIFF format is well-supported on both Macs and PCs (and TIFF images, unlike JPEGs, don't lose quality after repeated editing), we always recommend TIFF format.

3. **Choose whether to export every slide in your presentation or the just the currently active one.**

4. **Click Export.**

   PowerPoint creates a folder with the same name as your presentation (unless you changed the name in the Export As field at the top of the Export As dialog). In that folder, you find an individual file for each slide in the presentation.

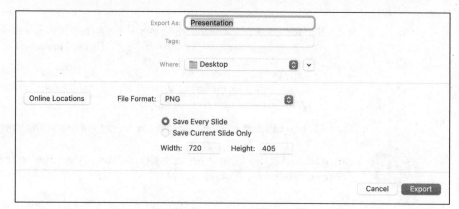

FIGURE 11-14:
Choose a file
format and click
Export, and
you're done.

Exporting a presentation as a PDF file

PDF, as you may already know, stands for Portable Document Format — the file format created by Adobe Systems for exchanging documents without regard for hardware, software, operating system, or installed fonts. So, a PDF file you create on a Mac will look exactly the same, regardless of the type of hardware, software, or operating system that's used to view it.

The PDF feature is built into macOS and is available in any app that has a Print dialog. The good news is that you have the same options as you have when printing hard copy. So, you can export a PDF file of slides, handouts (2, 3, 4, 6, or 9 slides per page), notes, or an outline. You can also select a subset of your slides and create a PDF that contains only those slides.

Exporting a PDF file couldn't be easier. To export your presentation as a PDF, follow these steps:

1. **Choose File⇨Print.**

The Print dialog appears.

2. **Set any print options in the Print dialog, as described in the preceding section.**

You're not going to print the presentation, but this is what you need to do to specify the following for your PDF file:

a. To include some (but not all) of your slides in the PDF, do one of the following:

To include a range of contiguous slides (such as Slides 6 to 9 or Slides 2 to 11), select the From radio button and specify the starting and ending slide numbers in the From and To fields.

To include noncontiguous slides (such as Slides 1, 2, 5, 6, 8, and 11), select the slides you want to print before you choose File⇨Print. Then select the Selected Slides radio button in the Print dialog.

    b. *Choose one of the options on the Output menu (Color, Grayscale, or Black & White).*

    c. *If you want a hairline frame drawn around each slide, select the Frame Slides check box.*

3. **Click the PDF button at the bottom of the Print dialog.**

4. **In the PDF pop-up menu, choose Save as PDF.**

The Save As dialog appears, as shown in Figure 11-15.

5. **Click Save.**

Save As:	Presentation
Tags:	
Where:	Desktop
Title:	
Author:	Dwight Spivey
Subject:	
Keywords:	
	Security Options...
	Cancel Save

FIGURE 11-15:
Click Save in the Save As dialog to create your PDF.

WARNING

Your PDF file doesn't include any fancy stuff, such as animations or transitions.

Saving your presentation online

Of course, you can save your PowerPoint presentation to any storage device on your home or office network, as long as you have the proper permissions — but saving that same presentation file to OneDrive and sharing it with others on the web involves cloud computing.

The basic *OneDrive* feature is offered by Microsoft for free, and it's pretty much Microsoft's version of another service you (as an Apple fan) probably already have: iCloud. Essentially, your OneDrive is much like a hard drive that exists online, which you can connect to from any PC or Mac with an internet connection. Think of the possibilities: You can access your Office files from just about anywhere in the world, just as though they reside on the computer you're using.

To save your presentation to your OneDrive, follow these steps:

1. **Click the Share button in the upper-right of your presentation's window to open the Share dialog, shown in Figure 11-16.**

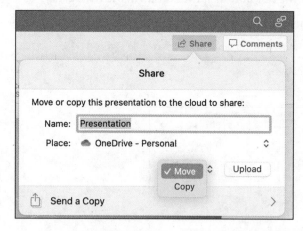

FIGURE 11-16:
Saving a presentation to OneDrive.

2. **(Optional) Type a new filename for your presentation.**

3. **If you have more than one account (such as one for personal and one for business), click the destination OneDrive account for the file.**

4. **On the pop-up menu to the immediate left of the Upload button, choose Move or Copy.**

   Move will move the file from its present location to your OneDrive account, and Copy will make a copy of it instead.

5. **To upload the file to your OneDrive, click Upload.**

To share your uploaded presentation with others, follow these steps:

1. **Click the Share button in the upper-right corner of your presentation's window to open the Share dialog, shown in Figure 11-17.**

   Note that the Share dialog offers different options than it did in Figure 11-16 because the file has already been uploaded to OneDrive.

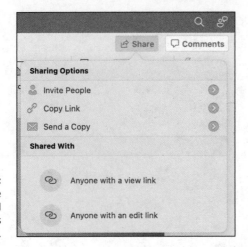

FIGURE 11-17:
You can share
your uploaded
file with others
via OneDrive.

2. **Choose a method for sharing your file with others:**

- *Invite People:* Click this option and you see the screen shown in Figure 11-18. Enter the names of people in your Apple Contacts app or type their email addresses. Add a message if you like. If you want them to be able to edit your presentation, be sure to select the Can Edit box. Then click the Share button.

FIGURE 11-18:
Check the Can
Edit box if you
want your
collaborator to
edit your slides.

- *Copy Link:* Copies a link for the shared file to your Mac's clipboard. You can then paste the link into documents, emails, websites, and more. Click Copy Link, then select View-Only (which allows others to only view the slides) or View and Edit (to allow others to edit the slides).

- *Send a Copy:* Lets you send a copy of the presentation file as a PowerPoint file or as a PDF to others via email.

Chapter **12**

Presentation Prowess

This chapter moves beyond merely creating a basic PowerPoint presentation and looks at ways to make the process better, faster, and easier, along with providing advice on how you can improve the presentations you create.

The bulk of the chapter describes a handful of tools that make PowerPoint easier to use or that help you create better PowerPoint presentations. The good news is that many of these tools work the same as their counterparts in Microsoft Word. So, if you're a Word user, you may already know how these tools work. (See Chapters 4 through 8 if you want to know more about working with Word.)

The chapter ends with some tips for adding panache and style to your live presentation.

Working with the Basic PowerPoint Tools

You may already be familiar with some or all of the tools discussed in the following sections: customization, spelling and grammar checking, researching, revision tracking, and templates. We remind you briefly of what each tool does and where to find more information in earlier chapters.

Ribbon and Quick Access toolbar customization

Customizing PowerPoint is easy: You can rearrange tabs and tab groups on the ribbon and add or delete most commands in custom ribbon tabs. You can also add, delete, or rearrange commands on the Quick Access toolbar. In Chapter 3, we cover customizing in all your Office apps, but in case you don't feel like flipping to that chapter, let's review it here.

Customize ribbon tabs and tab groups by rearranging them

Here are the steps for rearranging ribbon tabs or tab groups:

1. **Choose PowerPoint ⇨ Preferences to open the PowerPoint Preferences dialog.**

2. **Click the Ribbon & Toolbar button.**

3. **Select the Ribbon tab near the top of the dialog.**

   As shown in Figure 12-1, the dialog is divided into two sections: Choose Commands From and Customize the Ribbon.

4. **On the Customize the Ribbon pop-up menu, select an option.**

5. **Click the tab you want to move and drag it to its new location in the list.**

   You can also rearrange tab groups that reside in tabs. However, you can't rearrange commands or move them from one tab or tab group to another.

6. **Click the Save button in the lower right to save your changes.**

Note in Figure 12-1 that the main tabs in the tabs list might also include tab groups, which are subcategories within the tab. For example, in Figure 12-1, we expanded the Home tab so you can see the Clipboard, Font, Paragraph, and other tab groups listed below it.

FIGURE 12-1:
Rearrange ribbon tabs and commands in PowerPoint Preferences.

TIP

Display or hide ribbon tabs and tab groups by selecting or deselecting the check box to the left of their names.

Creating ribbon tabs and tab groups

Another level of customization is creating custom ribbon tabs and tab groups. To do so:

1. **Choose PowerPoint ⇨ Preferences to open the PowerPoint Preferences dialog.**

2. **Click the Ribbon & Toolbar button, and then select the Ribbon tab near the top of the dialog.**

3. **Click the + button at the bottom of the tabs list on the right, as shown in Figure 12-2, and choose New Tab from the menu.**

   If you want to create a tab group instead of a tab, choose New Tab Group from the menu.

4. **Select the New Tab (Custom) that now appears in the tabs list.**

5. **Click the options icon (circled ellipsis) at the bottom of the tabs list, and select Rename from the menu.**

6. **In the Display Name field, enter the desired name in and then click Save.**

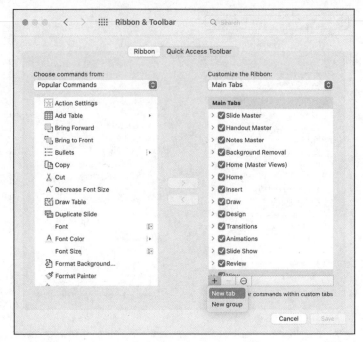

FIGURE 12-2:
Create a custom
ribbon tab by
clicking the +
button.

Customizing the Quick Access toolbar

The Quick Access toolbar is a holding place for tools you use frequently in your presentation. The tools it provides are the same in every window.

You can find the Quick Access toolbar, shown in Figure 12-3, at the top of every presentation window, just above the ribbon and to the immediate right of the red, yellow, and green buttons in the top left.

FIGURE 12-3:
The Quick Access
toolbar provides
quick access to
frequently used
tools.

Follow these steps to customize the Quick Access toolbar:

1. **Choose PowerPoint ⇨ Preferences to open the PowerPoint Preferences dialog.**

2. **Click the Ribbon & Toolbar button, and then select the Quick Access Toolbar tab near the top of the dialog.**

3. **In the Choose commands from pop-up menu, select an option. Scroll through the list of available commands, and then click to select the one you want.**

4. **Click the > in the middle of the dialog, shown in Figure 12-4, to add the selected command to the Customize Quick Access Toolbar commands list.**

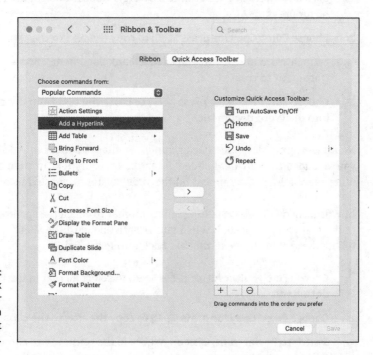

FIGURE 12-4:
Customize Quick Access toolbar commands in PowerPoint Preferences.

TIP

To remove a command from the Quick Access toolbar, select it in the Customize Quick Access Toolbar list and then click < in the middle of the dialog.

5. **Drag and drop commands in the order you would prefer them to appear in the Quick Access toolbar.**

6. **Click Save in the lower-right corner to save your changes.**

Proofing and reference tools

The spelling checker in PowerPoint works the same as the one in Word, as do many of the reference tools — the thesaurus, encyclopedia, dictionaries, and Translator tools. If you need help using any of these tools, refer to Chapter 6.

The one thing Word has that PowerPoint doesn't is grammar checking. If you aren't confident of your grammatical prowess, you might want to export your presentation in a format that Word can relate to and use the Word grammar checker on the text in your slide show. To do so, follow these steps:

1. **On the View menu at the top of the screen, choose Outline.**

2. **Click anywhere in your outline in the left sidebar and choose Edit⇨Select All (or press ⌘+A).**

3. **Choose Edit⇨Copy (or press ⌘+C) to copy the text to the clipboard.**

4. **Launch Word and, if you don't see a blank document, choose File⇨New Document to create one.**

5. **Choose Edit⇨Paste (or press ⌘+V) to paste the text from the clipboard into the Word document.**

No images, graphics, slide backgrounds, or shapes appear in Word, nor does text you've added to individual slides in text boxes. Only text in slide titles, lists, and other placeholders that appear on the slide master are pasted into Word.

In Word, choose Tools⇨Spelling and Grammar to check the spelling and grammar of the text you just pasted. When you're satisfied with the spelling and grammar, follow these steps to paste the text back into PowerPoint:

1. **Choose Edit⇨Select All (or press ⌘+A) to select all text in the Word document.**

2. **Choose Edit⇨Copy (or press ⌘+C) to copy the text to the clipboard.**

3. **Switch to PowerPoint, click anywhere in the outline, and choose Edit⇨Select All (or press ⌘+A) to select all text in the outline.**

4. **Choose Edit⇨Paste (or press ⌘+V).**

   This step replaces the old text in the outline (before spelling and grammar checking) with the text on the clipboard.

Commenting on slides

Working with others is a good way to get multiple viewpoints and solicit feedback for your presentation materials. PowerPoint offers the Comments feature, allowing each collaborator a way to leave comments that other collaborators can read and respond to.

Before you add a comment, determine whether it should apply to the entire slide or to a particular element on the slide (such as a graphic, link, or text). To comment on an entire slide, select the slide; to comment on an element in a slide, select the element.

After you select a slide or a slide's element, you can add a comment in multiple ways:

>> Choose Insert ⇨ Comment from the menu at the top of the screen. The Comments task pane opens on the right side along with a new comment box.

>> Click the New Comment button on the ribbon's Review tab. The Comments task pane opens with a new comment box.

>> Click the Comments button in the upper-right of the presentation window and then click the New button in the Comments task pane that appears (see Figure 12-5) to open a new comment box.

After the new comment box opens in the Comments task pane, simply begin typing your comment. Click the paper airplane icon or press ⌘+Enter (or ⌘+Return) to post your comment.

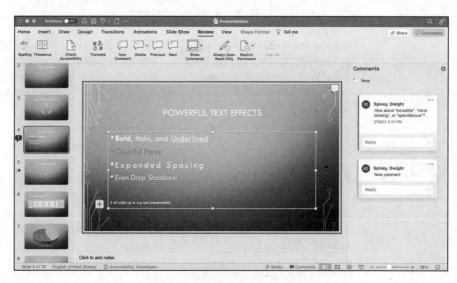

FIGURE 12-5:
PowerPoint comments look like this.

Here are your options for working with PowerPoint comments:

>> *To move a comment that applies to the entire slide:* Click and drag its speech bubble to a new location on the slide.

>> *To delete a comment:* Click the comment, click the Delete button on the Review tab, and then select Delete from the pop-up menu.

>> *To hide (or show) comments:* Click the Show icon (it's a toggle) on the ribbon's Review tab.

TIP

Comments don't appear when you present slides in slide show view, so you don't *have* to hide them before you make your presentation.

To review all comments in a presentation, click the Next Comment button until you've seen them all.

Templates and other miscellaneous tools

A few features that work the same in PowerPoint as in Word include templates, themes, AutoCorrect, and AutoFormat.

REMEMBER

Don't forget that you can create a presentation using the colors, fonts, images, and slide master items that you like and then save it as a template for reuse. If your business uses PowerPoint often, you can give a consistent look to your business presentations by creating a standardized design template for everyone to use. (If you need details on working with templates, see Chapter 7.)

AutoCorrect and AutoFormat (choose Tools ➪ AutoCorrect Options) are as useful in PowerPoint as they are in Word and work the same, as described in Chapter 6. In fact, Word, Excel, and PowerPoint share the same AutoCorrect and AutoFormat items. So if you create a new AutoCorrect entry in Word, it works in PowerPoint (and Excel) as well.

Using Hyperlinks

When you make a PowerPoint presentation to an audience, you might want to demonstrate a feature in another piece of software or show a web page as an example. You could pause the slide show by pressing the Esc key, switch to Finder or your web browser, and show the appropriate item. But that method would be tacky in the middle of a presentation.

The alternative solution that PowerPoint offers is to hyperlink to those items directly from the slide show. For example, if you want to display your website in the middle of a slide show, you add a clickable hyperlink to the slide. Then when you're ready to show the website, you click the link and — presto! — the website magically appears.

Here's how to add a hyperlink to a slide:

1. **In normal view, select the item you want to use as the hyperlink.**

In this example, we want to turn the first bulleted item on the slide, www.
boblevitus.com, into a hyperlink.

2. **Choose Insert⇨Hyperlink, or press ⌘+K.**

The Insert Hyperlink dialog opens.

3. **Click the Web Page or File tab.**

4. **In the Address field, type the URL of the web page.**

5. **(Optional) Click the ScreenTip button in the upper-right corner of the
Insert Hyperlink window and add a ScreenTip.**

A ScreenTip pops up in a little box when you hover the cursor over the link.

6. **Click OK.**

Now, whenever the slide appears onscreen during a presentation, you can click the
link (ours is shown in Figure 12-6) and the web page opens in your web browser.
When you're finished with the web page and close the web browser (or hide it
using ⌘+H, if you prefer to leave it open), you return to the slide show
automatically.

FIGURE 12-6:
The link as it
appears onscreen
in our slide show.

Simply closing the tab of your web page doesn't return you to your slide show; you must quit the browser or hide it.

The Hyperlink dialog has two other tabs — This Document and E-Mail Address — which let you create links to a document or to a preaddressed email message.

You can use hyperlinks also to navigate to other slides in a presentation. See the section on creating interactivity with action buttons in Chapter 11 for details.

Recording Narration

Sometimes you may want to add narration to your slide show — to supply information or provide a more personal touch or for use as an unattended slide show. To add narration, follow these steps:

1. **Click the slide where you want to begin the recording.**

2. **Choose Slide Show ⇨ Record Slide Show (or click the Slide Show tab on the ribbon and then click the Record Slide Show icon).**

   PowerPoint automatically enters presenter view, with recording tools at the top of the screen, as shown in Figure 12-7.

FIGURE 12-7:
Recording tools appear at the top of the screen when recording a narration for a slide.

3. To begin recording, click the red record button at the top of the screen.

4. Speak your narration as you click the mouse or use the arrow keys to advance the slides.

5. To stop the recording, click the red stop recording button at the top of the screen.

6. To exit presenter view, press the Esc key (or click the End Show button in the upper-left corner).

TIP

If you'd rather show your presentation without narration, you can turn it off as needed — for example, if you have to provide updated narration while your show runs. Click the Slide Show tab and disable the Play Narrations check box before starting your show.

Making the Most of Your PowerPoint Presentation

After you've done everything you want to do to your presentation, it's finally ready for the big screen. In this section, we cover some tools and tips that can help your presentation run smoothly in front of an audience.

Rehearsing and setting slide timings

Rehearsing a presentation in the privacy of your home or office — before you even *think* about doing it in front of a live audience — is always a good idea. You might even want to run through it more than once.

WARNING

Don't even consider standing in front of an audience and reading slides to them. Doing so is an insult to their intelligence and makes you look like an amateur presenter. Your job as the presenter is to weave a story around the bullet points on each slide — not to read the words verbatim.

If your presentation has a time constraint, you should also rehearse your timing, to ensure that you can present all material in the time allotted.

Fortunately, PowerPoint has a tool to help you to both rehearse *and* time your rehearsal. To use this tool, choose Slide Show➪Rehearse Timings (or click the Slide Show tab on the ribbon and then the Rehearse Timings icon). Your slide show starts immediately in presenter view. Pretend that you're standing in front of a room full of people and begin talking as though you were on stage. Click the mouse or use the arrow keys to advance to the next slide at the appropriate time.

When you're finished, click the End Show button in the upper-left corner to end the rehearsal. A dialog appears and informs you of the total running time for the slide show. It asks whether you want to record the new slide timings and use them when you view the slide show, as shown in Figure 12-8.

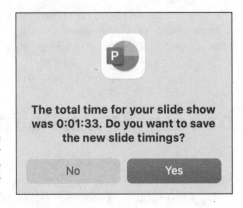

FIGURE 12-8:
Decide whether
or not to keep
your slide
timings.

The total time for your slide show was 0:01:33. Do you want to save the new slide timings?

No   Yes

Note the total time for your rehearsal. If it's too long or too short, click No in the dialog and try again. If your presentation is the right length, click Yes to save the timing for each slide. The next time you run the slide show, the slides advance automatically according to the timings you just used in the rehearsal. If you intend to manually click the mouse or use the arrow keys to advance the slides when you're ready (which we always do), click No. (This is ideal when you're pausing to answer questions from your audience.)

TIP

If you save the timings and later decide that you prefer to advance slides manually, choose Slide Show ➪ Set Up Show and select the Manually radio button in the Advance Slides section. Better still, turning off timings this way doesn't delete them, which means you can turn them back on at any time by selecting the Using Timings, If Present radio button in the Advance Slides section. (From the Slide Show tab on the ribbon, you can turn off timings by deselecting the Use Timings check box.)

TIP

You can also use the Rehearse with Coach option to have PowerPoint's Presenter Coach feature provide feedback to you. You'll be alerted if you use too many filler words (such as *um*) or if you use culturally sensitive terms, if you're reading the slides verbatim, and more. Give it a shot by clicking the Rehearse with Coach button on the ribbon's Slide Show tab.

HOW TO SET UP YOUR MAC FOR TWO DISPLAYS

If you're using a two-screen setup, here's how to make the presenter tools appear on your laptop screen and the slides appear on the projector (or the other screen). First, make sure that the second display or projector is connected to your Mac. Then choose Apple Menu⇨System Preferences and click the Displays icon. In the Displays System Preference pane, click the Arrangement tab.

The proxy icons represent the two available screens. Make sure that the Mirror Displays check box is deselected; then, if necessary, drag the menu bar to the display on which you want the presenter tools to appear. Close the Displays System Preference pane and you're ready to begin your presentation with presenter view appearing on the appropriate screen and the slides appearing on the other.

Using the presenter tools

PowerPoint offers a presenter view to help you hone your slide presentations. If your computer has two monitors connected, as it does when you're using a projector, you can see presenter view on your laptop screen and show slides on the second screen (the projector). But even if you have only one display available, presenter view is handy for rehearsing your presentation.

A picture is worth a thousand words, so Figure 12-9 shows presenter view in action.

Here's a blow-by-blow description of each tool:

>> **Thumbnails:** Enables you to gain immediate access to any slide in the show. Without thumbnails, you might have to click repeatedly, or even stop and restart the show, to display an earlier or later slide out of sequence.

>> **Current Time:** Displays the current time.

>> **Timer:** Keeps track of how long you've been speaking. Click the play/pause icon to start and pause the timer, or click the reset icon (circular arrow) to reset the elapsed time display.

>> **Audience view:** Shows the material being projected on the second screen in a two-screen setup.

>> **Next slide and previous slide arrows:** Displays the next and previous slides. (D'oh.)

>> **Preview window:** Shows the next slide or, if you've added animation to a slide, the next object.

>> **Notes:** Displays any notes you may have added to your slides.

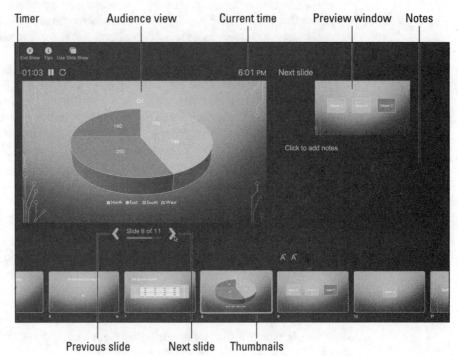

FIGURE 12-9:
The presenter
view screen.

Working with a single display

If you don't have two displays, don't fret. Although you can't use the Presenter Tools screen during your slide show, PowerPoint has some other tools you can use.

When you're presenting in slide show view, notice the little icons in the lower-left corner of the slide. If you don't see the icons, move the cursor and wait a few seconds for them to appear. The icons are tools to assist you if you're presenting on a single monitor (see Figure 12-10).

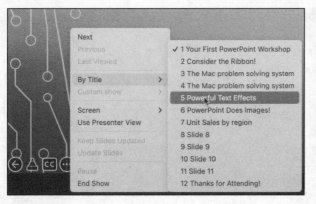

FIGURE 12-10:
Several handy
tools can assist
you while
working in
Presenter mode.

Most of the menu options are self-explanatory, but here's the scoop on what you can do with the ones that may not be crystal clear:

>> **Custom Show:** Link to another slide show.

>> **Black and White Screen (in the Screen menu):** Switch to a completely black or white screen. A black (or white) screen works great at the beginning of a presentation (when you don't want to reveal anything) — or in the middle of a presentation if you've paused to go on a tangent and don't want the current slide to distract the audience. Click anywhere on the slide to dismiss the screen and return to the current slide. Alternatively, you can press B on the keyboard to turn the screen black; pressing B again returns the screen to the current slide. If you prefer a white screen over black, the W key works similarly as a toggle to white and then back to the slide.

>> **Erase Pen:** Erase anything you've written on a slide with the Pen tool.

>> **Pointer Options:** The pointer is a bit more versatile than you might assume at first glance. Here's some of what you can do with it:

- *Automatic (⌘+U):* Automatically show the pointer cursor when you move the mouse, and hide the pointer after a few seconds of inactivity. This default setting is usually your best option.

- *Hidden:* Hide the cursor.

- *Arrow (⌘+A):* Display the pointer cursor all the time, even after a few seconds of inactivity.

- *Pen (⌘+P):* Switch to the pen tool, which you can use to annotate a slide, as shown in Figure 12-11.

- *Pen Color:* Choose the color of the pen.

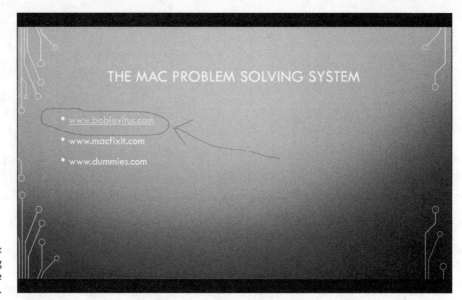

FIGURE 12-11:
Annotating
a slide with the
pen tool.

4

Crunching Data with Microsoft's Most Excellent Excel

Become acquainted with Excel by reading an overview and background information on what a spreadsheet is and what you do with one.

See how AutoFill and Error Checking can save you time, and sort, filter, find, and replace data like a pro.

Make your spreadsheets look cool and groovy by adding charts, formatting, special effects, and headers. Then, after taking a look at printing, sample more advanced Excel features, such as conditional formatting, multiple worksheets, and hyperlinking.

Chapter 13

Getting to Know Microsoft Excel

Microsoft *Excel* is the spreadsheet app of the Office suite. What is a spreadsheet? Well, here's a definition from Merriam-Webster's Dictionary (www.merriam-webster.com/dictionary/spreadsheet):

... a computer program that allows the entry, calculation, and storage of data in columns and rows.

Visually, a spreadsheet is a grid made up of cells defined by their row and column locations. A cell can contain numbers, text, or formulas that perform calculations. A spreadsheet can have just a handful of cells with data in them or "billions and billions" (shout out to Carl Sagan) of cells.

To be precise, a spreadsheet can have as many as 17,179,869,184 cells — 1,048,576 rows by 16,384 columns. If you can't get the job done with more than 17 billion cells, we don't know what to tell you, friend.

You can use Excel for all kinds of tasks, including creating reports, maintaining a check register, keeping lists of all types, and managing almost any data that can benefit from calculation. In this chapter, you discover the basics of using rows, columns, and cells, how to navigate within a spreadsheet, and how to use Excel views.

Interfacing with Excel's User Interface

We have good news for you. Most of what we cover in Chapter 3 regarding how to use menus, palettes, the Quick Access toolbar, and the ribbon applies also to these elements in Excel menus, toolbars, and palettes.

The Apple, File, Edit, Window, and Help menus are much the same in all Office apps. And the Excel View, Insert, Format, and Tools menus are a lot like Word's menus of the same names, though they contain a few items exclusive to Excel.

Following are a few basic concepts that work the same on Excel menus as they do on Word and PowerPoint menus:

>> A menu item with an ellipsis (. . .) opens a dialog with additional options on it.

>> A menu item ending with a right-pointing arrow has a submenu.

>> A menu item in gray type isn't available now.

A menu item is usually in gray for a logical reason, such as it works only when an image is selected or it requires a text selection.

TIP

Excel's ribbon, Quick Access toolbar, and palettes are also similar to their counterparts in Word and PowerPoint; see Chapter 3 for more details about how these elements work in all the programs.

In Excel, to change something— text, numbers, formulas, or whatever — you have to first *select*, or highlight, whatever you're changing. If it's text, you select it the same way you select text in Word and PowerPoint. When text is selected, you can modify it.

If the item you want to change is a graphical object, you click it to select it. When a graphical object is selected, handles appear around the frame. At that point, you can modify the object.

REMEMBER

Just remember that you need to select something before you can use most menu, ribbon, or palette commands.

Understanding the Concept of Rows, Columns, and Cells

In Excel, every cell has an address (sometimes referred to as a *name*), which is defined as the intersection of its column and row.

Rows have simple designations. They're numbered sequentially from 1 to more than 10,000: The first row is 1, the second row is 2, the 50th row is 50, and so on.

The way column addresses work isn't quite as simple. However, the first 26 columns are simple — they're designated by the 26 letters in the alphabet. So the first 26 columns are A through Z. But, at that point, you run out of letters and the situation grows a little more complicated — but not much: The 27th column is AA, the 28th column is AB, the 29th column is AC, and so on to the 52nd column, AZ.

After the alphabetical letters are all used up again, Excel starts anew, with B rather than A as the first of the two letters in the designation: The 53rd column is BA, the 54th column is BB, and so on.

Put 'em together, and what do you have? Cell addresses, of course. Figure 13-1 shows the cell addresses of 90 cells — the first 15 rows by the first 6 columns.

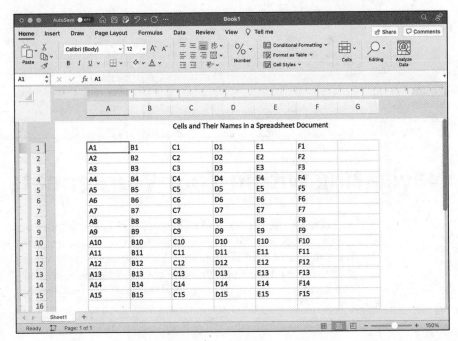

FIGURE 13-1:
Ninety cells containing their own addresses — in rows 1–15 and columns A–F.

Why are cell addresses important? Mostly because that's how you tell a formula which items it should use when performing calculations. For example, to multiply the number in cell A1 by the number in cell A2, the formula is =A1*A2, which translates into "Show me the product of cell A1 multiplied by cell A2."

Don't fret if this concept isn't making sense yet. As long as you understand how cell addresses are derived, you can get the hang of things as you explore Excel further in later chapters.

Using the Views

Understanding Excel views is simple. It has only two of them: normal and page layout. The big difference between them is that in page layout view, your worksheet looks like a page and appears basically the way it will print, whereas normal view just fills the screen with cells, using dotted lines to indicate where page breaks occur. Both are shown in Figure 13-2.

 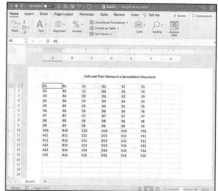

FIGURE 13-2:
Normal view (left) and page layout view (right).

Navigating within Your Worksheets

You can use the vertical and horizontal scroll bars to move around within worksheets, but as your sheets grow larger, using the mouse to scroll becomes less and less convenient. This section provides a few useful shortcuts for moving around in documents and selecting cells without touching the mouse. To become a true Excel whiz, memorize most or all of the shortcuts we describe.

Table 13-1 shows you how to move around a sheet and select cells using only the keyboard.

TABLE 13-1

Keyboard Selection

To Do This	Use This Keyboard Shortcut
Move one cell up, down, left, or right	Arrow key
Move to the next cell in a row	Tab
Move to the previous cell in a row	Shift+Tab
Move to the next cell in a column	Enter
Move to the previous cell in a row	Shift+Enter
Move to the beginning of the row containing the selected cell	Home
Move to the upper leftmost cell (cell A1)	Control+Home
Move to the last cell in use in the sheet	Control+End
Scroll to display selected cells	Control+Delete
Scroll down one screen	Page Down (fn+down arrow on some Mac keyboards)
Scroll up one screen	Page Up (fn+up arrow on some Mac keyboards)
Scroll one screen to the right	Option+Page Down
Scroll one screen to the left	Option+Page Up
Open the Go To dialog	Control+G
Open the Find dialog	⌘+F
Extend the selection by one cell	Shift+arrow key
Extend the selection to the last nonblank cell in the same column or row as the selected cell	Control+Shift+arrow key
Select the entire row containing the selected cell	Shift+spacebar
Select the entire column containing the selected cell	Control+spacebar

You can also select every cell in a sheet by clicking the little triangle that appears in the upper-left corner of every window. And you can select all cells in a column by clicking its column name (A, B, or C, for example) and select all cells in a row by clicking its row number.

One last thought: Excel and the concept of cells, rows, columns, and formulas may be new to you. If so, let us once again remind you about Office Help, which works the same in Excel as it does in Word.

TIP

See Chapter 3 for more about Office Help.

Chapter **14**

Crunching Numbers (and Data) with Excel

Excel's power as a spreadsheet derives from the flexibility it provides you in entering, formatting, deriving, analyzing, and presenting your data. Producing a bare grid of unformatted, manually entered text and numeric cells would make even the most compulsive Bob Cratchit exhausted, bored, and cross-eyed. Excel's powerful formula creation tools help you quickly and easily calculate results from your data, and Excel's formatting capabilities let you almost effortlessly draw attention to important data and results and, when desired, make supporting data fade into the background.

In this chapter, you find out how to use Excel's timesaving and effort-minimizing features to avoid exhaustion, boredom, and ocular fatigue.

Working with Templates

Traditionally, a spreadsheet (including Excel's) starts as an empty grid filled with identically sized cells. Although such a blank canvas offers incredible flexibility, many users instead consider it incredibly intimidating. Excel's templates let you avoid that vast expanse of emptiness by providing preconfigured and preformatted worksheets for a wide variety of common tasks that are just waiting for you to input your data into the indicated cells.

Just as it does for Word, PowerPoint, and Outlook, Microsoft Office offers Excel templates — these *local templates* are installed as part of Office and you don't have to be online to access them. Just as Word templates provide a starting point when you want to create a specific type of word processing document (for example, a newsletter or a flyer), Excel templates give you a head start and framework for creating specific spreadsheet documents or performing common spreadsheet tasks (such as managing a household budget or computing and structuring a home mortgage).

And don't forget that internet thing. Excel also offers *online templates* contributed by other Excel users. You can find a huge number of templates covering all sorts of common spreadsheet tasks. You can also find specific templates for movie collections, billing statements, timesheets, and more. Heck, you can find templates for purposes you'd never expect. Of course, you need an active internet connection to load these templates.

The following sections provide more details about finding and taking advantage of Excel templates.

Choosing a local template

The Workbook gallery collects all Microsoft-supplied local Excel templates and makes them available in a single location.

To create a document from a local Workbook gallery template, follow these steps:

1. **Choose File⇨New from Template or press Shift+⌘+P.**

2. **From the list on the left, click New.**

   The local templates fill the large pane on the right, as shown in Figure 14-1.

3. **Select the thumbnail representation of the template you want and click Create. (Alternatively, double-click the template's thumbnail.)**

Excel opens a new document based on the template you selected, and that's all there is to it. Now all you have to do is make the template your own document by entering data into the cells.

Click the Recent icon on the left of the Workbook gallery to display the Recent tab. There you'll find workbooks you've created, opened, or modified today, yesterday, or within the past week or past month.

TIP

Working with online templates

Online templates are maintained by Microsoft on its templates website, https://templates.office.com. You may be able to locate many of the internet-supplied templates by clicking the search field in the upper-right corner of the Workbook gallery and typing a name or category. Figure 14-2 shows a search for templates related to cards.

Microsoft continually changes and updates template categories and subcategories online, but you're always likely to find our favorite categories:

>> **Budgets** includes templates for tracking and managing your personal income and expenses as well as your business budget.

>> **Invoices** includes templates containing columns and formulas common to tracking and managing invoices.

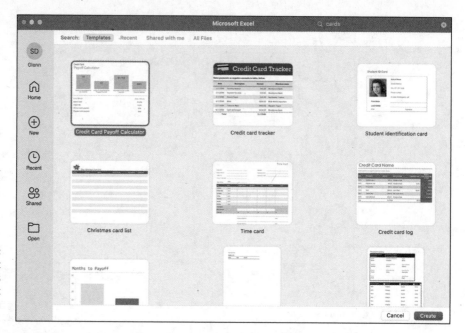

FIGURE 14-2:
Microsoft
provides dozens
of templates that
you can
search for.

>> **Lists,** as its name implies, includes numerous preformatted templates set to manage various common list types, including team rosters, chore charts, and grocery lists. Be sure to check out what's available in this category; you're bound to find at least one that comes in handy for helping to manage your everyday affairs.

>> **Reports** includes all sorts of templates designed to generate common reports.

TIP

You can find and download more templates from Microsoft by visiting `https://templates.office.com`. You'll find templates for just about any type of spreadsheet you can imagine, and then some.

Entering, Formatting, and Editing Data in Cells

Several decades ago, when Dan Bricklin's VisiCalc swept personal computers from the domain of hobbyists (read "nerds") into the realm of business, you selected a cell and then entered the spreadsheet data for that cell in a data entry box. This paradigm remains available to traditionalists by way of the traditional data-entry mechanism known as the Excel formula bar (see Figure 14-3). You specify the cell in the Name box on the left and then enter the data or formula in the Formula box on the right.

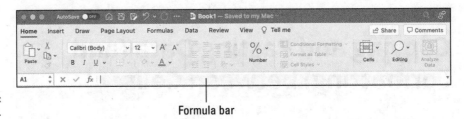

FIGURE 14-3:
The formula bar.

Formula bar

A modern graphical user interface (GUI), such as the one to which we Mac users are accustomed, begs us to enter our data directly into the cells where it belongs, and Excel obliges. Just click a cell (or navigate to it using your keyboard's cursor keys or by typing in the Name box in the formula bar) and start typing. Then move to the next cell and enter its data.

TIP

The cell data you enter or edit appears in the formula bar, but any formatting you apply via the Home tab on the ribbon or the Format menu appears only in the cell, as shown in Figure 14-4.

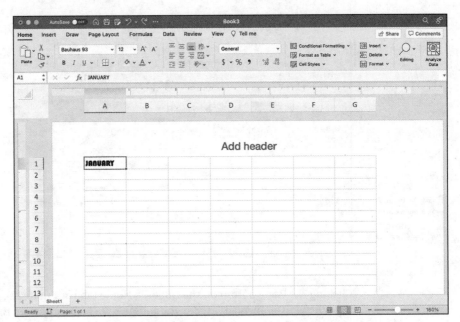

FIGURE 14-4:
Formatting isn't reflected in the formula bar.

All the usual editing techniques are available when working with a cell's contents. You can select all or part of the data and apply formatting via the ribbon; replace the selection by typing or pasting, and position the insertion point and then type or paste new data, for example.

Copying and Pasting Data (and Formatting) between Cells

We expect any Mac app that allows data entry to support copying (and cutting) and pasting data as well. Excel doesn't disappoint in that respect, but adds a few small wrinkles. For example, copying from one cell and then pasting in another brings the data, but you may not want to retain its original formatting. If you want to select which formatting is retained, right-click the destination cell, choose Paste Special from the contextual menu, and then select Paste Special again. You're presented with the dialog shown in Figure 14-5.

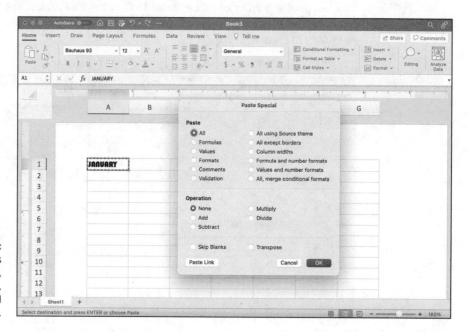

FIGURE 14-5:
Paste Special lets
you paste values,
formulas,
formatting, and
more.

Clicking the Paste button on the ribbon's Home tab isn't quite the same as choosing Edit ⇨ Paste. Instead, as shown in Figure 14-6, Excel pastes the data and displays a small paste options icon with a drop-down menu attached (Microsoft calls them *smart buttons*), in which you can choose to retain the formatting of the source being copied or to apply destination formatting (that is, any formatting you've already applied to the destination cell).

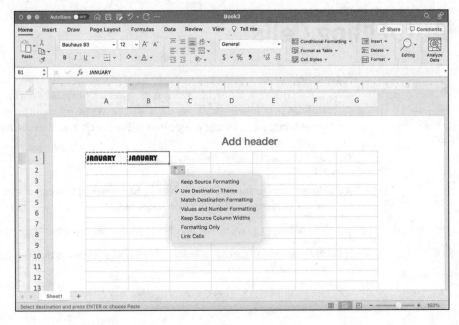

You might also be a little disconcerted the first time you choose Edit⇨Cut. Rather than make the data disappear, as this command does in most Office apps, it creates a dotted outline border on the selected cell. When you select another cell and paste, the data and the outline disappear.

TIP

You can make the outline stop shimmering without losing the selection by pressing Esc.

Finally, you can use the format icon (paintbrush) on the left side of the ribbon's Home tab to copy only a cell's formatting and apply it to one or more other cells. Follow these steps:

1. **Select a cell containing the formatting you want to use.**

2. **Click the paintbrush icon (format) on the Home tab of the ribbon.**

3. **Drag across the cell (or cells) to which you want to apply this formatting.**

You can lock the Format tool by double-clicking. Locking it lets you apply the selected formatting to multiple noncontiguous cells or ranges of cells. Clicking the locked Format tool unlocks it.

AutoFilling Cells

Spreadsheet users commonly want to fill a group of cells (rows or columns) with data. Sometimes, you need to work with a series of numbers (for example, 1–30) or common text labels (such as days of the week or months of the year), and sometimes, you need to use a repeated value (such as a default zip code).

To AutoFill a set of cells, follow these steps:

1. **Hover the cursor over the lower-right corner of the cell containing the initial value or the value to be repeated.**

   This action displays the fill handle, as shown on the left in Figure 14-7.

2. **Drag down (or across) a group of cells, as shown on the right in Figure 14-7.**

   Your values fill the cells you're dragging over.

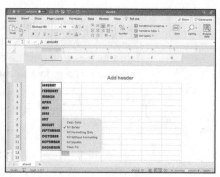

FIGURE 14-7:
Get a fill handle
(left) and drag
through the
cells you want
to fill (right).

Clicking the AutoFill smart button's drop-down arrow presents fill choices. The default is Fill Series.

An alternative to dragging with the mouse is to select a group of cells, type the information you want in one of them, and then press Control+Return to fill all the selected cells with that information.

TIP

If you don't want to have the smart button appear when you drag the fill handle, choose Excel⇨Preferences, click the Edit button, and deselect the Show Insert Options check box. Click OK to accept any preference changes you made.

Understanding Formulas and Functions

If all Excel allowed you to do was enter and format literal values in the sheet's cells, you would have a useful electronic implementation of a ledger book, but you would be missing out on a spreadsheet's real power — the capability to automatically calculate values in one cell based on the values in one or more other cells. The calculation that an Excel spreadsheet can perform is as basic as showing the sum or difference between two values or as advanced as working with a complex formula involving a variety of common statistical, trigonometric, financial, or date conversion functions. For example, in a Wedding Budget template, cell B9 might contain a formula (=B6-B8), telling Excel to calculate the available budget for your wedding by subtracting the actual expenses incurred to date from the total budget amount you've allotted.

Excel comes with hundreds of built-in functions, divided into categories. You can find a lengthy list, including descriptions of the functions, in Excel's Help system: Go to Help⇨Excel Help, type **Excel functions**, and then click either Excel functions (by category) or Excel functions (alphabetical) to explore them.

Many functions are general purpose, such as SUM, which totals the values in the referenced cells. Others are of interest only to users in specific fields. The ATANH function (which returns a value's inverse hyperbolic tangent, if that means anything to you!) is useful to mathematicians and engineers, and DDB (which returns asset depreciation based on the double-declining balance method) probably doesn't do much for you unless you're an accountant.

Creating a formula

When creating a formula, the first character in the formula must be the equal sign (=), which tells Excel that a formula follows, not text or numeric data.

TIP

Functions and formulas reference cells by name: for example, A1 or F10. You can also use a shorthand method to indicate a contiguous range of cells. For example, A1:A4 tells Excel that cells A1, A2, A3, and A4 are all arguments, and A1:B3 specifies that A1, B1, A2, B2, A3, and B3 are arguments. As you can see, using this shorthand for a cell range can significantly cut down on your typing time and make your intent clear. Furthermore, you can have multiple ranges in your argument list. (For example, A1:B3, D5:F7, A10:F10 specifies that all 21 cells referenced in the three ranges are the arguments to your function.) When referencing cells, you can use two forms of address — relative and absolute — to make a large difference. Check out the nearby "Absolute versus relative references" sidebar for the skinny on this important concept.

Keeping track of Excel formulas with Formula Builder

With the multitude of Excel built-in functions, many sporting somewhat cryptic names and taking multiple arguments, remembering just which function you need at any given time can be a daunting task. Excel eases the pain with Formula Builder. You can display the Formula Builder pane (shown in Figure 14-8) by choosing Formula Builder from the View menu. Also, you can click the More Help on This Function link in the Description box to call up Excel Help and display a full description of the selected function.

ABSOLUTE VERSUS RELATIVE REFERENCES

At first blush, cell references give the impression that the cell you name is the cell you get, but that isn't the case. For example, when you construct a formula in B1 that totals the values in A1:A10, you specify =SUM(A1:A10). But when you copy the formula in B1 into D1, the copy in D1 appears as =SUM(C1:C10). That's because Excel adjusts the cell references by their position relative to the cell containing the formula — this is what *relative references* means. This behavior is normally what you want, at least if you're anything like the generations of spreadsheet users who have preceded you. After all, you're likely to want to total or average multiple columns more often than you want to repeat a total or average in multiple places (and you can do that in the preceding example by just placing a formula such as =B1 in cell D1). Relative references also come in handy as you add or remove columns and rows because, even as a cell's address changes (for example, removing column E makes column F the new column E), the updated reference still points to the same cell.

Sometimes, though, you want an absolute address (for example, referencing a list of commission rates or sales tax percentages), and Excel obliges this desire at the cost of typing an additional character or two. The character you use is the dollar sign ($). For example, $A$10 always means cell A10, absolutely, and this gives you *absolute references.* You can even have *mixed references,* where the row is absolute and the column is relative (or vice versa), such as $A10 or A$10.

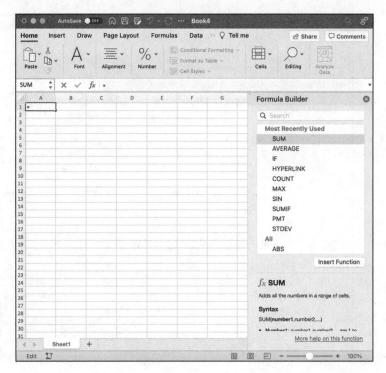

FIGURE 14-8:
Formula Builder makes finding and using Excel's built-in functions easy.

Selecting a function in the list gives you a brief description of it, as shown in Figure 14-8.

Formula Builder's window (see Figure 14-9) is ready for you to start plugging in argument values as Excel starts building your formula in the selected cell.

Another Excel feature that aids you in constructing formulas is Formula Auto-Complete. Formula AutoComplete kicks in when you start typing a function's name in a cell. A list of matching names appears, and you can select the one you want from the list to complete the name (by either clicking or selecting it with the arrow keys and then pressing Return or Enter). For example, if you type **=av** (you must type the equal sign first to engage Formula AutoComplete), as shown in Figure 14-10, Excel displays all functions whose names start with those two letters. After you select the function you want, the cursor is positioned in the function's argument list, awaiting your input.

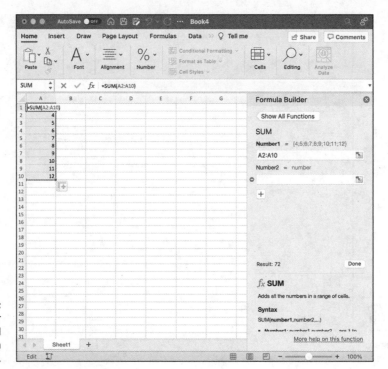

FIGURE 14-9:
Excel builds your
formula as you fill
in the blanks in
Formula Builder.

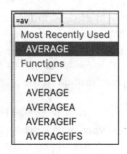

FIGURE 14-10:
Formula
AutoComplete
helps you cut
down on typing
by narrowing the
list of available
functions
as you type.

If AutoComplete isn't working for you, you need to turn on the feature:

1. Choose Excel⇨Preferences from the menu, or press ⌘+, (comma).

2. In the Preferences dialog, click AutoComplete in the Formulas and Lists section.

3. Select the Show AutoComplete Options for Functions and Named Ranges check box, as we did in Figure 14-11.

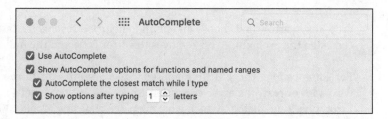

FIGURE 14-11:
Enable
AutoComplete in
Excel's
Preferences
dialog.

Using the Error Checking Feature

In Excel (or any other data presentation tool), the results can be only as accurate as the underlying data. Excel can't read your mind. If you create a formula that subtracts where it should add, your results will be erroneous and you can easily take incorrect action based on those erroneous results. Unfortunately, Excel can't save you from that class of error, any more than it can prevent you from entering 12 when you meant to enter 1.2 (assuming that both values are permissible for that cell). However, Excel can warn about some types of errors. The values that Excel checks are controlled in the Excel Preferences Error Checking pane, shown in Figure 14-12. To open this pane, choose Excel ➪ Preferences and then click the Error Checking icon.

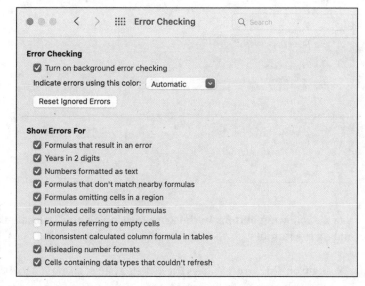

FIGURE 14-12:
Control the types
of errors Excel
checks for in
the Error
Checking pane.

When Excel spots an error, it displays a small triangle in the cell's upper-left corner. If you click the offending cell, a smart button containing a caution icon (an exclamation point in a yellow diamond) appears. Click the smart button's drop-down arrow and choose an option to help you resolve the issue. After you've corrected the problem, Excel removes the error code and the indicator.

For some people, those little menu triangles are difficult to see and, in a sheet with a lot of text, the error codes don't necessarily stand out. Excel provides the Error Checking dialog (which you open by choosing Tools⇨Error Checking), shown in Figure 14-13, to help you find and fix any problems. If Excel doesn't find any errors on the sheet, it tells you, "No errors were found." If it finds errors, it displays the Error Checking dialog, which displays errors one at a time, starting in cell A1 and going across each row in turn.

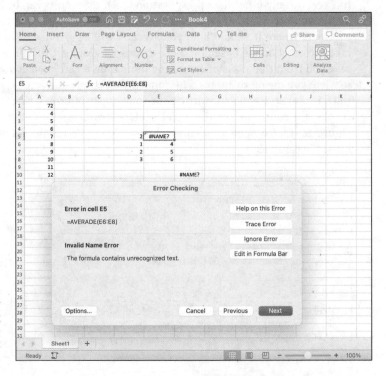

FIGURE 14-13:
Use the Error
Checking dialog
to easily locate
problematic
formulas.

Use the following buttons in the Error Checking dialog to locate the error's cause and fix the formula:

>> **Help on This Error:** Invokes Excel's Help system, taking you to the page discussing the particular error type

>> **Trace Error:** Draws a box around the cells in the argument list and an arrow pointing to the formula

>> **Ignore Error:** Does just what you'd expect from its name

Ignoring some errors, such as when a formula doesn't include adjacent cells containing data, removes the error indicator; however, if a real problem exists, such as a syntax error, the error indicator remains.

>> **Edit in Formula Bar:** Dismisses the Error Checking dialog and places your cursor in the formula bar so that you can make corrections

>> **Options:** Presents the Error Checking pane in the Excel Preferences dialog

>> **Cancel:** Dismisses the Error Checking dialog

>> **Previous/Next:** Moves to the previous or next error, if one exists

Error Checking works on only the active sheet in your workbook. If you want to check other sheets, select them and reinvoke the Error Checking dialog by choosing Tools ⇨ Error Checking.

Sorting and Filtering Data

One common use for Excel is as a list manager (a simple database). Every column is a field, and every row is a record. (Okay, every row other than the first is a record if the first is used to display field names. Excel calls it a *header row*.) Examples of such lists are inventories of personal possessions (for example, vinyl records, which are once again in vogue), membership lists, or bridal registries. In fact, many of the online templates discussed earlier in this chapter are simple databases (lists). Excel's powerful searching and sorting features that we're about to help you explore, along with Excel's formulas to calculate values based on the data you enter, make Excel an excellent vehicle for this type of list management.

Sorting data

When presenting list data, you often need to display it in a sorted order. For example, when listing contact information, occasionally you want to sort by surname, zip code, or company or department. Excel makes these types of sorts easy to accomplish. Just follow these two steps:

1. **Select a cell in the column you want to sort.**

If you select the column header rather than a cell, Excel gives you the option to sort only the contents in the selected column or to expand your selection so that data in other columns is sorted to track with the first column.

2. **Click the down arrow next to the Sort & Filter button on the ribbon's Data tab and choose Sort Smallest to Largest or Sort Largest to Smallest from the pop-up menu.**

   Your records (the rows) are now rearranged with the sort column controlling the order in which they appear.

If your sort column contains numbers, the sort order depends on whether the cells are formatted as text or numbers. If the data is simply text composed of digits (that is, it's left justified in the cells), you might not get the result you expect. For example, 11 precedes 2 when sorted textually. When you want to sort numbers, make sure that the cells in the column are formatted as numeric data.

Using filters to narrow your data searches

Another common database or list operation is to search for only those records that meet specific criteria. (For example, a library might use this type of operation to create a list of all its hardback books.) These searches filter out records that don't match your criteria, which is why Excel calls these searches *filters*.

To perform a simple filtering operation, follow these steps:

1. **Click in any cell in your list.**

2. **Click the Sort & Filter button on the ribbon's Home tab and click the Filter button. Or click the Filter button on the Data tab (shown in Figure 14-14).**

   Filter arrows appear at the top of each column.

3. **In the column heading for the data you want to filter, click the filter arrow.**

   A dialog appears, as shown in Figure 14-14.

4. **Click the Choose One pop-up menu and then click a criteria to select it.**

5. **Click the value pop-up menu and select a value from the list.**

   Rows that don't match your filter criterion are hidden until you choose to show them again (by clicking the filter arrow again and choosing Clear Filter).

The Filter arrow turns into a tiny filter icon for a column that has a filter applied. Also, the row numbers for those rows matching the filter are displayed in blue.

Filter arrows   Filter button

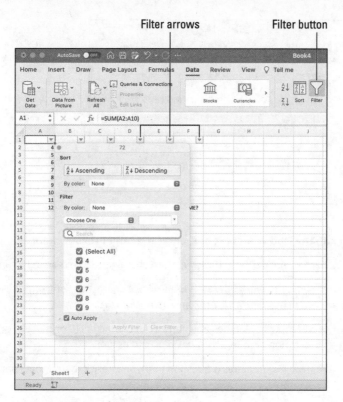

Finding and Replacing Data

As your worksheets fill with data, locating a particular number or piece of text can become problematic. Although Excel filters are useful for finding values in the columns of a list, not all worksheets are lists. If you want to find a particular number or text string wherever it occurs in your worksheet, a more generic searching capability is required. As usual, Excel provides commands to facilitate your searches.

You can search a cell range, sheet, or workbook for a target number or text. To do so, follow these steps:

1. If you want to search a cell range, select the range; otherwise, click in any individual cell to search either the sheet or the entire workbook.

2. Choose Edit ⇨ Find ⇨ Find.

The Find dialog (seeing a pattern yet?), shown in Figure 14-15, appears.

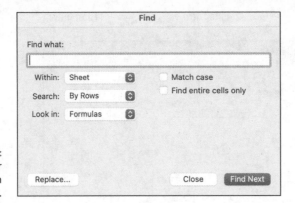

FIGURE 14-15:
Search for specific values in the Find dialog.

TIP

3. **In the Find What text box, enter the target text or number.**

   Excel supports these three wildcard characters in your search string:

   - *Question mark (?):* Matches any single character. For example, entering **a?m** matches *alm, arm, asm,* and *abm.*

   - *Asterisk (*):* Matches any number of characters (0 or more). For example, entering **a*m** matches *am, alm,* and *accum.*

   - *Tilde (~):* Precedes a question mark or asterisk to find that character. For example, enter **abc~?** to match *abc?.*

4. **(Optional) Choose from the following pop-up menus or check boxes to refine your search:**

   - *Within:* Specify whether to search only in the current sheet or all sheets in the workbook.

   - *Search:* Search by row or column.

   - *Look In:* Restrict your search to formulas, values, notes, or comments.

   - *Match Case:* Select this check box to make a text search case-sensitive.

   - *Find Entire Cells Only:* Select this check box to confine the search to exact matches — for example, a search for **Frank** doesn't match a cell containing *Frank Sinatra.*

5. **Click Find Next.**

6. **When you're finished, click Close.**

Closely related to searching text is replacing it. To find one piece of data and replace it with another, proceed as follows:

1. **To search a cell range, select the range; otherwise, click any individual cell to search either the sheet or the entire workbook.**

2. **Choose Edit ➪ Find ➪ Replace.**

   The Replace dialog appears, as shown in Figure 14-16.

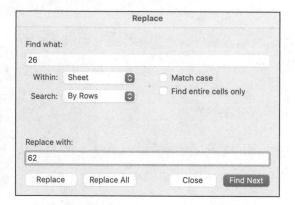

3. **In the Find What text box, enter the target text or number.**

4. **in the Replace With text box, enter the replacement value.**

5. **(Optional) Choose from the Within pop-up menu to specify whether to search only in the current sheet or all sheets in the workbook.**

   Choose from the Search pop-up menu to search by row or column. The Match Case check box makes a text search case-sensitive, and the Find Entire Cells Only check box confines the search to exact matches. (For example, a search for *Elvis* doesn't match a cell containing *Elvis Presley*.)

6. **Click Find Next.**

7. **If you want to replace the found value with your replacement value, click Replace.**

8. **Repeat Steps 6 and 7 as often as you want.**

9. **(Optional) To perform a blanket replacement without inspecting the found values, click Replace All rather than perform Steps 6 through 8.**

10. **When you're done, click Close.**

Chapter **15**

Enhancing and Printing Your Excel Spreadsheets

The devil may be in the details, but presentation is everything. Raw data underlies everything you do in Excel, but human eyes glaze as they pore over row after row, column after column, and sheet after sheet of numbers and text.

In every business meeting where results are discussed, both in real life and on TV or in the movies, the results are shown in charts: Business is bad and a jagged line moves down and to the right; business is good and the line climbs up and to the right; candidate Smith is leading candidate Jones 45 percent to 30 percent with 25 percent undecided, and you see a pie chart.

When data is presented in tabular form, the important numbers (usually totals or averages) are frequently displayed in a larger or bold font against a contrasting background, often with arrows pointing at them. And, contrary to the idealized concept of a paperless office, a few trees often must be killed to disseminate your data or report to clients or customers. Thus, you should print the report with all appropriate page numbering, authorship information, dates, and other types of information — and that's placed in the header or footer on each page.

This chapter walks you through using Excel features to help you achieve your presentation goals, whether they're electronic or printed.

Creating and Formatting Charts

Fred Barnard is credited with coining the maxim "A picture is worth a thousand words" and attributing it to a Chinese proverb. The proverb is even more appropriate in reference to numbers rather than words — at least in the opinion of the *USA Today* editorial staff (and most other mainstream media), in which charts and graphs abound when presenting statistical information.

Excel offers a wide range of chart categories. Each category includes two or more of the following variations on the theme, enabling you to graphically communicate your data:

>> A **column chart** illustrates a comparison of values over time, such as monthly receipts or expenses.

>> A **line chart** tracks trends, such as stock prices or inventory levels over time, where each data point is connected to the next one by a line.

>> A **pie chart** demonstrates which portion of a whole each category comprises (for example, which percentage of all vehicles sold were Fords).

>> A **bar chart** illustrates comparisons among individual items. Essentially, it's a column chart, rotated 90 degrees, that's less likely than a column chart to be time-based.

>> An **area chart,** which is essentially an aggregate line chart, shows a total and which portion of the total each subtotal contributes.

>> An **XY chart** (or scatter chart) shows data distribution and is handy for locating cluster points.

>> A **stock chart** illustrates opening, high, low, and closing stock prices.

>> A **surface chart,** which acts similarly to a complex area chart, demonstrates the interactions of multiple values, such as longitude, latitude, and elevation (for a topographic map).

>> A **sunburst chart,** like a pie chart, illustrates which portion of a whole each component comprises. However, in contrast to a pie chart, a sunburst chart can show the apportionment of multiple wholes in nested concentric rings.

>> A **treemap chart** displays hierarchical data using nested rectangles within categories.

» A **histogram chart** arranges numerical data by frequency.

» A **pareto chart** uses both bars and line graph to display data and is generally used to more easily identify areas of information that should be focused on first.

» A **box and whisker chart** displays the spread and the center of sets of data, with boxes demonstrating the center and two lines (whiskers) showing the minimum and maximum spreads.

» A **waterfall chart** visualizes the cumulative effects of adding or subtracting numerical data to or from an existing value.

» A **funnel chart** illustrates the stages of a process, such as sales over time.

» A **radar chart** plots each row's values along separate axes drawn from the center to the vertex of a regular polygon. (Four rows result in a quadrilateral, five result in a pentagon, eight in an octagon, and so on.)

The simplest way to create a chart in Excel is to use the Insert Chart group on the Charts tab. To do so, follow these steps:

1. **Select the data you want charted.**

2. **Click the Insert tab and then click the icon for a chart category.**

    You see thumbnail representations of available chart styles in that category.

    You can also click the Recommended Charts button to see charts Excel recommends for the type of data you've selected.

TIP

3. **Click the thumbnail representation for the specific chart type you want.**

4. **(Optional) Use the Chart Design and Format tabs to customize titles and labels, as well as other formatting.**

    These tabs appear only if the chart you created in Step 3 is selected, which it is by default the moment it's created.

If you move the cursor into the chart, the cursor turns into a *move* cursor (four-headed arrow). Click and drag to reposition your chart. Also, when the chart is selected, a small border surrounds the chart, with handles at each corner and the midpoints of each side, allowing you to click and drag to resize or reshape the chart. (Corners scale both height and width; hold down the Shift key while clicking and dragging to scale proportionally. Sides resize only the height or width.)

Excel maintains a link between the chart and its underlying data. Thus, if you modify the data, Excel updates the chart to reflect your change. Clicking a chart's border area causes Excel to highlight the underlying data in your worksheet by drawing borders around it, as shown in Figure 15-1.

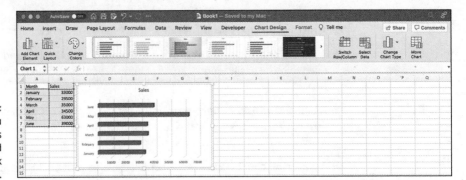

FIGURE 15-1:
Excel shows you
which data is
being charted
when you click
the chart area.

TIP

You can control the order in which your data series is plotted without rearranging the supporting data. Follow these steps:

1. **Click the chart to select it.**

2. **Click the Chart Design tab on the ribbon.**

3. **Click the Select Data button near the right end of the ribbon, as shown in Figure 15-2.**

The Select Data Source dialog appears. Note the list of data series items in the Legend Entries (Series) box on the left, as shown in Figure 15-3.

FIGURE 15-2:
The ribbon
provides full
configuration
control.

4. **Select the series you want to move and then click the up or down arrow until the list of series is in the order you want.**

Note that if only one series is being plotted, you can't reorder, and no data series appears in the list.

5. **Click OK.**

The chart redraws to display the series in your new order.

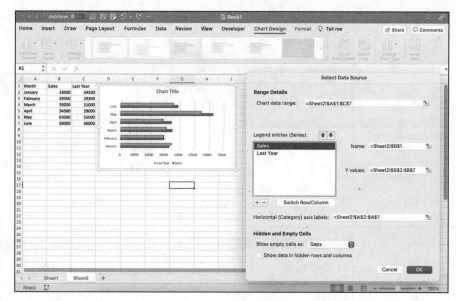

Including Pictures and Shapes

To paraphrase a proverb, "You can lead your audience to the data, but you can't make them understand." Charts, as described earlier in this chapter, give your audience a nudge toward comprehension, but sometimes you need to be less subtle. Including a line with an arrowhead leading from an important datum to its graphical representation can provide that proverbial slap upside the head, as shown in Figure 15-4.

Arrows aren't the only way to adorn your sheets. Using the Illustrations button on the ribbon's Insert tab (shown in Figure 15-5) gives you access to the Office shape library (click Icons to open the Stock Images pane, also shown in Figure 15-5), clip art, SmartArt, 3D models, and even images from your Photos library.

"Of what use," you might ask, "are photographs on a spreadsheet?" Well, Excel is used so often as a list manager (see Chapter 14 for details) that you can imagine a workbook that charts, for example, statistics for players on a Little League team. A snapshot of each player beside the player's row would be a nice presentational touch.

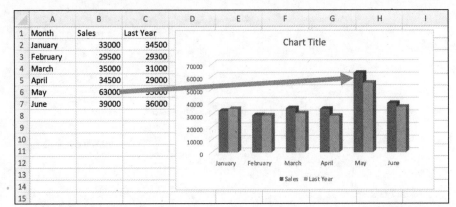

FIGURE 15-4:
Occasionally, you
have to make
your point truly
obvious, and an
arrow can do
the work.

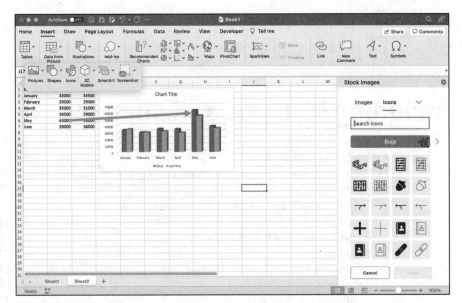

FIGURE 15-5:
The Insert tab's
Illustrations
button is your
graphics
one-stop-
shopping spot.

You can also use images in charts, which is particularly common in column charts to fill the bars. To do so:

1. **Select a data series in your chart.**

2. **Click the ribbon's Format tab, and then click the Format Pane button on the right side of the ribbon.**

   The Format pane opens on the right.

3. In the Format pane, select the fill & line icon (paint can), and then click Fill in the list provided to expand its options. as shown in Figure 15-6.

4. Select the Picture or Texture Fill radio button, click the Insert button in the Picture Source section, and place your chosen graphic in the chart.

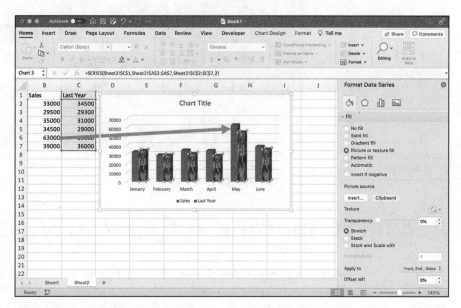

FIGURE 15-6:
Use the Format pane to change the fill for a data series in your charts.

Adding a graphic to your sheet — whether the image is a shape, a piece of clip art, or a photo— is as simple as selecting it using the options under the Pictures button. (To find the Pictures button, click the ribbon's Insert tab and then click the Illustrations button.) The image, as shown in Figure 15-7, appears with eight resizing handles around its bounding box. Drag any handle to resize. (The corner handles resize proportionally; the midpoint handles scale in just one dimension.) Move the cursor within the rectangle to display the repositioning arrows and then click and drag to move the image. The little green ball connected to the top of the image is your rotational handle; position the cursor atop the green ball (the mouse cursor changes to a circular arrow, as shown in Figure 15-7) and then click and drag to rotate the image.

Using the controls on the ribbon's Picture Format tab, you can recolor, crop, and adjust the appearance of any selected picture on your sheet. You can even right-click the picture and choose Change Picture to substitute a new image in place of the existing image without losing any other formatting you've performed on the old image. Or you can click the Reset icon on the Picture Format tab and remove any adjustments you've made to the image.

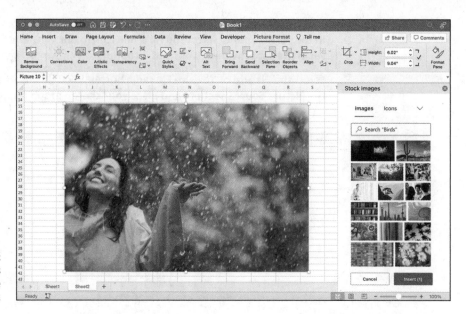

FIGURE 15-7:
Use the handles
to resize or rotate
an image.

Adding Formatting and Special Effects

macOS is a graphics powerhouse, and the Office ribbon takes extensive advantage of its available features. In addition to all the expected text formatting capabilities, the ribbon is *context-sensitive*, which means that when you select a chart or graphic on a sheet, you see tabs specific to that object, so you can tweak its appearance. The ribbon offers so many ways for you to adjust appearance that comprehensive coverage would far exceed the size of this book. We hit just a few high points here, but rest assured that the general techniques involved remain the same for all formatting features, with details tailored to the particular object you're formatting.

The Picture Format tab, shown in Figure 15-8, includes the following tools to let you alter a selected image:

>> **Color:** Adjust the image color.

>> **Crop:** Adjust the image size.

>> **Quick Styles:** Choose a different frame style for your image from a panoply of options.

>> **Set Transparent Color (from the Color pop-up menu):** Make a specific color transparent.

>> **Artistic Effects:** Apply a plethora of Photoshop-like special effects and filters.

>> **Reset picture:** Undo all applied formatting and effects.

FIGURE 15-8:
The Picture
Format tab lets
you apply both
fine and coarse
adjustments to
your graphics.

Reset Picture

TIP

If you need to replace the image with another, just right-click the picture and choose Change Picture from the pop-up menu.

The Crop to Shape item (which appears as part of the Crop pop-up menu) lets you apply a cookie-cutter shape to your content, but that bounding shape might not be immediately apparent if your image has a good amount of transparency (as does a great deal of clip art). To fix this problem, start by right-clicking the picture and choosing Format Picture. Then, in the Format Picture pane that opens on the right, click the fill & line icon (paint can pouring paint), select Fill, and specify a fill color or pattern to make the shape apparent.

When you select the Set Transparent Color item (available from the Picture Format tab's Color pop-up menu, as shown in Figure 15-9), the cursor turns into an arrow that you use to click a specific color in the image that you want to make transparent. Be aware that this command works best on solid blocks of color, not in photographs with subtle differences in shade, where it makes transparent only the specific tint you click.

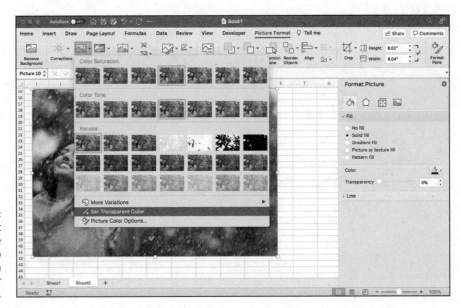

FIGURE 15-9:
Transparent
Color allows the
background to
show through
specific color
regions.

Clicking the effects icon (pentagon) in the Format Picture pane presents the options shown in Figure 15-10. The familiar shadow, reflection, glow, bevel, and 3D effects are available: Just select an item to apply the effect. Remember that you can always choose Undo from the Edit menu if an effect you've applied doesn't look right.

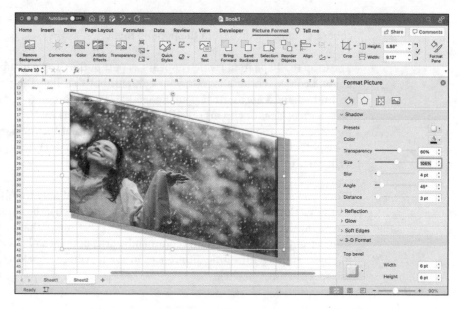

FIGURE 15-10:
The Format Picture pane's Effects tab is a treasure trove of filters and effects.

If you've used Photoshop or Photoshop Elements, you'll be familiar with the effects in the Artistic Effects category on the ribbon's Picture Format tab, shown in Figure 15-11; your image must be selected for this tab to appear on the ribbon. Most of these impressive effects are identical to the ones you find on the Photoshop Filters menu and in its Filter gallery. If you're unfamiliar with these powerful Photoshop-like tools, we strongly encourage you to play with them!

TIP

If, at any time, you want to return to square one, click the reset picture icon in the Picture Format tab (refer to Figure 15-8) and the image returns to its initial state.

FIGURE 15-11:
The Picture
Format tab's
Artistic Effects
option lets you
apply Photoshop-
style filters
to an image.

Creating and Sorting Custom Lists

Excel knows about four lists: months of the year and days of the week, in both
spelled out and abbreviated, three-character form. But those are just the seed corn
to lists in Excel. Choose Excel ➪ Preferences and click the Custom Lists button (in
the Formulas and Lists row). Doing so displays the Custom Lists pane in Preferences, as shown in Figure 15-12. Note that the months and days already appear in
the Custom Lists list box.

FIGURE 15-12:
In the Custom
Lists pane, create
and manage
the lists Excel
knows about.

Creating a custom list

You can define a list in two ways. First, if you have the entries on a sheet, you can just import them. Just click the Import List from Cells box near the bottom of the pane, enter or select the range of cells containing your list, and click the Import button.

Second, the manual method is a simple two-step process:

1. **In the Custom Lists dialog, click in the List entries box.**
2. **Type your list items, in order, pressing Return after each entry.**
3. **To add the new list to the Custom Lists pane on the right, click the Add button.**

Some candidates for custom lists include department names or codes, inventory item names or SKUs, state names or abbreviations, and commonly used categories such as Q1, Q2, Q3, and Q4. Anything you use for labeling columns is a candidate. Custom lists can be used for sorting as well as for AutoFill fodder.

Sorting a list

To sort based on a custom list, follow these steps:

1. **Click a cell in a table.**
2. **Click the Data tab, click the arrow next to the Sort icon, and then choose Custom Sort from the pop-up menu.**

   The Sort dialog appears.
3. **In the Order pop-up menu, choose Custom List, as shown in Figure 15-13.**
4. **Select a list to sort by and then click OK.**
5. **To dismiss the Sort dialog and perform the sort, click OK again.**

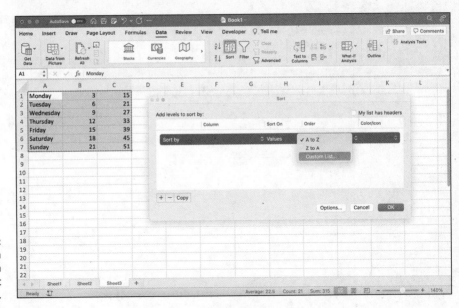

FIGURE 15-13:
Choose a custom list to specify a column's sort order.

Adding Headers and Footers

What would a report be without headers and footers on every page, telling you the title and page number and other pertinent information? The answer is that the report would be just fine, as long as you had only one or two pages to deal with and never got the pages out of order. Reality, however, dictates that you will have multiple reports to reference (maybe monthly reports that look very much alike) or will need to tell your boss that a particular data point can be found on page 18.

REMEMBER

Headers and footers appear only in page layout view, so they're out of the way when you're working on a sheet in normal view — Excel's only other view.

Creating a header or footer

When you're viewing your spreadsheet in page layout view, the words "Add header" appear above the first row, as shown in Figure 15-14. Similarly, the words "Add footer" appear in the area below the page's last row. Simply clicking in those boxes lets you add a header or a footer, respectively.

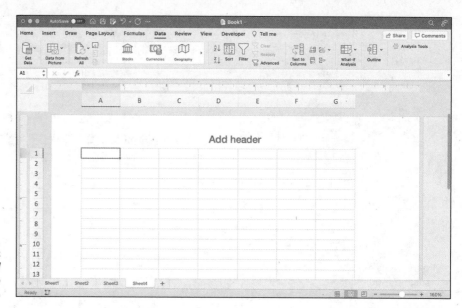

Editing a header or footer

Clicking within a header or footer allows you to edit the text within it.

When you're editing a header or footer, Excel displays the Header & Footer tab on the ribbon, as shown in Figure 15-15. You use this tab to insert codes for commonly used but variable items, as well as to format the text.

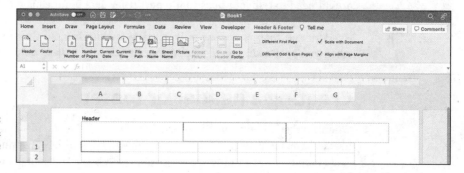

This list describes what happens when you click some of these tab buttons:

» **Page Number:** Inserts a code (&[Page]) for the page number that will appear in your document.

» **Number of Pages:** Inserts the number of pages. Its code is &[Pages].

- >> **Current Date:** Inserts the current date, using the code &[Date]. Note that the current date is the date at the time you're viewing or printing the sheet. If you want the creation or last-edited date to appear here instead, enter it manually.

- >> **Current Time:** Inserts the time of viewing or printing and is represented by the code &[Time].

- >> **File Path:** Inserts the path to the file of the document that's open, such as DrMacHD/Users/bobl/Documents/Office4Dummies/Chapter15.xlsx. The code is &[Path]&[File]. If you don't want the filename displayed, choose Edit⇨Undo (or press ⌘+Z), which toggles back and forth between including and not including the &[File] portion of the code.

- >> **File Name:** Inserts only the &[File] code described in the previous bullet.

- >> **Sheet Name:** Tells Excel to print or display the name of the worksheet. Its code is &[Tab]. (Did you expect &[Sheet], by any chance?)

- >> **Picture:** Presents a dialog in which you can navigate to any folder that contains the image you plan to use. Excel places the code &[Picture] where the graphic is to be displayed.

- >> **Format Picture:** Invokes the Format Header/Footer Picture pane on the right, letting you adjust the picture's size, orientation, and visual attributes.

TIP

Header and footer areas are divided into three pieces each: left, center, and right. You fill in each section separately, and the content of those sections is justified to match their position on the page. (The left is left justified, the middle is center justified, and the right is right justified.) You can move from one section to another by using the mouse or the keyboard. Pressing the Tab key lets you cycle through the sections by moving the cursor from left to right; pressing Shift+Tab moves the cursor from right to left.

Printing Your Spreadsheets

You've formatted your sheets, adorned them with charts and graphics to illustrate results and provide context, and added the header and footer information your audience needs to place your data in order and provide context. Now it's time to get down to the business of printing all this work you've accomplished. Read on to see how to set up your document by using the Page Setup dialog.

Preparing for printing with Page Setup

You've probably done much of your setup work on the ribbon's Layout tab (such as orientation, scaling, and printing gridlines or headings). Many of these same controls are available also in the Page Setup dialog.

Excel's Page Setup dialog is highly customized and bears little visual similarity to the standard Page Setup dialogs you encounter in other apps, such as TextEdit, Mail, or Music. To open the dialog, choose File ⇨ Page Setup. Figure 15-16 shows this dialog with the Sheet tab selected.

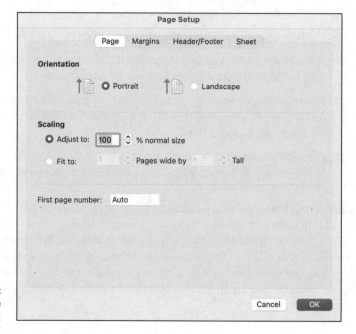

The four tabs in the Excel Page Setup dialog reveal panes that enable you to choose various settings for your page's appearance:

>> **Page:** Includes controls for orientation, scaling, and page numbering.

>> **Margins:** Controls the left, right, top, and bottom margins for the sheet and any header or footer, as well as whether the printout should be centered horizontally or vertically — or both or neither.

>> **Header/Footer:** Almost makes irrelevant the header/footer discussion that appears earlier in this chapter. You can choose from a number of canned header and footer samples on the Header and Footer pop-up menus, or you can create your own header or footer by clicking Custom Header or Custom Footer. Both present a dialog with instructions and buttons that duplicate the Header & Footer ribbon tab buttons. The Header dialog appears in Figure 15-17.

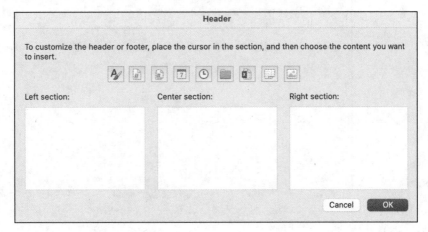

FIGURE 15-17:
The Header
dialog.

Header

To customize the header or footer, place the cursor in the section, and then choose the content you want to insert.

Left section:

Center section:

Right section:

Cancel   OK

>> **Sheet:** Divided into various sections:

- *Print Area:* Specify which portions of a sheet to print.

- *Print Titles:* You can include column headers and row labels on subsequent pages. For example, by specifying **$A$1:$D$1** in the Rows to Repeat at Top text box, you tell Excel to print the column headers at the top of every new page. Similarly, if you have category labels in column 1 that you want repeated on every page, you specify that cell range in the Columns to Repeat at Left text box.

- *Print Options:* These controls let you specify that you want gridlines, row or column headings (such as A–Z, 1–9), or comments to print. (See Chapter 16 for more details about comments.) Additionally, you can specify that the printing be in black-and-white or draft quality.

- *Page Order:* Specify the order in which the pages print when the sheet is too large to fit on one page. You can choose whether to print from left to right and then down (choose Over, then Down) or from top to bottom and then across (Down, then Over).

Ready, set, print

Choosing File ⇨ Print (or pressing ⌘+P) presents the standard macOS Print dialog. As is the case in virtually every Print dialog on either Mac or Windows, some variation of what you see depends on the printer and printer driver you're using, as shown in Figure 15-18.

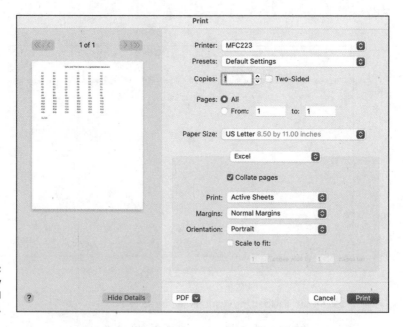

FIGURE 15-18: Excel's slightly customized Print dialog.

Click the Excel pop-up menu in the Print dialog to access other print features of Excel, macOS, and your specific printer.

TIP

You can ⌘+click sheet tabs to make multiple sheets active. The Quick Preview is quite useful, in this case, to peruse and verify that you've selected all the sheets you want printed.

Chapter **16**

Advanced Spreadsheeting

E xcel is the industry standard spreadsheet application — the one to which every other spreadsheet is compared — for a reason. Thus far, all challengers have come up short. Microsoft introduced Excel (on the Mac, first) back in 1985, replacing its Multiplan spreadsheet. One of Excel's biggest features in the early days was that it was the first to let the user alter a sheet's appearance by supporting multiple fonts, character attributes, and shading. Microsoft continued adding features, allowing users to control more of Excel's functionality, including extensive automation capabilities.

In this chapter, you find out how to customize Excel to make it work like you want it to, use multiple sheets in a workbook, and add hyperlinks to spreadsheets. You also learn how to collaborate with others to combine your spreadsheet talents.

Customizing Excel

Microsoft has gone to great lengths to make Excel look, feel, and behave like a natural part of your macOS experience. Tailoring Excel's appearance and behavior to fit your work style and sense of aesthetics falls into two major areas: preferences and the Excel toolbar and menu system.

Preferences

The Excel Preferences dialog (choose Excel⇨Preferences or press ⌘+comma), shown in Figure 16-1, bears a strong resemblance to the macOS System Preferences window. You can find most customization options in this dialog's various panes (which appear when you click the corresponding icon in this dialog).

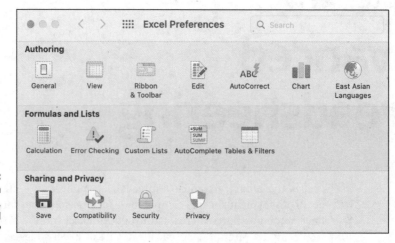

FIGURE 16-1:
Is it System
Preferences,
or is it Excel
Preferences?

Excel lets you tune its appearance and behavior to suit your style and usage. You get a plethora of choices in the various categories.

Covering every option in detail would add so many pages to this book that you'd need a crane to lift it. We hit only a few of the preferences you might want to find quickly. Besides, every preference pane has a Description box, which displays useful information about any option over which you hover the cursor.

General pane

The General pane, which you can access by clicking the leftmost button on the Authoring row (labeled General), includes a few especially useful preferences:

- » **Use R1C1 Reference Style:** Unless you're incredibly comfortable with alternative numbering systems, you probably think C1024 is a more comprehensible name for the 1024th column than AMJ. Selecting the R1C1 check box bypasses the mental gymnastics of performing base 26 arithmetic (with letters substituting for numbers) to specify a column name and lets you use standard decimal numbering preceded by R (for row) and C (for column) when designating a cell (or row or column).

- » **Default Font:** As its name implies, use this text box (or the associated pop-up menu) to specify your preferred font. The default is the aptly named Body Font — better known as Calibri. (You can also specify a default size for your chosen font by using the Font size text box and pop-up menu.)

- » **Show Workbook Gallery when Opening Excel:** If you work primarily with existing documents and find the Workbook gallery an unnecessary addition when you first launch Excel, deselect this check box and the application immediately displays a new, blank workbook.

- » **Confirm before Opening Other Applications:** We like to enable this option so that if we don't intend to open another application (such as opening a web browser by accidentally clicking a hyperlink in a spreadsheet), we can simply deny the action and stay in Excel.

View pane

The View pane controls what Excel features are visible and how some features are displayed. You find options in these boxes to establish default behaviors:

- » **Show in Workbook:** You can hide or show the formula bar, sheet tabs, headers, and other items, as well as specify whether new sheets appear in normal or page layout view. Excel's default is to display new sheets in normal view.

- » **For Cells with Comments, Show:** Controls whether and how comments are shown. See the section "Collaboration and Revision Tracking (a.k.a. Change Tracking)," later in this chapter, for a discussion of comments.

- » **For Objects, Show:** Controls whether non-cell data, such as graphics, charts, text boxes, and others, are shown in their entirety, displayed as gray rectangles (indicators), or hidden.

- » **In Ribbon, Show:** Hide or show the Developer tab and Group Titles. Selecting the Developer tab check box displays the Developer tab on the ribbon, from which Excel pros can utilize Visual Basic and other advanced tools.

Ribbon & Toolbar pane

You're unlikely to find a model home in which every aspect is exactly the way you want it. The home might be slightly more expensive than is comfortable, you might want to repaint a room, or you might decide to replace the living room carpeting. A perfect match is rare. Like the model home, Excel might be close to what you want but still leave you feeling the need to tweak it. For example, you might find Excel's ribbon and its menus cluttered with features you don't need (if, say, you use Excel almost exclusively as a list manager, you probably don't need pivot tables). Similarly, you might want a single location that contains the tools and commands you use most often. Look no further than the Ribbon & Toolbar pane for such customizations.

As discussed in Chapter 3, you can customize the dickens out of the ribbon and toolbar in Microsoft Office apps, and Excel is no exception. This preferences pane affords two tabs: one for customizing the ribbon itself and its commands, and another for customizing the Quick Access toolbar, which resides at the top of every Excel workbook window.

Edit pane

The Edit pane controls how Excel behaves while you're editing a sheet (for example, when you enter data and how you interact with cells). One option on this pane allows you to specify how Excel interprets two-digit year values when you enter a date. By default, Excel interprets 00 to 29 as 2000 to 2029 and 30 to 99 as 1930 to 1999.

AutoCorrect pane

In the AutoCorrect pane, you can access the Excel subset of Word's AutoCorrect preferences. Check out Chapter 6 for the scoop on Word's AutoCorrect.

Chart pane

The Chart pane has only two options, and both pertain to showing information in charts when you roll your cursor over the various elements within them. One option allows you to see the names of elements, and the other displays data point values.

East Asian Languages pane

Microsoft Office supports the use of East Asian languages, but the feature must be enabled from this pane. Choose Japanese, Simplified Chinese, or Traditional Chinese from the Select a Language pop-up menu, and then restart Excel to apply language-specific features.

Calculation pane

The Calculation pane, which appears when you click the Calculation button in the Formulas and Lists row, has two sections:

» **Calculation Options:** Specify whether formulas recalculate automatically (for example, when any referenced cell's value, name, or formula changes). The default is Automatic, but you can choose Automatic Except for Data Tables or Manual. Use the Iteration controls to limit how many calculations Excel performs when it encounters a circular reference or performs a goal-seeking calculation. (The default is 100.) Similarly, you can tell Excel to stop recalculating when results differ from the previous result by less than a set limit. (The default is 0.001.)

» **When Calculating Workbooks:** Specify whether to use the 1904 date system (the date system based on the Macintosh system clock, in which time began at midnight, January 1, 1904). You can also have Excel store values retrieved from external links (the default setting). By default, Excel stores everything to 15 decimal places; however, if you select Set Precision as Displayed, Excel stores only as many decimal places as you set for display precision. (The default display precision can be set in the Editing preferences pane.)

WARNING

If you're not absolutely sure you need it, we suggest that you don't use the Set Precision as Displayed option. You could end up losing data you later find you needed.

Error Checking pane

The Error Checking pane controls which errors are flagged. (See Chapter 14 for more details about error checking.)

Custom Lists pane

In the Custom Lists pane, you can add to the four custom lists with which Excel ships. See Chapter 15 for a fuller discussion.

AutoComplete pane

AutoComplete preferences tell Excel when and how to suggest values while you type, such as for function names (see Chapter 14) and text values.

Tables & Filters pane

By default, Excel references table names in formulas and resizes tables automatically if they span more than one column or row. You can turn off this perfectly legitimate behavior from the Tables section of this preferences pane. The Filters section of this pane has just one setting: By default, Excel displays dates grouped by year/month/day in a filtered column. Disable the Group Dates when Filtering check box to turn off this feature.

Save pane

The third preferences category, Sharing and Privacy, includes the Save preferences pane, in which you can tell Excel whether you want Autosave enabled by default (we'd heartily recommend that you leave this option selected) and whether you want it to save a preview picture for new files.

Compatibility pane

The Compatibility pane is a major destination, especially if you plan to share your workbooks with other users. In addition to pointing out when you use features not available in other Excel versions on either the Mac or Windows, the pane enables you to specify the default file format in which Excel saves workbooks. By default, Excel saves workbooks in .xlsx format (an XML-based format introduced in Excel 2007 on Windows), but if you need to interact with users of much older versions (which is fairly rare these days), you should probably opt for the older .xls format, used by Excel 97 through Excel 2004. (Other formats are available, including various interchange formats, such as comma-delimited text.)

Security pane

In the Security pane, you can set Excel to remove personal information (such as the authorship information on the File Info Summary tab), and activate a warning that appears when you're opening a workbook that contains macros. If you use the Enable All Macros option, you can be a Typhoid Mary, passing on macro viruses to others who may use macro-enabled files.

Privacy pane

The Privacy pane allows you to opt in or out of cloud-based connected experiences across the devices with which you use Microsoft Office products.

Conditional Formatting

Excel, like other spreadsheets, has its genesis in VisiCalc, an electronic ledger. One common practice in ledgers is to use different ink colors to highlight specific characteristics. For example, red ink can indicate a loss or negative value, and black ink can indicate a positive value. These color uses have become part of common English vernacular — something's "in the red" when it's losing money and "in the black" when it's showing a profit.

Excel takes the "in the black/in the red" metaphor a little further with *conditional formatting*, with which you can specify formatting attributes that you want to apply to a cell's contents based on the cell's value or on a formula you define.

To apply conditional formatting to a cell, proceed as follows:

1. Select the cell(s) to which you want to apply conditional formatting.

2. Choose Format⇨Conditional Formatting.

The Manage Rules dialog appears (see Figure 16-2).

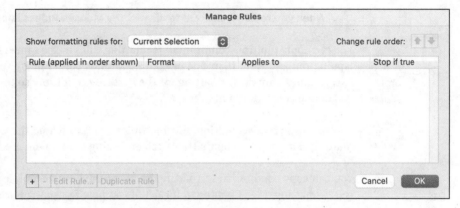

FIGURE 16-2: Use the Manage Rules dialog to add conditional formatting rules.

3. To add a new formatting rule, click the + (add) button.

4. To change the default two-color scale, click the Style pop-up menu to specify icons, data bars, the three-color scale, or Classic style (a single color).

The settings you see change according to the style you're using.

5. If necessary, to specify the target values for the cell, use the options in the Minimum and Maximum sections.

Again, Excel displays different settings depending on the choice you made on the Type pop-up menu in the Minimum and Maximum sections. Figure 16-3 illustrates the default rule, which is based on lowest and highest values in a cell — therefore, you don't have to enter a minimum or maximum value for the default rule.

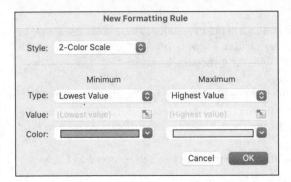

FIGURE 16-3:
In the New Formatting Rule dialog, you can configure conditional formatting.

6. **Click each of the Color pop-up menus and select colors.**

7. **Click OK.**

8. **(Optional) To set additional conditions, click the + (add) button.**

9. **When you're done, click OK to dismiss the Manage Rules dialog.**

REMEMBER

You can apply multiple conditional-formatting rules to the same range or to overlapping ranges. More than one of your conditions can evaluate to true; however, Excel applies only the formatting for the first true condition, so the order in which you define your criteria matters.

TIP

You can also create conditional formatting rules by clicking the Conditional Formatting icon on the ribbon's Home tab and using the pop-up menus that appear.

You can copy conditional formatting by using the Format tool, as with any other cell formatting. (See Chapter 14 for details on how to use the Format tool to copy a cell's formatting.) So, after you have a set of criteria you like, you can apply them to additional cells by selecting the cells with the conditional formatting, clicking the Format tool, and dragging across new cells to which you want to apply the formatting.

To modify or remove a conditional formatting criterion, choose Format⇨Conditional Formatting and make your changes in the Manage Rules dialog that appears. (You can change the applied formatting by clicking Edit Rule.) To delete a conditional formatting rule, click it in the list to select it, and then click the – (delete) button.

TIP

To completely remove conditional formatting from cells, select the cells and choose Edit⇨Clear⇨Formats.

Naming a Cell Range

A cell's name is called a *cell reference.* Cell reference nomenclature can be either R1C1 (for example, R31C27) or column letter/row number (for example, AA31 for column 27, row 31) format, depending on your General preferences setting. However, when you're working with your data, you probably think of a group of cells that contain inventory unit costs as something like Unit_Costs, not as B5 through H5. You might even place a text label in A5 that says Cost_per_Unit so that when other people look at your sheet, they know what the numbers mean.

You can assign a name to a cell or a range of cells and use that name in formulas rather than use the less descriptive cell references. To name a cell range, follow these steps:

1. **Select the cells you want to name.**

2. **In the formula bar's Name box (the box at the far left end of the bar), type a descriptive name for your selection.**

   Names must start with a letter or an underscore; consist of only letters, digits, periods, or underscores; be different from any cell reference; and be no longer than 255 characters. You can use both uppercase and lowercase characters, but Excel treats names as case-insensitive, so unit_cost and Unit_Cost are considered the same name.

You can now reference the cell range by name in formulas. For example, entering =AVERAGE(Unit_Cost) in the preceding example is the same as entering =AVERAGE(B5:H5), but you can more easily recognize which cells the first formula is describing.

Working with Multiple Worksheets

Excel workbooks can contain more than one sheet. In fact, previous versions of Excel defaulted to three sheets in newly created workbooks. (Excel defaults to one, but you can change that number in Excel's General preferences pane by typing a new value into the Sheets in New Workbooks text box.) Also, you can add sheets to your existing workbooks when you have the need (or desire). You may wonder why you'd want multiple sheets in a workbook. There are as many answers to that as there are to why you'd want to have multiple pages in a notebook. A teacher might want a grade book that contains one sheet for every class taught — keeping related data in one file is surely more convenient than managing multiple files. Or you might want to consolidate your financial data into one book, with separate sheets for checking accounts, savings accounts, brokerage accounts, and credit cards.

Excel offers many ways to add sheets to an existing workbook:

>> Choose Insert⇨Sheet and then choose the type of sheet from the submenu that appears: Insert Sheet (Blank) or Chart Sheet.

>> Click the + (plus) tab near the bottom of the workbook window to add a new, empty sheet.

>> To add a new, empty sheet, right-click any sheet's name tab and choose Insert from the shortcut menu that appears.

TIP

You don't have to live with only the generic Sheet-*n* name that Excel provides. You can double-click the text on the sheet's name tab to highlight it and type a new name. Or you can choose Rename from the shortcut menu that appears when you right-click the sheet's name tab. Again, the name becomes highlighted, and you can type a new name.

Excel cell reference notation can handle references to cells on other sheets and even in other workbooks. For example, you can reference cell C2 on Sheet2 in a formula on Sheet1 by using the notation Sheet2!C2. In other words, precede the cell reference with the sheet name (enclosing it in quotes if it contains spaces) and an exclamation point. To reference cells in another workbook, you can enclose the workbook name in square brackets, followed by the sheet name, an exclamation point, and then the cell reference. For example, "[GradeBook]SecondPeriod!C2" references cell C2 on the sheet named SecondPeriod in the workbook named GradeBook.

REMEMBER

For workbooks that aren't open, the full file system path to the workbook precedes the filename. Thus, the following line:

```
'BobsLion/Users/BobLevitus/Documents/Workbooks/[DVDs]Backups!Latest'
```

might refer to a cell in which you record the disk name, date, and time of your last data backup (yes, backing up your data is important!) in a workbook that contains your DVD inventory.

Hyperlinking

As with the other apps in Microsoft Office, you can insert hyperlinks in Excel. These links can redirect you to a web page; create a preaddressed email message; or open another Office document, prepositioned to the referenced text (in Word), cell (in Excel), or slide (in PowerPoint).

Creating a hyperlink to an Excel cell or object is easy. Just follow these steps:

1. **Select the cell or object that you want to become the hyperlink.**

2. **Choose Insert⇨Hyperlink (or press ⌘+K).**

   The Insert Hyperlink dialog appears (see Figure 16-4).

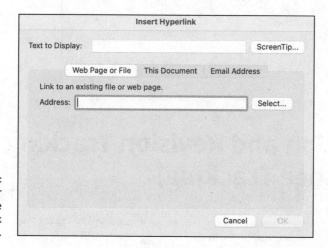

3. **Select the tab for the type of link you want to create.**

   For the purpose of this example, we're linking to a specific cell in the Excel workbook we're working in, so we select the This Document tab. The options in the Web Page or File and Email Address tabs work similarly.

4. **Type the cell reference (or select from the named documents and defined names in the dialog's lower list), as shown in Figure 16-5.**

5. **(Optional) In the Display text box, make the display text more descriptive, such as Total Assets or Stock on Hand, if you want.**

   You can also attach a ScreenTip that appears whenever the cursor hovers over the link. Click the ScreenTip button in the upper right of the Insert Hyperlink window. In the dialog that appears, type the text you want displayed in the ScreenTip.

   TIP

6. **Click OK to dismiss the Insert Hyperlink dialog.**

Removing a hyperlink is simplicity itself. Right-click a cell that contains a hyperlink and select Remove Hyperlink from the shortcut menu that appears. Similarly, if you want to modify or otherwise edit an existing hyperlink, right-click the cell containing the hyperlink and choose Edit Hyperlink.

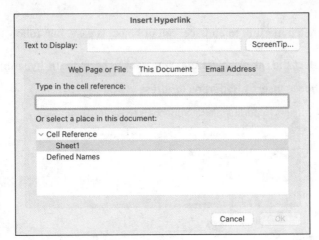

Collaboration and Revision Tracking (a.k.a. Change Tracking)

Sometimes, it takes a village (or, at least, a group) to create a spreadsheet. If your project requires input from multiple parties, you'll truly appreciate Excel's support for collaboration and revision tracking.

When you share a workbook, Excel automatically disables a number of Excel features, including

>> Creating or modifying conditional formatting

>> Merging cells

>> Adding or changing charts, pictures, shapes, and hyperlinks

So, if you want to perform any of these tasks, do so before you turn on change tracking and workbook sharing (or simply don't even turn them on).

Saving a workbook online

You can save your Excel workbooks to any storage device on your home or office network, as long as you have the proper permissions — but saving that same workbook to OneDrive and sharing it with others allows them to collaborate with you.

To save your workbook to your OneDrive, follow these steps:

1. **Click the Share button in the upper-right of your workbook's window to open the Share dialog, shown in Figure 16-6.**

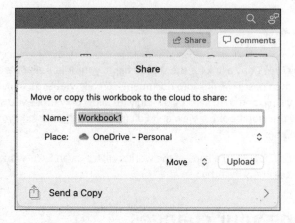

2. **(Optional) Type a new filename for your workbook.**

3. **Click a destination OneDrive account for the file (if you have more than one, perhaps for personal use or business).**

4. **Choose Move or Copy from the pop-up menu to the immediate left of the Upload button.**

   Move will move the file from its present location to your OneDrive account, while Copy will make a copy of it instead.

5. **Click Upload to upload the file to your OneDrive.**

To share your uploaded workbook with others:

1. **Click the Share button in the upper-right of your workbook's window to open the Share dialog, shown in Figure 16-7.**

   Note that the Share dialog offers different options than it did in Figure 16-6. That's because the file has already been uploaded to OneDrive.

2. **Choose a method for sharing your file with others:**

   - *Invite People:* Click Invite People, enter the names of people in your Apple Contacts app or just type their email addresses, add a message if you like, and then click the Share button. If you want them to be able to edit your workbook, be sure to check the Can Edit box before clicking Share.

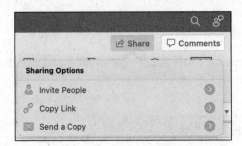

FIGURE 16-7:
Share your
uploaded
workbook via
OneDrive.

- *Copy Link:* Copy a link for the shared file to your Mac's clipboard, which you can then paste the link into documents, emails, websites, and so on. Click Copy Link, and then select View-Only (to allow only those you share with to view the workbook) or View and Edit (to allow others to edit your workbook).

- *Send a Copy:* Send a copy of the workbook file as an Excel workbook or as a PDF to others via email.

Tracking your changes

To track changes, choose Tools ⇨ Track Changes ⇨ Highlight Changes. In the High-light Changes dialog that appears (see Figure 16-8), make sure that the Track Changes While Editing check box is selected. (Otherwise, Excel doesn't save changes for you to view, accept, or reject later.)

FIGURE 16-8:
The Highlight
Changes dialog
lets you highlight
changes during a
specific period, by
a specific user or
users, or to a
specific cell
range.

When the Highlight Changes on Screen check box is selected (which it is by default), the changes appear in a ScreenTip whenever you hover the cursor over a change. A changed cell has a dark blue triangle in its upper-left corner, similar to the triangle indicating a formula error. (See Chapter 14 for more about Excel's error checking and marking.) Selecting the List Changes on a New Sheet check box tells Excel to create a history sheet for the change log (a textual history of all changes made).

REMEMBER

You can't log changes to a new sheet until the workbook has been saved with the Track Changes While Editing check box selected. After you turn on change tracking, save the workbook by clicking OK in the Save dialog that appears and then choosing Tools⇨Track Changes⇨Highlight Changes again. In the dialog that appears, select the List Changes on a New Sheet option. Yeah, this procedure is cumbersome, but not everything in life (or Excel) is easy.

Accepting and rejecting your changes

Now comes the payoff. You can review your changes and accept or reject them, either individually or all at the same time. Here's how:

1. **Choose Tools⇨Track Changes⇨Accept or Reject Changes.**

   Excel might prompt you to save your workbook at this point. If it does, go ahead and save your workbook.

   The Select Changes to Accept or Reject dialog appears, as shown in Figure 16-9.

FIGURE 16-9:
Specify the group
of changes you
want to check for.

Select Changes to Accept or Reject

☑ When: Not yet reviewed

☐ Who: Everyone

☐ Where: |

Cancel   OK

2. **Specify the types of changes you want to consider.**

   The default is All, but you can limit the considered changes to a specific user, time frame, or cell range by choosing from the pop-up menu and clicking OK.

   The Accept or Reject Changes dialog appears (see Figure 16-10).

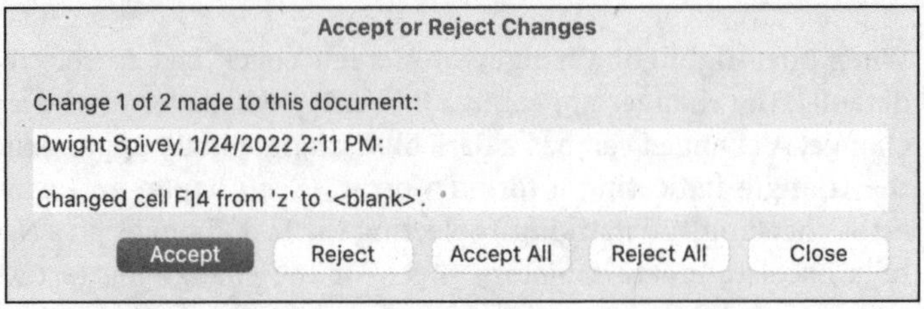

FIGURE 16-10:
Step through the
change history in
the Accept or
Reject Changes
dialog.

3. **Click the Accept or Reject button for each change.**

   Excel proceeds to the next change. Alternatively, you can click Accept All or
   Reject All to have Excel perform a blanket acceptance or rejection of all
   subsequent changes, without your input for each individual change.

4. **Click Close when you finish.**

   The Accept or Reject Changes dialog closes, and you return to your worksheet.

With this sort of control, you can relate to the Mel Brooks line in *History of the World, Part I* — "It's good to be the king!"

5

Microsoft Outlook: Miraculous Manager of Most Things

Review Outlook's five unique modules for managing email, news, people, events, notes, tasks, and more.

Discover how you can add email accounts to Outlook, send and receive email, spruce up your emails with fonts and images, add attachments, and more.

Learn how to keep track of events and appointments with Calendar, manage your contacts with Address Book, stay on top of your to-do lists with Tasks, and jot down your great ideas with Notes.

Synchronize data with other Mac apps and set up the Outlook modules so that they're all just the way you like them.

» Taking a tour of the major Outlook features

» Checking out all five Outlook modules

Chapter **17**

Getting to Know Outlook

One member of the Office for Mac quartet is Outlook. Compared to the others, it's an odd duck. You see, whereas each of the other three Office for Mac apps excels (pun intended) at a single task — word processing for Word, slideshows for PowerPoint, and spreadsheets for Excel — Outlook is more like five apps in one. To be precise, it includes five modules:

» An email client

» An appointment calendar

» A contacts manager

» A task manager

» A repository for notes

Put 'em together and what do you have? Microsoft Outlook, the Swiss army knife of Office for Mac apps. If we had to come up with a single name for everything Outlook does, we'd call it a personal information manager. In this chapter, you take a quick look at each of the five modules and how you might want to use them.

Taking a Quick Tour of Outlook

In contrast to the other Office apps, Outlook's five "views" don't appear on the status bar or on the View menu. Rather, you switch between them using the icons in the view switcher (at the lower left side of the window) or keyboard shortcuts.

Because each of the five modules has a slightly different interface, ribbon, and menu items, we offer the following sections to help acquaint you with the look and feel of each one.

The Mail module

The Mail module is a lot like the Apple Mail app that comes with your computer, as you can see in Figure 17-1. To activate it, press ⌘+1 or click the envelope icon in the view switcher (in the lower-left corner).

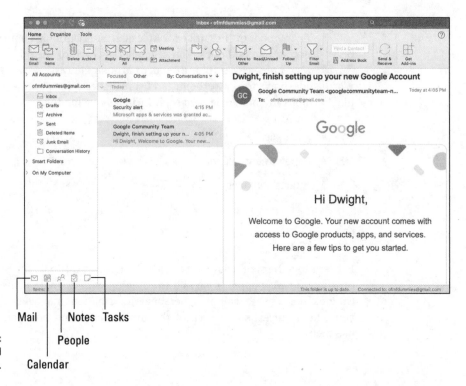

FIGURE 17-1:
Outlook Mail module.

As Apple Mail does, the Outlook Mail module offers a variety of folders for your mail and a junk mail filter. Instead of a toolbar, however, Outlook offers icons on the now-familiar ribbon.

TIP

Feature for feature, Outlook and Apple Mail are more alike than different. Why use one instead of the other? Mostly, it's a matter of preference. If you're accustomed to using Outlook for Windows or you're using the other Office for Mac programs extensively, you might prefer Outlook for its similarities and integration with those apps or to make use of Outlook rules and categories. (You can find out more about these features in Chapters 18 and 19, respectively.) On the other hand, if you've been using Apple Mail for a while, switching to the Outlook Mail module may be more trouble than it's worth.

For details on the Mail module, see Chapter 18.

The Calendar module

The Outlook Calendar module (shown in Figure 17-2) is a lot like the macOS Calendar app that comes with your Mac. You activate the Calendar module by pressing ⌘+2 or clicking the calendar icon in the view switcher.

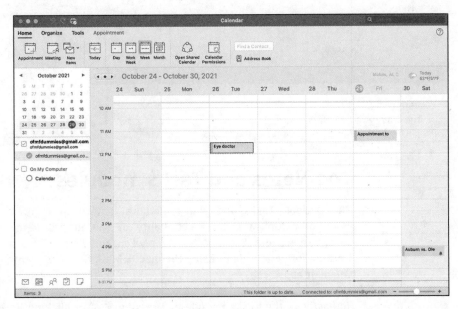

FIGURE 17-2:
The Outlook
Calendar module.

And, once again, the choice of which to use — the Outlook Calendar module or the macOS Calendar app — comes down strictly to your preference. There's no huge advantage to using one or the other. Try both and use whichever one you prefer.

You can find out more about the Calendar module in Chapter 19.

The People module

The People module is a lot like the Apple Contacts app that comes with macOS, as you can see in Figure 17-3. You activate it by pressing ⌘+3 or clicking its icon in the view switcher.

You can learn more about the People module in Chapter 19.

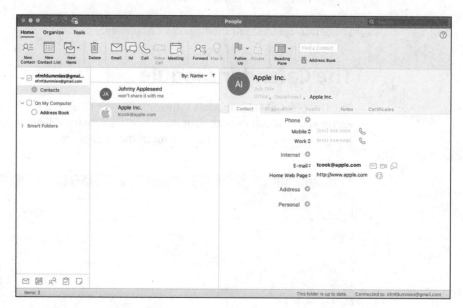

FIGURE 17-3:
The Outlook
People module.

The Notes and Tasks modules

The Outlook Tasks and Notes modules, shown in Figures 17-4 and 17-5, essentially duplicate the functionality of the macOS Reminders and Notes apps, respectively. See *MacOS Monterey For Dummies,* written by Bob "Dr. Mac" LeVitus, for details about using the macOS Mail, Contacts, Reminders, Notes, and Calendar apps.

You activate the Tasks module by pressing ⌘+4 or clicking its icon in the view switcher. Chapter 19 tells you much more about creating and using tasks in Outlook. As for the Notes module, you activate it by pressing ⌘+5 or clicking its icon in the view switcher. You can read more about the Notes module in Chapter 19 as well.

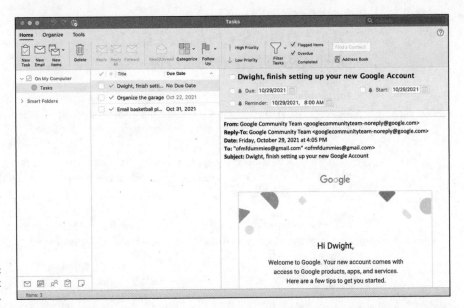

FIGURE 17-4:
The Outlook
Tasks module.

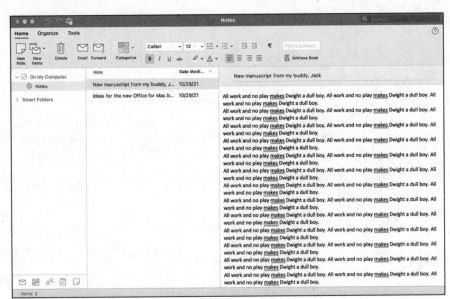

FIGURE 17-5:
The Outlook
Notes module.

OUTLOOK'S CHAMELEON MENUS AND RIBBON

You might notice that the fifth menu from the left in the Mail module is named Message. But in the Calendars module, the same menu is named Event; and in the People module, it's Contact.

Note also that the ribbon changes depending on which module is active. In fact, only a few items are common to all five modules, including the search field and the module icons in View Switcher.

We just want to make sure you know to expect that some menus and most ribbon icons are different in the different modules as you delve deeper into Outlook in later chapters.

Onward!

Chapter **18**

Emailing with Outlook

S ure, Outlook is a full-featured email client, but it's about as useful as a pound of dirt until you set things up correctly. Luckily, Microsoft has made the configuration process for most of us as automatic as possible, and even the folks who have to resort to setting things up manually will find the process easier than configuring Outlook's previous iterations. (That's our idea of progress — limiting the amount of technobabble required to make something work.).

This chapter shows you how to set up Outlook for email, and you'll also find out how to use Outlook to send, receive, and manage email. We present it all with a minimum of fuss and no splitting headache — promise.

Setting Up Outlook for Email

When sending and receiving email are working properly, we take them for granted. But you must configure your mail client software (Outlook) properly before any sending or receiving can occur.

That's the bad news. The good news is that after you've configured Outlook properly, you'll probably never have to do it again (unless you change your internet service provider or your account information changes).

The first thing you need to do is get Outlook and your mail server connected. You can start by configuring Outlook for email. Outlook supports IMAP and POP email accounts, as well as Outlook.com, Google, iCloud, Exchange, Yahoo!, and other popular email providers.

You have two ways to set up your email: automatically and manually. The automatic way is, as you might expect, much easier and the best way to set up the aforementioned providers, so we suggest that you try it first. As a matter of fact, Outlook is going to try hard to set things up automatically, as its prompts during the account setup process do their best to hide the fact that a manual option is even available. In case the automatic process doesn't work for you, or if your email provider requires you to set things up manually, we tell you how to perform a manual setup.

Setting up your email automatically

You use the Outlook Account Setup Assistant to configure your email access automatically. To do so, follow these steps:

1. **Choose Tools⇨Accounts.**

    The Accounts pane appears in the Outlook Preferences dialog.

2. **Click + (add account) at the bottom of the window, and then click New Account.**

    The Set Up Your Email dialog appears, as shown in Figure 18-1.

    In this chapter, we cover how to set up a typical ISP or web-based email account. If you need to connect to your company's Microsoft Exchange server, ask your network administrator for the specific configuration settings it requires.

3. **Type the email address for the account you want to configure, and then click the blue Continue button.**

4. **Follow the prompts to complete your account authentication.**

    The steps vary, depending on the type of email account you're adding. (Sorry, but there are simply too many variations at this stage of the process to cover in this book.) You may be whisked away to another window, or perhaps even your default web browser, to enter your password information and allow Outlook permission to access your account and its features.

    After you've successfully authenticated your account, Outlook lets you know that it's been added, as shown in Figure 18-2.

    If the automatic configuration wasn't successful, Outlook displays a dialog with an error message, possibly indicating why it couldn't access your account. Double-check that your email username and password information are correct, and then give it another try. If you continue to be unsuccessful, you'll want to reach out to your email provider for assistance.

FIGURE 18-1:
Enter your email
account
information here.

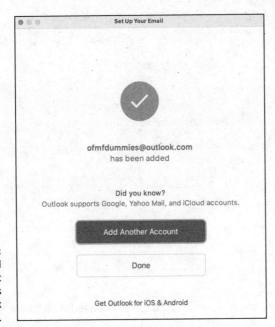

FIGURE 18-2:
A successful
automatic
configuration has
set up an Outlook
account.

5. **(Optional) To add another account, click the blue Add Another Account button.**

Follow the prompts, as you did in Step 4.

6. **When you've finished adding accounts, click Done.**

7. **Verify that all information on the screen is accurate.**

Note that your new account appears in the left sidebar of the Accounts pane, as shown in Figure 18-3.

If this was the first account you added to Outlook, it's marked as the default account. If you've added multiple accounts and the wrong one is set as the default, click the one you want to make the default, click the options icon (circle with an ellipsis) at the bottom of the sidebar, and click Set as Default.

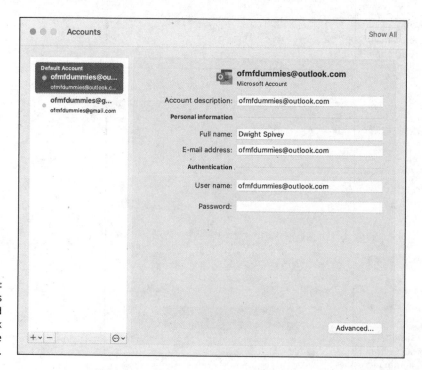

FIGURE 18-3:
Email accounts that you've added to Outlook appear in the Accounts pane.

Don't worry if you don't understand some of the technical babble you may see in the Accounts pane (again, what you may see varies widely depending on the email provider). Settings such as Incoming Server and Use SSL to Connect are correct already if automatic configuration was successful. Make sure, however, that your full name appears as it should — if not, click in the Full Name field and type a moniker.

TIP

Do you have a number of different email accounts from the same email provider (such as two iCloud accounts)? If so, you might want to add a descriptive name to each account so that they're easier to tell apart (for example, Dwight's Work Account and Dwight's Personal Account). Simply click in the Account Description field and type the new name.

8. **To close the Accounts pane and return to the main Outlook Mail window, click the red circle in the upper-left corner.**

TIP

If you ever want to change anything about this account, simply click its name in the Accounts pane (which you open by choosing Tools⇨Accounts). But because you just verified that everything about this account is working properly, you probably don't want to change anything at this time.

Setting up your email account manually

A few email providers require you to manually add email accounts to email apps like Outlook. To do so:

1. **Choose Tools⇨Accounts to open the Accounts pane.**

2. **Click the down arrow next to the add icon (+) at the bottom-left of the Accounts pane and choose New Account from the pop-up menu.**

   The Set Up Your Email dialog appears.

3. **Type your email address for the new account, and then click the Continue button.**

   If Outlook is unable to configure the account automatically, the screen shown in Figure 18-4 appears, with a list of email providers and an IMAP/POP option.

4. **To continue manually, click the IMAP/POP button.**

5. **In the Type pop-up menu, choose the type of account you want to set up: IMAP or POP.**

   See the nearby sidebar "How to find information about your email account" for tips on locating your account type and other information.

6. **Fill in the fields shown in Figure 18-5:**

   - *Email Address:* The email address for this email account, which you entered earlier.

   - *Username:* The name you use to log in to your email account (not your full name, most likely). It appears in the From field in outgoing email messages, so don't get cute here.

   - *Password:* The password for this email account, which you entered earlier.

- *Incoming Server:* The name of the mail server that receives your mail.

- *Outgoing Server:* The name of the SMTP server that sends your mail.

  Filling in the Incoming and Outgoing Server fields might be tricky. If you don't know the name of your mail and SMTP servers, refer to the nearby sidebar "How to find information about your email account."

7. **When you've finished filling in these fields, click the blue Add Account button.**

Alas, when you set up an account manually, Outlook will attempt to verify the account information and refuses to add the account if anything is wrong.

1. **Choose File⇨New⇨Email (or press ⌘+N).**

   You can instead click the Home tab on the ribbon and then click the New Email icon (it's the first icon in the Home group).

2. **If you have more than one account, in the From pop-up menu choose the one you just set up manually.**

3. **In the To field, type the email address of the same manually added account.**

4. **In the Subject field, type** Test.

   You don't need to type anything in the body of the message, unless you want to.

5. **Click the Send icon in the message window (near the upper-left corner).**

HOW TO FIND INFORMATION ABOUT YOUR EMAIL ACCOUNT

In case you don't know what type of account you have or you don't know any of the information you need to set up your account manually, here are some ways to find it:

- Look in the documentation or paperwork you received with your cable or DSL modem or router.

- Search on your email provider's website.

- Call your email provider on the telephone.

Wait a few minutes and then choose Tools ⇨ Send & Receive, or press ⌘+Control+K, or click the Send & Receive icon on the Home tab of the ribbon.

At this point, one of the following should have happened:

>> The test message arrived safely in your Outlook inbox.

>> The test message is still sitting in your outbox, and an error message has appeared on your screen.

If you received an error message, go to Tools ⇨ Accounts and double-check the settings for the account. If you're convinced they're correct, get in touch with your email provider's support team to get help.

TIP

The Use SSL to Connect (Recommended) option is frequently the cause of issues with sending and receiving email. In the settings for your account, you'll see one check box for the incoming server and one for the outgoing server. Select or deselect one or both to see if that resolves the error message.

Sending, Receiving, and Managing Your Email

The Outlook Mail module offers everything you need to send, receive, and manage email from one account or many. This section tells you how to do all these things and more.

Creating and sending messages

One primary purpose of an email program is, of course, to create and send email messages. If you sent yourself a test message, as described earlier in this chapter, you know how to create a message already. We describe the task here as well, and show you some cool things you can do to messages you create, such as format and beautify the text, add attachments, and create and use multiple signatures.

To create a message, follow these steps:

1. **Choose File ⇨ New ⇨ Email to open a new email window.**

You can instead press ⌘+N or throw caution to the wind and click the New Email icon on the Home tab of the Outlook ribbon.

2. **If you have more than one email account, choose from the From pop-up menu the one you want to use to send this message.**

3. **Address your message in one of these ways:**

   - *Click in the To field and type a recipient's email address.* If the recipient is in your contacts, simply click the person's name when it appears as you type. Repeat as necessary to add other recipients.

   - *Click the little address book card icon (shown in the margin) to open the Search Contacts and Rooms window, as shown in Figure 18-6, and then drag and drop the contact into the To field. When you've finished adding recipients, click the little red circle in the upper-left corner of the Search Contacts and Rooms window.*

TIP

   To restrict your search to just contact names, click the Search All Fields pop-up menu and click Search Names Only.

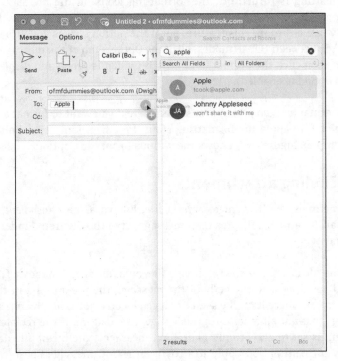

FIGURE 18-6: Dragging and dropping is one way to add a recipient.

4. **Adding a subject line to any email you send is considered good form, so type a subject in the Subject field.**

5. Click in the body of the email and type your message.

If you're a good typist and prefer to use the keyboard instead of the mouse, press the Tab key to move forward from field to field or press Shift+Tab to move backward from field to field. Try it — you'll like it.

At this point, you can click Send in the toolbar and send the message, but read on if you want to make your message prettier first.

Formatting your message text

To format the text in your message, HTML formatting must be turned on, which, luckily, it is by default. If it's turned on (and we remind you that it is by default), you can select a portion of the text and choose a font, size, style, and justification and all the other items in the Message tab above the body of the message. But if formatting is turned off, the formatting icons on the message window ribbon appear dimmed and are unavailable. Honestly, we can't think of a good reason why you'd turn off this feature, but if the notion strikes you, it's simple to do. To toggle between HTML modes, click the Options tab of the message window ribbon and then click the Format Text switch (which is green and displays HTML when the option is enabled).

To format text, you must first select the text you want to format and use the Message tab to apply the formatting (font, font size, font color, bold, and italic, for example). Figure 18-7 shows the various formatting options.

Including attachments

Sometimes, you'll want to send a file, known as an *attachment*, to someone by email. To attach a file to a mail message, drag the file from Finder to the message window.

If the file is a media file (an image file, an audio file, or a movie file, for example) and you drag it to the body of the message, the file appears in the body of your message, where it can be seen or played — an *embedded* attachment. (Note, however, that not all email programs allow this feature. If the recipient's email program is set to accept only plain-text messages, the media file doesn't show up. Any formatting you apply to text in an HTML message doesn't show up if the recipient is using a text-only email app.)

As with text formatting, adding an attachment to a message increases the amount of data that has to be sent, resulting in longer transmission times. If you're sending a high-resolution photo or a long video clip, for example, you can easily add several megabytes of data to a single email message. If the message is returned by the recipient's email server as undeliverable because it's too large, you know that the attachment added too much bulk.

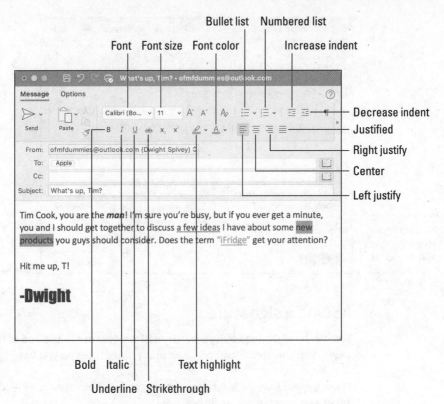

Bullet list　Numbered list

Font　Font size　Font color　Increase indent

Decrease indent

Justified

Right justify

Center

Left justify

FIGURE 18-7:
The Message tab
and its options
for formatting
text.

Bold　Italic　　Text highlight

Underline　Strikethrough

You can also click the Attach File icon on the Message tab to select one or more files from the familiar File Open dialog. After you've attached one or more files to a message — in other words, without embedding them in the body of the text — they appear in the Attachment line under the Subject field, as shown in Figure 18-8. To the right of the filename is its size.

To remove a file from the Attachment line, click the small arrow to its right and then click Remove, as shown in Figure 18-8.

TIP

Click the tiny arrow to the right of any file in the Attachment line and choose Preview to open the Quick Look display for that file. Outlook doesn't have to launch the app. For example, you can view a Word document without waiting for Word to load.

REMEMBER

The names and sizes of media files embedded in the body of the message don't appear in the Attachments line, and you can't remove them by selecting them from the menu shown in Figure 18-8. To remove a media file from the body of your message, select it in the body of the message and then press Delete.

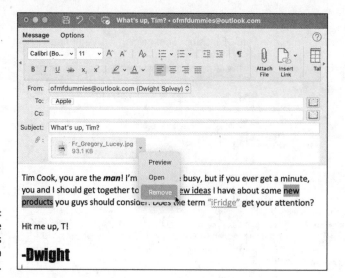

Adding a signature

You can have Outlook automatically add a signature to the end of your email messages. You can create and reuse as many signatures as you like.

Many people have at least two signatures for their messages — one for personal email and another for business.

Here's how to create and use signatures:

1. **Choose Outlook⇨Preferences and then click the Signatures icon.**

   The Signatures pane appears in the Outlook Preferences dialog.

2. **Click + (add a signature) in the middle left of the pane, and a new window appears for you to customize the signature.**

3. **In the Signature Name field, type a new name for the signature.**

   Your name is used as the starting point for all new signatures.

4. **Type the signature in the body portion of the window, as shown in Figure 18-9.**

5. **(Optional) Select the text in your signature and use the familiar tools on the Signature window's ribbon to format the text to your liking.**

6. **To add the new signature to your Signatures list, click the red circle in the top-left corner of the Signature window, and then click Save when prompted.**

   You're then returned to the Signatures pane of the Outlook Preferences dialog.

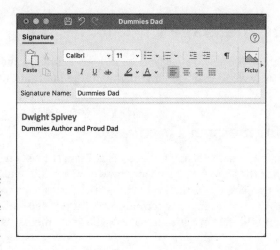

FIGURE 18-9:
A signature is
great way to spice
up and personal-
ize your emails.

7. **(Optional) To specify which signature will be added automatically to your messages:**

   a. *In the Choose Default Signature area, click the Account pop-up menu and select an account.*

   b. *Click the New Messages menu, the Replies/Forwards menu, or both, and select a signature.*

   To turn off the automatic default signature feature, click the pop-up menu and choose None.

8. **Close the Signatures pane by clicking the red Close button in the upper-left corner.**

That's it. To add a signature to a message manually, click the Message tab in the email window and then click the down arrow next to the Signature icon. It's just under the Picture icon on the ribbon, and its icon looks like a tiny pen writing on paper. If the icon is hidden, you might need to click the arrow on the right side of the ribbon or expand the email window by clicking and dragging its right edge. On the menu that appears, choose the signature you want to use. It's then inserted in the message at the current insertion point.

To give you an idea of how versatile the Outlook signature feature can be, we have created five signatures— Consulting, Long, Short, XLong, and XShort. Each is slightly different from the others, and we select the one that's the most appropriate before we send a message.

TIP

No law says that this feature must be used for *only* signatures. If you have other boilerplate text you use often, you can create a signature of it. Then to insert it into a message, click the Signature icon on the message window's ribbon and choose the boilerplate signature from the pop-up menu.

Receiving messages

This section shows you how to get your mail both manually and automatically. Then you look at ways to manage junk mail with the built-in Outlook junk mail filter.

Checking for messages manually

You can receive mail manually any time you like. From the ribbon, click the Home tab and then click the Send & Receive icon toward the right. Menu lovers can click Tools⇨Send & Receive. From the keyboard — the fastest method, of course — simply press ⌘+Control+K. In a few seconds (or minutes, depending on your connection speed and the size of your messages), your new messages appear in your inbox.

But who wants to remember to go fetch email a dozen times a day? Fortunately, Outlook lets you set up schedules for automatically sending and receiving mail.

Scheduling an email to be sent later

Sometimes you may prefer to go ahead and write an email but have it sent at a later time. An example of this type of email is a weekly newsletter.

REMEMBER

This is a great feature, but it's limited to Microsoft Exchange email accounts, including Outlook.com and Microsoft 365 accounts.

To schedule an email:

1. **Create your email message.**

2. **Click the tiny arrow next to the Send button and then click Send Later.**

TIP

   If you don't see the tiny arrow next to the Send button, your email account doesn't support this feature. Try selecting a different email account in the From field, if you have multiple accounts.

3. **In the fields provided, shown in Figure 18-10, select the date and time you'd like this email to be sent.**

4. **To set the scheduled deliver, click the Send button.**

If you want to cancel or reschedule the delivery, go to the Drafts folder for the account, select the scheduled email, and click the Cancel Send button. You can then send the email immediately, reschedule the date and time for delivery, or cancel the email.

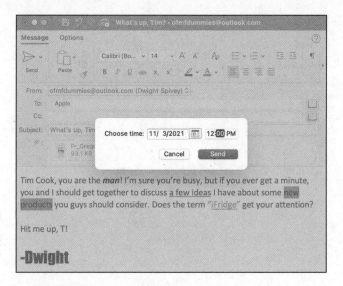

Dealing with junk mail

Nobody likes it, but everyone gets it. We're talking about junk mail, also known as *spam*. Fortunately, Outlook has tools to filter spam before it arrives in your inbox and quarantine it in a special Junk Email folder.

The junk email feature has changed a bit over the years. Outlook used to act as the main traffic cop of your email messages for most, if not all, account types. That's no longer the case, because Microsoft now believes that your ISP or email provider should bear some or all of the load. That's why the junk email feature works for only IMAP and POP email accounts.

TIP

If you enable IMAP or POP for an email account such as Google (check with Google or your ISP or email provider to find out how to do this), you'll need to add the account to Outlook manually for Outlook's junk email feature to work with it.

Here's how to set up and use the junk email tools.

1. **Choose Tools⇨Junk Email Preferences to open the Junk pane, as shown in Figure 18-11.**

    If the Junk Email Preferences option is dimmed, your email account doesn't support it. And if your accounts are not IMAP or POP, you won't see them in the Junk pane under the "These Settings Only Apply To" section on the left.

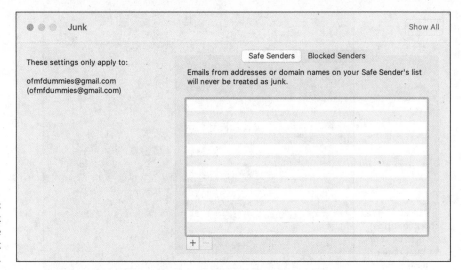

FIGURE 18-11:
Allow and block senders using the tabs in the Junk pane.

2. **To make sure that email from specific senders is always delivered to your inbox and not filtered by the junk email tool:**

   a. *Click the Safe Senders tab.*

   b. *Click + at the bottom of the window.*

   c. *Type the email address of the sender you want to allow.*

   You can also simply add a domain to this list, which allows any email from that domain to come through unscathed. For example, if you want to allow all emails from dummies.com, just type dummies.com in the field.

TIP

   If an email address is in your Outlook contacts, it's never classified as junk (unless you add that address to your Blocked Senders list, which we cover in the next step).

3. **To make sure that email from specific senders is always filtered by the junk email tool and sent to the Junk Email folder for the account they're sent to:**

   a. *Click the Blocked Senders tab.*

   b. *Click + at the bottom of the window.*

   c. *Type the email address of the sender you want to thwart.*

   You can also add a domain to this list, to block all email from that domain. For example, if you want to keep out all emails from dummies.com, just type dummies.com in the field.

4. **Click the red circle in the upper left to close the Junk pane.**

Now Outlook will evaluate all your incoming mail for the affected accounts and direct to the Junk Email folder any message it thinks is spam.

Each email account has its own Junk Email folder, so be sure to check them all if you have multiple email accounts. When you first start using this feature, you probably should look in all your Junk Email folders regularly, just in case a piece of good mail has been misclassified.

If you receive a junk mail message in your inbox, you can get rid of it in several ways:

» Select the message and choose Message⇨Junk Mail⇨Mark as Junk, or press ⌘+Shift+J. Or from the ribbon's Home tab, click the Move button, click the Junk button, and then select Junk, Not Junk, or Block Sender.

» Right-click the message directly in the list and choose Junk Mail⇨Mark as Junk from the contextual menu.

Either method helps train the junk mail filter so that the next time you receive a similar message, Outlook is more likely to automatically classify it as junk.

Conversely, if a piece of good mail accidentally ends up in a Junk Email folder, select the message and choose Message⇨Junk Mail⇨Mark As Not Junk (or press ⌘+Shift+Option+J). You can also toggle off Junk Email status by right-clicking the email and selecting Junk Mail⇨Mark as Not Junk in the contextual menu. This action alerts the filter that messages similar to this one are probably okay.

Sometimes, Outlook suspects that a message is junk mail but isn't sure. In these cases, the mail appears in your Junk Email folder with a note that says something like "This message appears to be Junk. Links and other functionality will not work." You also see a Mark as Not Junk button. If you click this button, the message is marked as Not Junk and returned to the proper folder from whence it came.

Finally, to add a sender to your Blocked Senders list, select the message from that person and choose Message⇨Junk Mail⇨Block Sender. The sender's address is added to the Blocked Senders tab in the Junk pane. (And yes, as you may have guessed, you can right-click any message in the list, choose Junk Mail, and then click Block Sender. You're so predictable, Microsoft!)

To remove a domain or address from the Safe Senders or Blocked Senders tabs in the Junk pane, just select it and press Delete, or click the — icon below it.

Managing your email

It's an immutable law of nature: The longer you use an email account, the more mail you'll receive. We've had multiple email accounts for more than a dozen years, and our email programs now store more than 60,000 messages. Although most people don't keep that much old email around, you still need to manage however much you have. So here are some tips, hints, and techniques for managing the email you send and receive.

Organizing your messages in folders

Outlook lets you create unlimited folders and subfolders, so take advantage of this feature. As the number of messages you have increases, it makes sense to start organizing them into folders rather than let them all sit in your inbox.

To create a new folder, choose File⇨New⇨Folder. If you want the folder to appear as a subfolder of another folder, first select the parent folder and then choose File⇨New⇨Folder. (You can also right-click the parent folder and choose New Folder from the menu that appears.) When the folder appears in the folder list, double-click it and type a name for it. You can create as many or as few folders and subfolders as you like.

Later, if you want to change the name of a folder or subfolder, click the name, click the name a second time (this isn't a double-click; pause between the first and second click), select the old name and delete it, and then type a new name.

Now, after you read a message in your inbox, drag it to the appropriate folder, where it is saved forevermore. You can also right-click the message, select Move from the pop-up menu, and choose the folder you want to move the email to.

Searching your messages

In the upper-right corner of the main window's toolbar is the search field, which you can use to search for email messages or any other item in Outlook (contacts, events, to-do items, or tasks, for example). The search field is your friend, so use it often. Following are some tips for using it effectively.

You can limit your search to a single folder, if you want. Just click the folder before you start typing in the search field. Or click the On My Computer folder to search all messages you've saved in folders or subfolders.

When you type text in the search field, a couple of things happen. First, Outlook displays the Search tab on the ribbon and immediately makes that tab active. Also, a set of very useful filters appear on the ribbon below the search field (shown in Figure 18-12), allowing you to specify search criteria. Our favorite filters include

>> **Current Folder and Subfolders:** Include just the parent folder or all subfolders.

>> **All Items:** Delve through all the data in Outlook, including other modules such as People and Notes.

>> **Attachments:** Check for messages with attachments of a certain size (helpful for searching and deleting old messages that are taking up too much disk space).

>> **Date Received and Date Sent:** "I *know* I sent that last Friday, but where is it?" If you organize by using subfolders and you've moved that message out of your outbox, these options are your ticket.

>> **Advanced:** Click this icon to build your own, custom search.

FIGURE 18-12: The Search ribbon provides an abundance of tools to narrow your searches.

The advanced search feature is especially powerful. Figure 18-13 shows the advanced search header, which appears under the ribbon when you click the Advanced icon — each button in the header is a pop-up menu, allowing you to build such criteria as *Priority Is High* or *Read Status Is Forwarded*. Click the first button to choose the base criterion, and then click the second button to choose the corresponding modifier.

Note that to the far right of the buttons are two more buttons: a minus sign (−) and a plus sign (+). The + lets you specify additional search criteria, allowing you to build some truly specific searches. Click the minus sign to remove a criterion.

FIGURE 18-13:
An advanced
search lets you
apply a multitude
of filters at
one time.

Finally, the Save Search icon on the Search tab lets you save a search in the Smart Folders folder, which appears in the Navigation pane to the left of the window. If you find yourself searching for the same thing over and over again, click the Save Search icon, and the next time you want to run that search, you can just click its name in the Smart Folders folder. Sweet!

TIP

The items in the Smart Folders folder are saved searches. To prove it, right-click any item in the Smart Folders folder and choose Edit. The criteria for the search appears, which you can change if you want.

Creating rules for received messages

Wouldn't it be nice if Outlook were smart enough to play a sound and display a dialog to alert you whenever new mail from your mom arrives? No sweat — it can do that and much more by using rules.

Rules work on the if-then principle: If something is true (or false), then an action occurs (or doesn't occur). A specific example will help you understand, so here's how to create a rule that makes a sound (three times) and presents a dialog every time new mail from Mom arrives:

1. Choose Tools⇔Rules to open the Rules pane in the Outlook Preferences window.

2. Click + (add) at the bottom of the pane.

The Edit Rule dialog appears, as shown in Figure 18-14.

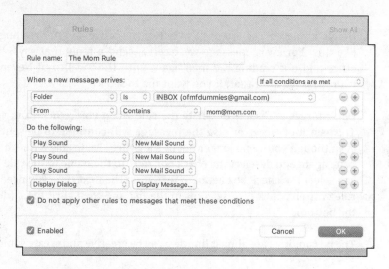

FIGURE 18-14:
Set up conditions
for your rule.

3. **In the Rule Name field, type** The Mom Rule.

4. **Make the choices shown in Figure 18-14 from the pop-up menus, clicking Add Action to add the second, third, and fourth items.**

   The only item in the When a New Message Arrives section should look like From Contains mom@mom.com.

   The items in the Do the Following section should look like this:

   • Play Sound — New Mail Sound

   • Play Sound — New Mail Sound

   • Play Sound — New Mail Sound

   • Display Dialog

5. **Click the Display Message button next to the fourth item (Display Dialog) and type** An email from your mother has arrived.

6. **Click OK to close the Dialog Text dialog.**

7. **Click OK to close the Edit Rule dialog.**

That's it. Note that the rule now appears in the Rules list next to the proper classification (typically IMAP, POP, or Outgoing). The next time an email message from Mom arrives, the New Mail sound plays three times and a dialog with the message "An email from your mother has arrived" appears onscreen.

That's one example of a rule, and a simple one at that.

Here's a rule we use often: "I'm out of the office and not reading mail." It goes like this: For every message we receive, send a reply that says, "I'm out of the office and not reading my mail again until the Twelfth of Never. Please resend your message after that, if you want me to see it."

Don't forget to disable or delete the rule when you return from your trip on the Thirteenth of Never or else the message will continue to be sent automatically, even though you're no longer out of the office. To disable a rule, display the Rules pane again and deselect the check box next to the name of the rule in the list. (You can select the check box again to turn it on the next time you need it.) To delete a rule entirely, click it to select it in the list and then click the – (delete) button at the bottom.

The possibilities are almost limitless, so be creative and create some rules yourself.

Chapter **19**

Managing Your Affairs with Outlook

The Outlook modules covered in this chapter — Calendar, People (formerly Contacts), Tasks, and Notes — share a common theme: They're designed to keep you and your stuff well-organized.

You don't have to use all these modules. Instead, feel free to pick and choose the ones that work for your organizational style. For example, you might rarely use the Notes module, preferring instead to put anything you need to remember on either your Calendar or to-do list (Tasks).

You also don't need to use every feature in every module. For example, you might not find assigning categories to tasks or events useful — if most of the things you do are short, stand-alone projects with a single deadline, you probably don't need all the follow-up and due date features offered by Calendar.

You should also consider compatibility and communications between your apps and devices. For example, some apps and hardware may not sync directly with Outlook because they were designed to work with Apple's Calendar or Contacts apps.

Finally, some features may overlap, and it might be better to pick one or the other rather than feel obliged to use both. You see an example of what we mean in the first section of this chapter, when we explain how groups and categories work and why you might choose to assign groups but not assign categories to your contacts.

REMEMBER

The bottom line is to keep an open mind as you explore these four modules and their features. Some parts will appeal to you more than others, so feel free to use the ones that make sense to you or the ones that you believe will save you time or effort. For us, having one more type of thing to keep track of (Notes, for example) just doesn't make sense. And, categorizing events, contacts, and tasks seems to be more effort than it's worth, most of the time.

Your mileage, of course, may vary.

Scheduling Events with Calendar

When you work with Calendar in Outlook, you need to first activate the Calendar module by clicking the Calendar icon (shown in the margin) in the view switcher or by using the keyboard shortcut ⌘+2.

Calendar is ideal for storing time- or date-sensitive information such as meetings and appointments. The module is easy to use and has many useful features to help ensure that you never miss an event again.

Switching views

Calendar's Home tab contains four view icons, each of which provides a slightly different take on your calendar and its content. This list describes what these icons display (or open), from left to right:

>> **Day:** A single day. (The keyboard shortcut is ⌘+Control+1.)

>> **Work week:** A five-day work week. (The keyboard shortcut is ⌘+Control+2.)

>> **Week:** A seven-day week. (The keyboard shortcut is ⌘+Control+3.)

>> **Month:** An entire month at a time. (The keyboard shortcut is ⌘+Control+4.)

Figure 19-1 shows examples of the Month, Work Week, and Day views.

The same views are also available on the View menu, so you can switch to them by using that menu, if you prefer.

Click the Today button on the ribbon's Home tab to see the current day on the calendar in whichever view is active. (The keyboard shortcut is ⌘+T.)

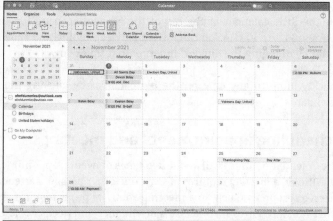

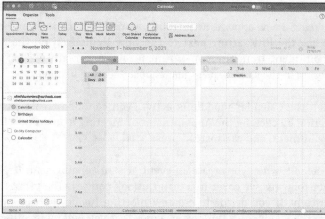

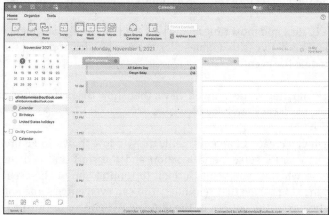

FIGURE 19-1:
Month (top),
work week
(center), and day
(bottom) views.

See the little calendar at the top of the Navigation pane (on the left side of the views in Figure 19-1)? You can switch between hiding and showing this little calendar by dragging the divider underneath it up or down.

Quickly jump to any date on the big calendar by clicking the date on the little calendar.

Scheduling appointments and meetings

The Calendar module is all about two types of events: appointments and meetings. In Outlook, a *meeting* requires at least one other person's attendance, and you can reserve resources (such as a meeting room or projector). An *appointment*, on the other hand, requires no one else's attendance and needs no resources.

To create a new appointment from any module, choose File ➪ New ➪ Appointment or click the little arrow next to the New Items icon on the ribbon and choose Appointment from the pop-up menu. As you might expect, you create a new meeting in the same way — just choose Meeting instead.

When the Calendar module is active, you can also create an appointment or a meeting by clicking the Appointment or Meeting icon on the Home tab. Or for an appointment, you can instead press ⌘+N.

By default, when you create an event, it's an appointment. If you decide to invite other folks (as we cover in a bit), Outlook converts the event to a meeting automatically. If you decide to create a meeting (using the icon on the Home tab or from the File menu), Outlook assumes that you will invite others from the start.

The easiest and most timesaving way to create an appointment when the Calendar module is active is to double-click the day or click and drag the time you want to schedule the event.

Click and drag works only on views that show the hours in the day — namely, the week, workweek, and day views.

When you create an appointment, the window shown in Figure 19-2 appears. Fill in the event's subject and location and the start and end times. Also, you can choose whether you want Outlook to remind you of the event and how long in advance to provide that reminder. You can even enter some notes about the event in the box at the bottom of the window. When you're finished with the appointment details, click the Save & Close button on the ribbon to save your event, an example of which is shown in Figure 19-3.

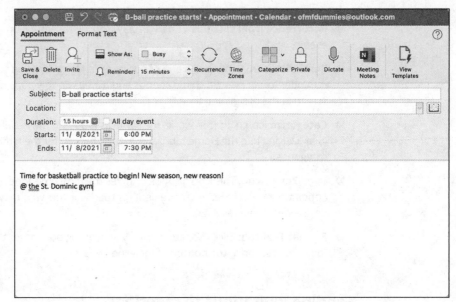

FIGURE 19-2:
The Appointment
window is where
you get down to
the nitty-gritty
of your
appointment info.

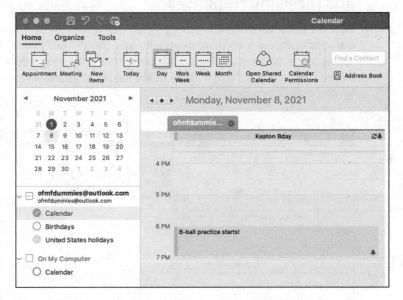

FIGURE 19-3:
After you click
Save & Close in
the Appointment
window, the
event appears on
your calendar.

Here are more details about some of the items in the Appointment window:

>> **All-Day Event check box:** Selecting this option causes the start and end times and duration to disappear. This makes sense, but it can be disconcerting if you're not expecting those details to vanish.

- » **Recurrence icon:** Click this icon to display a dialog for setting up recurring events.

- » **Reminder icon:** Reminder is one of our favorite features. If you set up a reminder for an event, a chime sounds and a little window pops up on your screen at the designated time.

- » **Categorize icon:** This icon works the same as it does in the People module. (See "Delving into the Home tab," later in this chapter, for the nitty-gritty on categories.)

- » **Time Zones icon:** This icon displays or hides the local time zone for an appointment or a meeting (convenient for road warriors who may change time zones while traveling).

- » **Format Text tab:** Click this tab to display formatting options for the text in the notes section at the bottom of the window.

Sending invitations to meetings and receiving responses

Click the Invite icon to invite other people to attend an event — as mentioned, this action transforms a mere appointment into (drum roll, please) a meeting. The appointment window is also transformed into a meeting window, as shown in Figure 19-4, adding To and From fields for email addresses of invitees and the inviter, as well as a Send icon.

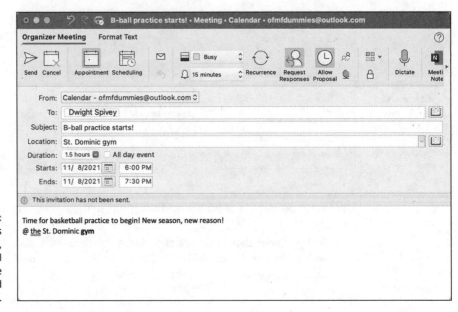

FIGURE 19-4: To invite others to your meeting, add their email addresses to the To field and click Send.

Click Send and the invitation is emailed to the recipients as an enclosure in an email message. The enclosure that controls the invitation and response mechanism works optimally if the recipient is using a Microsoft Office email program — Outlook for Windows or Mac — but should also work with most other platforms (such as Google). The email message includes links that allow the recipients to simply click a link to accept, decline, or accept tentatively. You'll typically be notified in the original email invitation that your recipients have accepted.

If you create a meeting event and add attendees (or invite others to an appointment), a new icon appears in the window — Check Names, which automatically verifies the contact information for your attendees. (This feature is A Very Good Thing when you're heading an important meeting with a dozen co-workers.)

TIP

If you're using Microsoft Exchange on your company's network, you can use Scheduling Assistant to view the availability of each person you're inviting — as long as they are using the same Exchange system. Click the Scheduling icon to check whether your attendees are marked as Busy or Out of Office during your meeting. After you've sent the invitation, Scheduling Assistant also allows you to check on the status of the folks you've invited.

Printing the event

Click the Quick Print icon at the top of the Appointment or Meeting window to send the event information to your default printer. Before the printing kicks off, however, the standard macOS Print dialog appears, as shown in Figure 19-5 — in it, you can set the number of copies, or even create a PDF instead of a hard copy. (Click the PDF pop-up menu at the bottom of the Print dialog and choose Save as PDF from the menu.) Naturally, you can also print from the menu by choosing File ⇨ Print or by pressing ⌘+P.

Deleting an event

To make an event go away altogether, just click the event and choose Cancel Meeting or Delete Event (for an appointment). The appropriate window appears (both options are shown in Figure 19-6), depending on the type of event you're cancelling. If you indicate that you want to cancel a meeting, Outlook even sends a cancellation email to your attendees!

Quick Print icon

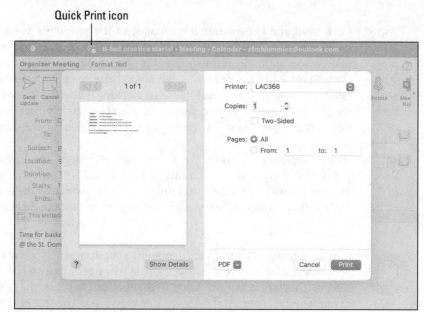

FIGURE 19-5:
The Quick Print
button opens the
Print dialog.

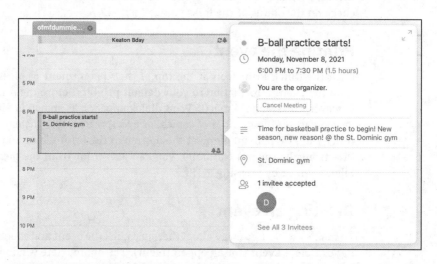

FIGURE 19-6:
A quick click will
cancel your
meetings or
appointments.

Managing Your Crew with the People Module

The People module is a complete solution for storing and viewing your business and personal correspondence. This section starts with the basics: adding and removing contacts. Later in this section, we show you how to work with the contacts you've created — how to find them as well as how to create and use views and groups. Finally, we offer some timesaving shortcuts and organizational tools that can make you more efficient and effective.

 You need to activate the People module by clicking the People icon in the view switcher (shown in the margin) or pressing ⌘+3 to follow along in this section.

TIP If you need to import a vCard (short for virtual business card) that you've received as an email attachment (or exported from another app), just drag the vCard file to the contacts list in Outlook to import the data. You may have to adjust the size of the Outlook window to see both the contacts list in Outlook and the vCard (wherever it may reside in Finder).

Adding and removing contacts

In this section, we show you how to create contacts, add senders of email messages as contacts, and remove contacts.

Creating a contact

To create a contact from any module, you can choose File ⇨ New ⇨ Contact.

When the People module is active, you can also create a new contact by

>> Clicking the New Contact icon on the Home tab

>> Pressing ⌘+N

When the New Contact window appears, as shown in Figure 19-7, just fill in the blanks (such as first and last names, email, phone numbers, and address).

TIP Press the Tab key to move the cursor from field to field; press Shift+Tab to move the cursor from field to field in the opposite direction. You can also click a field to jump to it.

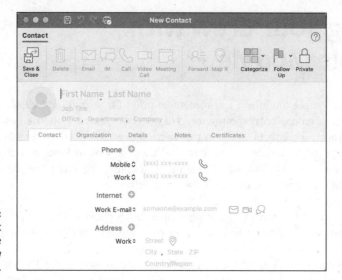

FIGURE 19-7:
Create a contact
by filling in the
blanks in the New
Contact window.

Many fields allow you to add additional information, such as the contact's home address and other phone numbers, and personal information, such as the contact's age, birthday, names of family members, and (we love this one) their blood type! To enter additional information, click one of the buttons bearing a plus sign in the window and then click the alternative information you want in the pop-up menu that appears.

Or, if you don't want to add anything else right now, click the Save & Close icon at the top of the window. If you later decide that you want to add more information to a contact, click the contact in the list on the left side of the main Outlook window to display the information and then add data in the same fashion.

Adding the sender of an email message as a contact

We often receive email from someone we expect to have contact with in the future. To store that person's address, you can, of course, select and copy the person's email address, create a contact, and then paste the address in the appropriate field in the New Contact window — but there's an easier way to accomplish this task.

To add the sender of an email message to your contacts list, right-click the email in the Mail module's message list and choose Sender ⇨ Add to Contacts from the menu that appears, as shown in Figure 19-8.

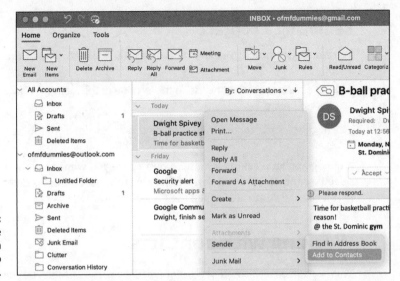

FIGURE 19-8:
Adding the
sender of an
email message to
the contacts list.

Alas, if the person included a snail mail address or phone number in the message, you have to copy and paste that information into the appropriate fields in the New Contact window (or paste it into the appropriate fields in that person's contact information window, if the person is already in your contacts list). Outlook is smart, but it's not *that* smart.

This is one place where Apple Mail and Contacts (in macOS) have Outlook beat, hands down. If someone sends you an email and the person's snail-mail address appears somewhere in the body of the message, Mail offers to add it to Contacts. Furthermore, if the person's snail-mail address is already in your Contacts, it's added as another address. Apple Mail can also discern phone numbers and dates and offer to add them to Contacts and Calendar, respectively.

By the way, it would behoove you to note the other things you can do from the pop-up menu that appears when you right-click a message. In addition to adding the email address to your contacts list, you can

>> Send a reply, forward the message, or print the message.

>> Mark the message as unread or read.

>> Set a category for the message to help identify it later.

>> Set a priority for the message (high, normal, or low).

>> Save or preview all attachments the message contains.

>> Mark the message as junk or block the sender.

Removing a contact

To remove a contact from the Outlook contacts list, do one of the following:

>> Select the contact in the list on the left side of the main window and press Delete.

>> Right-click the contact in the list and choose Delete from the contextual menu.

A dialog appears, asking whether you're sure you want to permanently delete the selected contact. If you click the Delete button, the contact is deleted immediately. If you change your mind, click the Cancel button.

Working with contacts

This section covers the cool stuff you can do with contacts. Of course, you have to know how to find the contacts you want to do the cool stuff with, so we cover that, too. You also find out about views and groups — two different tools that can help you manage your ever-expanding contacts list.

Finding contacts

Finding contacts is something you do almost every time you use the Outlook People module. The most basic way to find a contact is to scroll down the list until you see the contact's name. Although this technique works, it's not efficient, and the more contacts in your contacts list, the less efficient it becomes.

If you click the By column heading at the top of the list (shown in Figure 19-9), a pop-up menu allows you to choose which field Outlook uses to sort the list. So, if you know that someone works for, say, Apple, a faster route might be to click By, select Company, and then scroll down (especially if the contact's last name starts with Z).

TIP

Here's an even *faster* way to find a contact whose name starts with Z. Suppose that you have the list arranged by name, which is the default. At the top of the contacts list, see the upward-pointing arrow (labeled in Figure 19-9)? Click the arrow and it changes to a downward-pointing arrow, indicating that the sorting order of the list has changed from ascending (*a* to *z*) to descending (*z* to *a*). Click the arrow again to reverse the sort order. This technique works with any sort criterion you choose from the By menu.

But when you have hundreds of contacts in your list, scrolling — even when you change the sort order — isn't usually the best or most efficient way to find a contact or contacts. The fastest way to find a person in your contacts list is to type the contact's name in the Find a Contact box on the Home tab and then press Return. This search opens the Search Contacts and Rooms window and focuses on the names in your contacts list. The results of a typical Find a Contact search are shown in Figure 19-10.

Click to change sort order (ascending or descending)

Click to sort

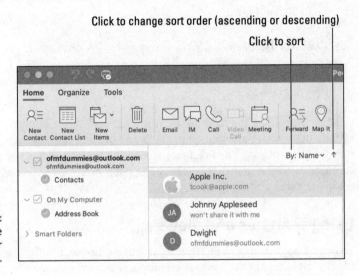

Selected contact   Find a Contact box

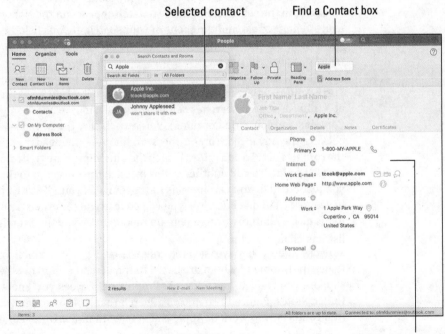

Contact details area

However, you're not limited to searching just names: Click the Address Book icon on the Home tab to open the Search Contacts and Room window and you can search *all* fields in each record.

Here are a couple of other features of the main People module window that you can see in Figure 19-10:

>> **Contacts list:** Displays a list of all contacts in the database

>> **Contact details area:** Shows the details for the selected contact (Tim Cook in Figure 19-10)

TIP

Click the Reading Pane icon on the Home tab and select Bottom (it's set to Right by default), which puts your contacts list on top and the Reading pane below. You may find that placing the Reading pane on the bottom allows you to display more contacts at a time and that it's easier to get a bird's-eye view of details such as company name and category in your list.

Using searches and views

You can find contacts (and other items) using the search field on the toolbar (at the top-right end of the Outlook window), which offers a more comprehensive set of options than the Search Contacts and Rooms window. As soon as you type a character in the search field, the Search tab appears on the ribbon, offering several icons to limit or expand the scope of your search. If you click the All Items icon on the Search tab, for example, Outlook searches every module for every item that matches your criteria.

Furthermore, whereas the simple search is a solo affair and can be used only one at a time, advanced searches can have more than one criterion (such as Company Contains and Job Title Contains). You can display the advanced search header by clicking the Advanced icon on the Search tab — the header appears at the top of the contacts list. To add criteria, click the plus sign at the right side of the advanced search header. To add another criterion, click the plus sign to the right of the item you just created. You can have as many items as you like or as few as one. If you have more than one criterion, you can choose whether the search is for any of the items or for all items from a pop-up menu just below the Search Results bar.

Suppose that you have several contacts at Apple (a small computer firm in Cupertino), some of whom are based in the US and others in other countries. Now suppose you want to see a list of all Apple employees you know who work in the United States. Figure 19-11 shows a search that looks through your contacts list to find contacts who work at Apple *and* who work in the United States.

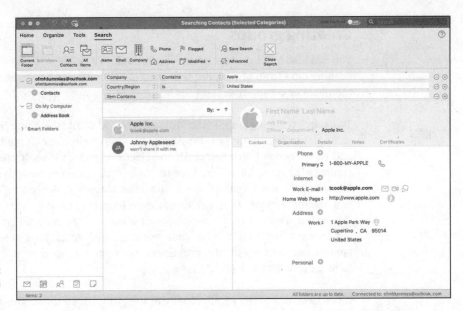

FIGURE 19-11:
A search with
multiple criteria.

Next, let's suppose that you perform this search often and don't want to re-create it from scratch every time. To save a search so that you can use it later, just follow these steps:

1. Click the Save Search icon on the Search tab.

An Untitled entry appears under the Smart Folders heading in the Navigation pane (to the left of the Outlook window).

2. Type a name for this search and press Return (or Enter).

To use your saved search, just click its name in the Smart Folders section of the Navigation pane.

If you decide that you want to modify the saved search's criteria, right-click its name and choose Edit from the contextual menu. Or, to get rid of that search completely, right-click the name and choose Delete. A warning dialog appears; if you click the Delete button, your saved search is gone forever.

TIP

The nice thing about saved searches (also known as *Smart Folders*) is that if you later add to your contacts list another person who meets the same criteria as that of a saved search, the next time you use this saved search, it automatically includes that person. Go back to the Apple example: Whenever you designate a person's company name as *Apple* and Country/Region as *United States,* that contact is automatically added to your *Apple US* saved search when you run it again.

Creating groups

You can also build contact groups in Outlook — a *group* is a convenient method of sending email and organizing sets of contacts that belong together, such as family members or company employees.

To easily create a group, select all contacts you want to include in the group. For example, to create a group for Apple US, simply click the Apple US saved search and then choose Edit ⇨ Select All to select everyone. (At least one contact in the contacts list must be selected for the Select All option to be active.) Then choose File ⇨ New ⇨ Group. Options from this point may vary, depending on what license you use for Outlook. (You might not even have permission to create a new group if your business or organization doesn't allow it.) Typically, a Create a Group dialog appears. From there, give your group a name, email, and description, choose appropriate settings for the group, and then add members to it. Finally, click the Save & Close icon to save the new group.

TIP

If you need to add folks individually to the group, open the group, select Members, type the first few letters of a name, select that name when it appears, and then click the Add Members button. Later, rinse and repeat with this technique — if you want to add someone who's not in your contacts list, type that person's email address instead.

TIP

If you don't want anyone in the new group to know who else is receiving the message, select the Use Bcc to Hide Member Information check box.

The group is saved in your contacts list. Now whenever you want to send an email message to all those Apple US contacts, address the message to the Apple US Group, which is a heck of a lot easier than trying to remember everyone's names (or resorting to a saved search) every time you need to send them all a message.

If you need to add or remove a member, double-click Apple US Group in the contacts list and the Apple US Group window opens. Use the plus (+) and minus (−) buttons in the Group window to add or remove contacts. Or you can add them by dragging them from the contacts list to the Apple US Group window, and remove them by selecting them in the Apple US Group window and then pressing Delete.

Delving into the Home tab

The previous sections of this chapter cover basic techniques for creating and searching for contacts. In this section, we show you some ways to use your contacts list in the People module even more effectively by using some of the unique (to Outlook) tools on the Outlook ribbon.

Because Outlook is an integrated suite of separate modules, many of the actions you can initiate from the People module can be done in other modules as well. That's a good thing because after you know how to do something in one module, you don't have to learn much (if anything) to use it in other modules — and sometimes you don't even have to switch modules to accomplish that task.

In addition to the New Items icon and its menu that you use to create a contact or group (as well as the Home tab icons we've already used in this chapter), the Home tab contains a number of other icons, including Delete, Email, IM (Instant Messaging), Meeting, Forward, Map It, Categorize, Follow Up, and Private.

The one thing they have in common is that they all work on the selected contact(s). So, if you select a contact or contacts and then click the Email icon, a blank email message addressed to that contact (or those contacts) appears.

Groups let you hide all email addresses in the group automatically. On the other hand, clicking the Email icon in the People module puts them all in the To field of the message. You can still hide the addresses by dragging them to the BCC (Blind Carbon Copy) field, but the group method does it automatically.

The IM icon opens a Microsoft Teams chat window (assuming you have the app installed on your Mac and configured for the same account) with the selected contact if the contact has a valid chat address in the IM address field.

The Categorize icon and its menu let you assign categories to contacts. You can also assign them by choosing Contact ⇨ Categorize. Categories are available throughout Outlook — in Mail, Calendar, and Tasks — so they can be useful in organizing your information. Outlook comes with a handful of categories, each with an assigned color. You can keep them, delete them, or change their name and color, as you see in a moment.

Items may have none, one, or many categories. To assign a category to a contact or contacts, select the contact(s) and then either click the Categorize button on the ribbon's Home tab or choose Contact ⇨ Categorize. Scroll down to the category you want to assign and then click. Repeat if you want to assign more than one category to a contact or contacts.

To create additional categories, either click the Categorize button on the ribbon's Home tab and choose Edit Categories, or choose Contact ⇨ Categorize and choose Edit Categories. Outlook displays the Categories preference pane, shown in Figure 19-12. Now click +, type the new category name, click the arrow next to the color circle to select a color to assign to the category, and then click Add to accept the new category.

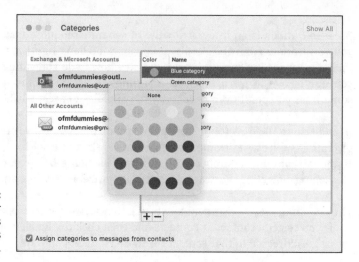

FIGURE 19-12:
Edit, add, or delete categories in the Categories preference pane.

Finally, to edit a category, choose Edit Categories from the Categorize icon (or choose Contact➪Categorize➪Edit Categories). When the Edit Categories window appears, click the colored circle to the left of the category's name to change the color; double-click the name of a category to change its name. To delete a category, select it and press Delete or click –.

The Forward icon is just plain neat. Select one or more contacts and then click this icon to create an email message that you can send to anyone with that person's vCard as an attachment! For example, an employee might have requested your current contact information for a vendor — rather than manually creating a message, exporting the vendor's vCard file, and then attaching it, everything is done for you.

Click the Map It icon to open your web browser and display a Bing map for that person's address. The Private icon allows those who share contacts with others through Microsoft Exchange to hide specific contacts — private contacts are essentially invisible to other Exchange users when they're using Outlook.

Another way to use items in your contacts list is to select them and then right-click to display a contextual menu. Most items on the contextual menu perform the same function as the ribbon icons. We talk about using Delete, New Email to Contact, New Meeting with Contact, New IM to Contact, Categorize, and Forward as vCard in previous sections of this chapter. Follow Up is covered later in this chapter.

The rest of the items on the contextual menu are self-explanatory: Open, Print, Choose/Copy to Folder, and Copy Contact Details.

TIP

You can use the Organize tab on the ribbon (which you can display no matter which module you're using) to create folders in the Navigation pane — a great way to, well, organize things! A folder can hold items that belong together, such as the contacts, events, and tasks that make up a project. To create a folder from the Organize tab, just click New Folder — Outlook creates a new heading in the Navigation pane under the account you're currently using, and you see the entry for your new folder under it. Type a descriptive name for the new folder, and then start dragging items to it. (Alternatively, right-click an item and choose Move from the menu that appears. You can move the item by using the Choose Folder option or create a duplicate item in the folder by using the Copy to Folder option.)

Tracking Progress with the Tasks Module

To use the Tasks module, you must first activate it by clicking the Tasks icon (shown in the margin) in the view switcher or by using the keyboard shortcut ⌘+4.

The Tasks module is a sophisticated to-do list manager. Tasks can have a start date and a due date, reminders, categories, and recurring schedules. In other words, a task is a lot like an event, but rather than appear on the calendar, it appears on the tasks list (as shown in Figure 19-13).

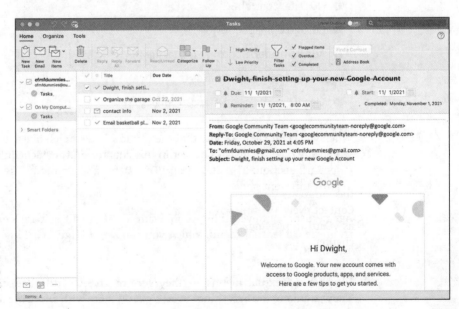

FIGURE 19-13:
The Tasks module helps you keep track of what needs to be done.

TIP

You can display and hide completed or uncompleted items in the tasks list by selecting the Completed check box on the Home tab. Likewise, you can show and hide tasks you've flagged for follow-up (using the Follow Up icon, which we discuss in the next section) and tasks past the due date you assigned.

To create a new task from any module, choose File ⇨ New ⇨ Task or click the little arrow next to the New Items icon in the ribbon and choose Task from the pop-up menu. When the Tasks module is active, you can also create a new task by

>> Clicking the New Task icon on the ribbon's Home tab

>> Pressing ⌘+N

When you're using the Mail or People module, you can add a message or contact to your tasks list by clicking the little arrow next to the Follow Up icon on the Home tab and choosing available items (these may vary by module) from the pop-up menu. Those items are listed here, with their keyboard shortcuts:

>> Today, Control+1

>> Tomorrow, Control+2

>> This Week, Control+3

>> Next Week, Control+4

>> No Date, Control+5

>> Custom Date, Control+6

>> Add Reminder, Control+= (equal sign)

>> Mark As Complete Control+0

>> Clear Flag ⌘+Option+' (apostrophe)

When you create a task, note that the window looks much like a new Appointment window, which we discuss earlier in this chapter, in the "Scheduling Events with Calendar" section. The Start Date, Due Date, and Reminder fields appear, in a slightly different style.

Again, just about everything you'd want to set or edit in a Task entry is available from the contextual menu, which you can see by right-clicking the item in the Tasks list.

We love contextual menus — they sure are handy little boogers, aren't they? They're among the best things ever, right up there with sliced bread, guitar amplifiers, exotic cars, and pizza.

Understanding Notes

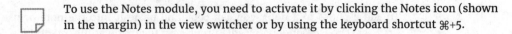

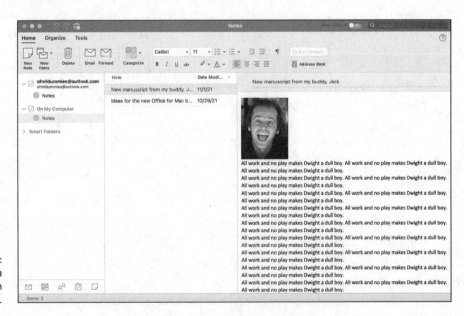

To use the Notes module, you need to activate it by clicking the Notes icon (shown in the margin) in the view switcher or by using the keyboard shortcut ⌘+5.

The Notes module provides a place where you can store bits of text and images that don't quite fit anywhere else. You might use a note to save a recipe, boilerplate text, or images that you expect to reuse someday, notes to yourself, and almost anything else that isn't an email message, an event, a contact, or a to-do item.

To create a new note from any module, choose File ⇨ New ⇨ Note or click the little arrow next to the New Items icon on the ribbon's Home tab and choose Note from the pop-up menu. When the Notes module is active, you can also create a new note by

>> Clicking the New Note icon on the ribbon's Home tab

>> Pressing ⌘+N

Figure 19-14 shows a note with an embedded photo — one reason to embed photos in notes is that you can use them at a later time in a Word document, if you like.

FIGURE 19-14:
A note with a picture from a pal, JT.

The other items you see on the Home tab — the formatting tools, Categorize, Delete, and Find a Contact — work the same as in other modules.

To add a photo to a note, you can copy and paste it into the note or use Media Browser (choose Window⇨Media Browser in the menu at the top of the screen) to browse photos from your macOS Photos and Photo Booth collections. After you've found the photo you want to include in your note, just drag it to the note's pane (refer to Figure 19-14).

Chapter **20**

Getting Advanced with Outlook

This chapter shows you some Outlook tips and tricks not covered elsewhere in this book. First, we cover some ways you can customize Outlook to suit your own style and needs. We also discuss some app preferences and how you can use them, too, to customize Outlook. Finally, you find out how to synchronize your contacts, events, and notes in Outlook with macOS Contacts, Calendar, and iCloud, and we tell you why you might want to do so.

Customizing: It's Not Just for Hot Rods Anymore

Like the other apps in Office for Mac, Outlook sports a ribbon interface — along with the familiar toolbar and menu system, you're often confronted with a huge number of various icons, pop-up menus, and check boxes. Sure, Outlook is powerful, and having all these options is useful, but do you truly need *all* of them? Taking care of simple tasks can sometimes seem overwhelming, even after you finish reading these chapters. Wouldn't it be helpful if you could redesign portions of the Outlook window to match the way *you* work?

In fact, you can! Feel free to bend and shape the Outlook interface to suit your personal style of computing. Read on to see how.

Would you like to use Outlook as the default email client on your Mac? If so, open the macOS Mail app and choose Mail⇨Preferences. Under the General tab's Default Email Reader option, click the pop-up menu and select Microsoft Outlook.

Reducin' the ribbon

You can't change the icons on the ribbon, but you can save some screen real estate by reducing the ribbon to just its tabs and eliminating icons until you need them again. (This trick is useful if you're working on an Office document on your Mac-Book, which doesn't have the same elbow room onscreen as an iMac.) To hide the ribbon icons in any of the modules, simply click the active tab (which is denoted by a blue line under the tab name). For example, Figure 20-1 shows the ribbon in the Tasks module, with the Home tab active. Click the active Home tab and the ribbon will be hidden from view (as shown in the lower half of Figure 20-1).

FIGURE 20-1:
The ribbon
playing
peek-a-boo.

To restore the ribbon to its pristine condition, click any of the available tabs to reopen the ribbon and make the tab active.

Concentrating on columns

Here are three things you should know about the columns in Outlook in any module:

>> You can display or hide columns by choosing View⇨Columns or right-clicking any column header. For example, when you're in the Tasks module, you might not care about the start date or the date completed — you just want to see the due date. In that case, turn off the Start Date and Date Completed columns, as shown in Figure 20-2.

The items on these menus are *toggles,* which means that you select an item to reverse its current state.

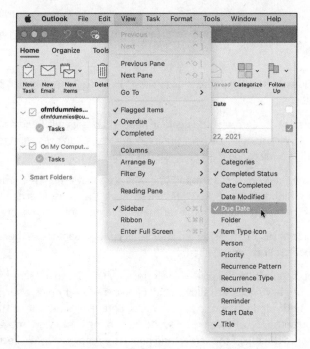

FIGURE 20-2:
Display and hide
columns by using
the View menu or
by right-clicking a
column header.

» You can rearrange the order of columns by clicking and dragging their headers. In the Tasks module, for example, to display the Due Date column before the task name, you would click the Due Date column header, drag it to the left of the Task column, and then release the column header. As you drag a column it appears much lighter, kind of like a ghost of itself, until you drop it into place.

» You can reverse the sort order of a column by clicking its header. A little black arrow denotes the column's current state. If the arrow points upward, the sorting order is from *a* to *z* (or ascending, if the column contains numerical data); if the arrow points downward, the sorting order is from *z* to *a* (or descending, if the column contains numerical data). This trick works also on dates and times, with entries appearing chronologically or in reverse chronological order.

Hiding, showing, and rearranging interface elements

If you have a small display, you may find yourself wishing that you could create additional room for all or part of the Outlook window. The good news is that you can, by hiding interface elements such as the Reading pane and sidebar, or by rearranging elements.

To show, hide, or rearrange interface elements in Outlook, you can do the following:

» To hide the Reading pane, choose View⇨Reading Pane⇨Hidden or press ⌘+\.

» To display or rearrange the Reading pane, choose View⇨Reading Pane⇨Right or Below (depending on your preference). Or you can press ⌘+\ to display the Reading pane to the right or ⌘+Shift+\ to display it below.

» To hide the icons on the ribbon (the tabs are always shown), choose View⇨Ribbon or press ⌘+Option+R to toggle the icons. Alternatively, you can just click the active tab's name, as mentioned earlier in this chapter.

» To hide or display the sidebar, choose View⇨Sidebar, or use the trusty keyboard shortcut ⌘+Shift+[.

» If you need a bit more screen real estate, try Outlook in full screen, which (as you may have guessed) allows Outlook to crowd everything else out and hold your undivided attention. Choose View⇨Enter Full Screen. In full screen, the menu at the top of the screen is hidden; to bring it into view, move your cursor to the top of the screen and hold it there for just a split second and the menu will reappear. Then you can choose View⇨Exit Full Screen to do just that. You can also press ⌘+Control+F to toggle between Enter Full Screen and Exit Full Screen.

TIP

Note that all these menu options that control the display of window elements are toggles: If the option does not display a check mark beside it in the View menu, the item is hidden and choosing the menu option makes it appear. Conversely, if the option displays a check mark beside it, the item is displayed, and choosing the menu option hides it.

The fast way to start an advanced search

We discuss some advanced search options in Chapter 19, but Outlook offers another, even easier and faster way to start an advanced search with multiple criteria: Choose Edit⇨Find⇨Advanced Search (or press ⌘+Option+F). This command starts an advanced search directly below the ribbon, as shown in Figure 20-3.

When you need to fine-tune a search and use more than one criterion, an advanced search is usually the fastest way to go.

TIP

Advanced searching is particularly useful in the People module, in which you can specify separate criteria for every field used by the Contacts database.

FIGURE 20-3:
Get to the
Advanced Search
screen by
pressing
⌘+Option+F.

What's Your Preference?

Outlook has a huge number of preference settings you can tinker with to change various aspects of the program's behavior. The Outlook Preferences window contains dozens of items, which are divided into three major categories — Personal Settings, Email, and Other — and then subdivided into seven Personal Settings panes, five Email panes, and three Other preference panes.

To open the Outlook Preferences window, choose Outlook⇨Preferences or press ⌘+comma.

Describing every one of the options in the Outlook Preferences window is far beyond the purview of this book, even though we'll at least touch on a brief description of them. In the following sections, we point out a few that you should definitely check out.

Your personal preferences

The seven Personal Settings preference panes deal with settings that affect the entire program or modules other than Mail. We cover them in the order they appear in the window.

TIP

Click the Show All button in the upper-right corner of the preferences window to exit the preferences you're currently viewing and see all the others.

General pane

The General pane, shown in Figure 20-4, offers settings that affect how Outlook operates. For example, you can hide folders in the sidebar to reduce clutter and allow Office files stored on a Microsoft online service such as OneDrive or SharePoint to be opened by the Office apps installed on your Mac (Word, Excel, and the like).

Accounts pane

As you might recall if you've read previous chapters, the Accounts pane lets you add and manage your email accounts — it's the repository of All Things Technical for all your email providers.

Notifications & Sounds pane

The Notification and Sounds pane lets you determine which kind of alert (if any) you want when new mail arrives. You can also turn on or off individual sounds (new message, mailbox sync error, or reminder, for example).

Categories pane

You can manage your Outlook categories from the Categories pane: Add, edit, and delete categories; change the color associated with them; and specify which categories should appear in the Navigation pane.

Fonts pane

The Fonts pane lets you choose default fonts for new mail, replies, forwards, and plain-text email messages.

AutoCorrect pane

Good ol' AutoCorrect — it's great when it works, but not-so-great when it does-n't. Luckily, Outlook lets you use the settings in the AutoCorrect, AutoFormat, and Text Completion tabs of this preference pane (shown in Figure 20-5) to customize how this feature works for you.

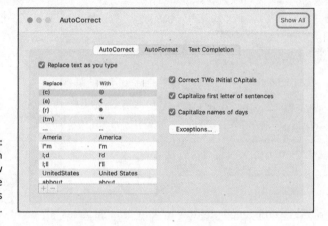

FIGURE 20-5:
Teach AutoCorrect new tricks using the options in this preference pane.

TIP

The Replace Text as You Type list, found on the AutoCorrect tab, is shared among the Office apps. Make changes in one app and they're available in the others.

Spelling & Grammar pane

The Spelling & Grammar pane gives you just two options, and we bet you can guess what they are. That's right, you can enable or disable the spelling check and the grammar checker!

Roll over, Beethoven, and catch the email preferences

The following five panes deal specifically with the Mail module.

Reading pane

The Reading pane lets you specify when to mark messages as read and what happens after you delete or file an open message. You can also configure how Outlook handles threaded conversations and whether Mail should automatically download embedded pictures that appear in email messages (note the Security section in Figure 20-6).

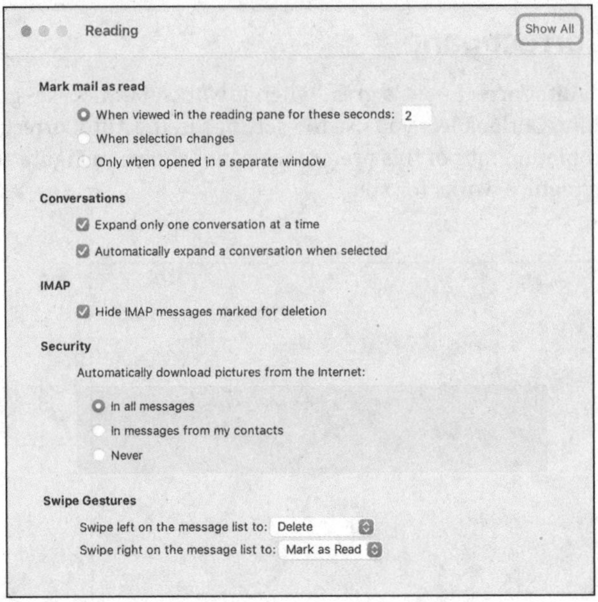

FIGURE 20-6:
Decide how
to handle
messages here.

Why not allow embedded pictures in your emails? After all, email does look rather plain with nothing but text and empty placeholder boxes where the pictures should be. While we allow all messages to download pictures, there are good reasons for some folks not to. Some pictures embedded in emails contain elements that allow spammers to know when you've viewed their messages. We allow them because we're rather tech-savvy and know that some images can be nefarious, but if you're not too adept at this tech stuff or are simply worried that the black helicopters flying over your house will pounce on your roof if you click a certain image in your email, you may want to not allow this option.

We recommend choosing the In Messages from My Contacts option as a happy medium between the In All Messages option and the Never option. You can always click the Download Pictures button in a message that has blocked them, preferably once you've determined that the message is friendly rather than hostile.

Composing pane

You use the Composing pane to specify how to format replies and forwarded messages and whether to add attribution text to mail automatically. This pane also offers options that specify Outlook's default behavior when handling replies and forwarded email messages. (Note that the two tabs let you separately configure HTML and plain-text messages.)

Signatures pane

Refer to Chapter 18 for the skinny on adding signatures to your email messages using the settings on the Signatures pane.

Rules pane

You can use the settings on the Rules pane to help automate message handling within Outlook — Chapter 18 demonstrates rules in action.

Junk pane

Why not allow Outlook to take care of mundane chores such as filtering emails from those you decide who can and who cannot send you email? You can automate these tasks by using rules, as we demonstrate in Chapter 18.

Everything but the Kitchen Sync

The last section of the Outlook Preferences window lumps together a number of panes that address specific modules and features — we guess they don't fit anywhere else. (We'll have to leave a note in Outlook to ask Microsoft.)

Calendar pane

Customize the Calendar module, shown in Figure 20-7, to match your workday and the duration of your workweek, set the default reminder time, and set the default time zone.

Contacts pane

The Contacts pane lets you customize the format of addresses and phone numbers. It also has several options for sorting and verifying email addresses.

Privacy pane

The Privacy pane allows you to opt in or opt out of cloud-based connected experiences across the devices with which you might use Microsoft Office products. An example is the weather for your local area being available on both Outlook for your Mac and your iPhone.

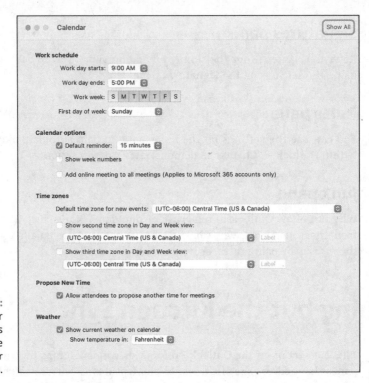

FIGURE 20-7:
The Calendar
pane allows
you to customize
your calendar
for your needs.

"New" Outlook? Yes, Please!

We can hear you asking, "New Outlook? What is this new Outlook of which you speak, dear author?" Friend, it's exactly what it sounds like — a new and different version of Outlook.

After a moment of bemusement, we're sure your next question goes along these lines: "Why the devil are you mentioning this now, after three chapters of the old Outlook?" Fine question, and a fair one, at that.

Here's the deal: Yes, Microsoft is introducing a new version of Outlook for Mac, but it isn't quite ready for prime time, meaning the new Outlook can't quite do everything the old Outlook can do. That being the case, this book is more concerned about the full-fledged version of Outlook that can offer you, dear reader, everything you paid for (and more), as opposed to simply offering you information for a product that's good but not yet great. That's not to say new Outlook isn't something you'd be interested in; it just might not cut it for most users.

Microsoft maintains a support website to update you on the progress of new Outlook, and even lists features offered by old Outlook that the new version doesn't yet support. The URL for that site is miles too long for this book, but if you go to support.microsoft.com and search for *new Outlook for Mac*, you'll find the site in a snap.

To give you an idea of how early in the game new Outlook still is, Microsoft lets you toggle between the old and the new (and back again, if you like) with the flip of a switch. To try out new Outlook:

1. **Open Outlook and note the New Outlook switch in the upper-right corner of the window (labeled in Figure 20-8).**

Click for the New Outlook experience

FIGURE 20-8:
A new Outlook
awaits if you but
click this switch.

2. **Click the New Outlook switch.**

   A dialog appears that includes a blurb about what things the new Outlook may not be able to bring over from the old.

3. **Click Open New Outlook if you want to continue.**

   New Outlook opens in all its glory, as shown in Figure 20-9.

If you're not thoroughly impressed after poking around a bit, you can easily return to old Outlook (which is still quite new, mind you) by clicking the New Outlook switch again in the upper-right corner of the window.

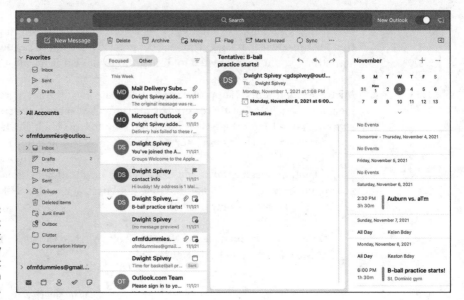

FIGURE 20-9:
New Outlook
looks great, but
you'll want to play
around a bit
before making a
full commitment.

6

The Part of Tens

IN THIS PART . . .

Pore over ten things you need to know that didn't fit elsewhere in the book.

Discover ten shortcuts guaranteed to improve your productivity.

Learn ten techniques for customizing Office to work the way you want it to work.

IN THIS CHAPTER

» Discovering tips for using little-known features in your Office apps

» Finding online resources for getting help with apps

» Checking out other apps that Microsoft develops for Apple devices

Chapter **21**

Ten Unsung Office Features and Microsoft Apps for Mac

As you know, *Microsoft Office* is a huge suite of apps and ancillary items, such as templates and clip art. The first five parts of this book do the heavy lifting and familiarize you with the four major programs. In this chapter, you look at items that aren't covered elsewhere or are covered only briefly but perhaps deserve a closer look.

The Developer Ribbon Tab

Very briefly touched on in Chapter 16, the Developer tab in Word and Excel is a playground for Office uber-geeks (or anyone else who likes to dabble in the dark arts of macros, content controls, and the like).

You can add the Developer tab to Word and Excel by following these steps:

1. **Open the Preferences dialog in your chosen app.**

2. **Click the View button in the Preferences dialog.**

3. **In the ribbon section of the View dialog, select the box for the Developer tab.**

4. **Close the Preferences dialog, and the Developer appears on the ribbon.**

"What can I do with the Developer tab?" we hear you asking. Great question! We could answer by saying, "If you don't already know, you probably don't need to know," which is probably accurate but not polite. So, here's a bit of what you can do with it:

>> **Create, record, edit, and delete macros.** Macros are tools to automate frequently used tasks, such as formatting you use throughout multiple documents.

>> **Open and work with the Visual Basic editor.** Visual Basic for Applications (VBA) is the programming language used for Office apps. Although you can't use it to make programming changes to the apps themselves, you can use it to create and customize very complex macros.

>> **Build forms that other users can fill out by using tools such as check boxes, combo boxes, text boxes, scroll bars, and more.**

A Multitude of Fonts

You might not have noticed, but when you installed Office, your font collection grew by quite a lot. That's right: One bonus feature in Office is that its installation includes a sweet little collection of fonts for all occasions.

The collection includes a number of useful typefaces, such as

>> **Gill Sans:** If you're tired of using Helvetica or Arial (yuck) as your headline font, try this one. It's available in five weights (Bold, Bold Italic, MT, MT Italic, and Ultra Bold).

>> **Edwardian Script:** This elegant font replicates flowery calligraphic handwriting and is perfect for invitations, thank-you notes, and monograms.

>> **Stencil:** This big, blocky font looks as though it were spray-painted on by using a (gasp) stencil.

The fonts are installed in a hidden folder in each app. You can view them by right-clicking the name of the app (such as Microsoft Word) in the Applications folder and selecting Show Package Contents. From there, go to Contents ⇨ Resources ⇨ DFonts and you'll find your Office fonts hiding there.

Do not attempt to add or remove anything to the files when viewing the package contents of an app! Doing so could damage the installation and potentially cause you to have to reinstall the app.

You can preview these font files by clicking the Font menu on the ribbon's Home tab of each app and perusing the list of fonts. Each font name is presented in the font itself. If a font name has a cloud icon next to it, the font isn't currently installed. You can download and install the font by selecting it.

Icons Gallery

Although Office is well known as a suite of business productivity apps, it also includes a nice collection of clip art, which Microsoft now refers to as *icons*. And, even though much of this artwork is indeed business oriented, the Stock Images Icons pane also contains a good number of images you can use in documents that have nothing to do with business.

So the next time you're looking for a way to spice up a document, pop open the Stock Images Icons pane and insert a bit of art. In Word, PowerPoint, or Excel, choose Insert⇨Icons to open the Stock Images Icons pane on the right side of the current window. In the search window, type the name or description of the art you're looking for and prepare to be amazed by the plethora of options you'll discover. Click to select the image you want, and then click the Insert button to place the image in your document, spreadsheet, or slide.

Here are a few tips for getting the maximum benefit from the Stock Images Icons pane:

>> When you initially add an image to a slide in PowerPoint, a new pane called Design Ideas opens on the right. This pane offers help for those of us who are design-challenged. Check out the suggestions, and if you see one you like, simply click to use it.

>> You're not stuck with the initial colors and the look of the image you inserted. Right-click the image and select Format Graphic from the menu. The Format Graphic pane opens on the right, and you can change all sorts of characteristics.

>> You can't open the Stock Images Icons pane directly from Outlook. However, you can open the pane from another Office app, and then drag and drop an image from the pane to an email message you're composing.

Import Outlook Archives

Let's say you've used Outlook for years on a PC and want to move all your emails, contacts, tasks, notes, and calendar items to your newly installed Outlook for Mac. Or perhaps you'd like to do the same except you're moving from an older Mac with an older version of Office. Microsoft's got you covered!

The first thing you'll need to do is export your content from Outlook on your PC or old Mac to an archive file. Outlook archive files are in the .pst format (Windows) or the .olm format (Mac). Both formats are supported by the newest version of Office for Mac.

Here's how to import those archives into your new installation:

1. **Open Outlook.**

2. **Choose File⇨Import.**

   The Import dialog appears.

3. **Select the type of archive you're importing and click Continue.**

4. **In the Choose window, browse your computer to find and select the archive file, and then click the Import button.**

5. **Allow the process to complete and then click Finish.**

   The imported content appears in the On My Computer section of the navigation pane on the left.

Microsoft Teams

Microsoft Teams is an all-in-one collaboration tool. You can use it to communicate via voice, text, or video conference. Teams is also a file- and app-sharing tool. All considered, it's an excellent app for anything from one-on-one conversations to all-hands-on-deck departmental meetings.

Teams is available for all major platforms: Mac, PC, Linux, iOS, iPadOS, and Android. Visit www.microsoft.com/en-us/microsoft-teams/ to learn more about Teams (including plans and pricing information) and to download it.

Teams can be acquired as a stand-alone app (for free or otherwise; more on that in a moment) or as part of a subscription if you sign up for the Microsoft 365 Personal or Family edition.

The basic version of Teams is free but limited in some functionality compared to other versions. You still get:

>> Group calling for up to 1 hour and up to 100 participants

>> Unlimited chat

>> Access to tools such as tasks and polling for event planning

>> 5 GB of OneDrive storage

>> Secure data encryption

Sounds pretty good, especially for free! Frankly, the free version is about all most individual users need. But if you find that it won't suit you, check out the Microsoft 365 Personal and Family plans. They include everything the free version offers, plus the following:

>> Group calling for up to 30 hours and up to 300 participants

>> The big three Office apps and more

>> Technical support for the life of your subscription

There is still one more option for business users that doesn't require purchasing a version of Microsoft 365 Business. Microsoft Teams Essentials gives you everything that comes with the free versions, plus:

>> Group meetings for up to 30 hours

>> Up to 300 participants per meeting

>> 10 GB of OneDrive storage per user

>> 24x7 phone and web support

Microsoft Teams Essentials is a good bundle but will set you back $4 per user per month. For just $1 more per user, you could go with Microsoft 365 Business Basic, which gives you the big three Office apps, Outlook, web versions of Office apps, and more. Something to think about.

Outlook Profile Manager

Outlook Profile Manager (previously known as Microsoft Database Utility) is a companion program that allows you to manage multiple profiles for Outlook. If you're someone who uses Outlook in multiple capacities that you'd like to keep separate (for example, if you use it for both work and personal reasons), you can create a profile for each. Profiles store sets of emails, calendars, tasks, contacts, account settings, and more.

Your main profile is created automatically when you first launch Outlook. To manage your profiles:

1. **Go to your Applications folder.**
2. **Right-click the Microsoft Outlook icon and select Show Package Contents.**
3. **Open the Contents folder and then the SharedSupport folder. Double-click Outlook Profile Manager to open the app.**
4. **Use the + and − buttons in the toolbar at the bottom of the Outlook Profile Manager dialog to add or delete selected profiles, respectively.**
5. **(Optional) Set a profile as the default by selecting it in the profiles list and clicking the three dot icon (set default profile button).**
6. **To quit Outlook Profile Manager, click the red dot in the upper-left corner of the dialog window.**

Microsoft Remote Desktop

Let's say you have a PC running Microsoft Windows (sorry, but the reality is that sometimes we Mac users have to swim in those murky waters) in your lab at work and there's a document on it that you really need to review. However, you're at home and don't want to make that long trek to the office, and to make things even more interesting, you only have a Mac in your humble abode. That's where the little gem that is Microsoft Remote Desktop demonstrates its quality.

TECHNICAL STUFF

Only the Pro and Enterprise versions of Windows have the Remote Desktop feature that enables the PC to accept incoming connections.

Remote Desktop is an app you can install on your Mac or iOS device (it's free to download and use), but it's not just any app. This app allows you to remotely connect to and control Windows PCs from anywhere in the world. You can

>> Open and use any app installed on the remote PC

>> Access network resources local to the remote PC

>> Access files and folders

>> Print documents to printers in the remote PC's location

>> Run apps from the remote PC that don't support direct installation on your Mac or iOS device

>> Do just about darned near anything else you could do if you were sitting right in front of the remote PC

For links to documentation for getting set up and started, visit https://aka.ms/rdclients and click the links for iOS or macOS under the *Remote Desktop Clients* section. Learn how to set up your PC for remote access at https://aka.ms/rdsetup.

Then, download and install the Microsoft Remote Desktop app for macOS or iOS by searching for it in the App Store on your device.

TIP

You can use Remote Desktop also to access virtual machines that your company or organization may use. Ask your IT department for assistance with setting these up for remote access.

Microsoft Edge

Microsoft Edge is Microsoft's latest incarnation of a world-class web browser. It replaced Internet Explorer (thank goodness!) a few years back on Windows. These days, Edge has been retooled and made available for other platforms, including macOS, iOS, and iPadOS.

You already have a great web browser on your Mac and other Apple devices (Safari), so why bother with another one, right? Well, in our opinion, it's a great idea to always have more than one browser installed just in case you run into hiccups with certain websites. Sometimes a website may be troublesome in one browser and completely trouble-free in another. Also, web-based apps — such as Microsoft's Office 365 versions of Word, Excel, PowerPoint, and Outlook — might work better or support more functionality when using a browser developed by the same company.

Edge is free, fast, secure, and reliable — using it is truly a next-level experience when compared to the days of Internet Explorer — and it will serve you well as an alternative browser or even as your (gasp!) default browser.

Learn more about and download Edge for Mac at www.microsoft.com/en-us/edge. You can check it out in the App Store to do the same for your iPhone or iPad.

Microsoft To Do

Most of us have a to-do list as long as our arms (we know some folks who literally write the list *on* their arms!), and we also have our computers or smart device screens in front of us constantly. Microsoft saw an opportunity to develop an app that would marry the to-do list with the computing device: Microsoft To Do. (Appropriate name, yes?)

To Do lets you create lists and reminders to keep you on track all day long, it's beautifully designed, and it's free to boot! We know some diehard Apple fans who prefer Microsoft's To Do app over Apple's own Reminders app, which is similar in functionality. We can't honestly claim to be in that camp, but we have used To Do and heartily recommend it, especially if you're someone who appreciates the Microsoft aesthetic.

You can find Microsoft To Do in the App Store for macOS, iOS, and iPadOS.

Microsoft OneNote

We've all had this experience: A great idea pops into your head but you lose it because you can't jot it down in the moment or you think you'll remember it later only to forget it the very next minute. Wouldn't it be wonderful (and more prudent, frankly) if you had a notebook with you that you could instantly open and use to record that idea? Yep, Microsoft's thought of that, too, and thankfully someone there had the foresight to write it down before the idea was lost in the ether. That's how we got OneNote.

OneNote acts as a digital notebook for your Mac, iPhone, or iPad. You can write down your ideas, upload images, draw plans and other illustrations, share your ideas with others, and even capture audio recordings using OneNote.

OneNote is free to download in the App Store for macOS, iOS, and iPadOS. It may also have come with your Office installer, depending on the version of Office you've purchased or subscribed to.

Chapter **22**

Ten Timesaving Shortcuts and Tips for Enhanced Productivity

We've been Office users since time immemorial. We still remember Microsoft's first effort at a spreadsheet, MultiPlan, and the pain of writing using version 1.05 of Word for the Mac.

We also remember the good qualities of Office. And, over the years, we've developed quite a few time- and effort-saving techniques that we share with you now. These tips and hints are all over the board (and all over the Office suite), but the one characteristic they have in common is that they all can save you time, keystrokes, or effort — or all of the above.

Memorize Keyboard Shortcuts

If you do only one thing to speed up your use of the Office apps, memorize frequently used keyboard shortcuts. The more you keep your fingers on the keyboard keys (and off the mouse), the more efficient you will become while using the Office apps.

The keyboard shortcuts in Table 22-1 have saved us lots of time and effort over the years.

TABLE 22-1

Common Office Shortcuts

Command	Keyboard Shortcut
New Document	⌘+N
Save Document	⌘+S
Open File	⌘+O
Cut, Copy, or Paste	⌘+X, ⌘+C, and ⌘+V, respectively
Undo Last Action	⌘+Z
Increase or Decrease Font Size	⌘+Shift+> and ⌘+Shift+<, respectively
Jump to the Beginning or End of a Document	⌘+Home (alternatively, ⌘+Fn+Left Arrow) and ⌘+End (alternatively, ⌘+Fn+Right Arrow), respectively
Cycle through windows in the active app	⌘+~
Open the Editor pane (Word only)	⌘+Option+L
Use Thesaurus	⌘+Option+Control+R
Open the Font dialog (Word only)	⌘+D

TIP

Create a helpful printed list of keyboard shortcuts to memorize whenever you begin using a new program. We keep a list taped to the desk or monitor until the shortcuts become second nature to our fingers.

Get to Know Your Preferences

We mention app preferences several times throughout this book, but in almost every case we direct you to a specific preference setting that's germane to the discussion at hand.

Direct your attention to the Preferences dialog in each app (choose *App Name* ➪ Preferences or press ⌘+comma to open it) and try various settings to determine which ones suit your style.

For example, we don't like to see the paragraph marker included when we select a paragraph in Word and we don't like entire words to be automatically selected rather than just the text we drag the cursor over. If you feel the same way, you can fix both default behaviors by deselecting them in the Word Preferences Edit pane.

Here's another example: We rarely want to convert URLs (internet addresses) to hyperlinks in our Office documents so we can avoid accidentally opening web pages by clicking, rather than selecting, links. So we always turn off that option in an app's AutoCorrect preference pane.

We have no way to climb into your brain to figure out which preference settings will make your life better, so we encourage you to find some time to try them all.

Save a Document as a PDF File

Sometimes you want to send someone Word, Excel, or PowerPoint *documents* but, for some reason, not the actual Word, Excel, or PowerPoint *files.*

Why might you not want to send the file? Maybe you're not sure that your recipients have a copy of Office. Perhaps you don't want them to be able to edit (change) the document. Or you might have used fonts that you don't think the recipients have installed and you want to ensure that the document looks right when it's opened.

The solution to all these dilemmas is to send a PDF file. The Portable Document Format (PDF), invented by Adobe in 1993, has become the de facto standard for sharing documents among different apps, operating systems, hardware configurations, and installed fonts. A PDF file always looks exactly the same, regardless of your computer type (such as Dell, HP, or Apple), operating system (macOS, Windows, or Linux, for example), app software (such as Adobe Reader or Preview), or fonts used in the original document.

To be sure that recipients see what you intended for them to see, your best bet is to send a PDF file instead of a Word, Excel, or PowerPoint document. To create a PDF document from one of these document types, follow these steps:

1. **Choose File ⇨ Print.**

   The Print dialog appears.

2. **Choose Save As PDF from the menu that opens when you click the PDF button in the lower-left corner of the dialog.**

   The standard Save File dialog appears.

3. **Name the file.**

4. **Navigate to the folder in which you want to save the file.**

5. **Click the Save button.**

TIP

To email the file to someone, you can choose Send in Mail instead of Save As PDF from the menu that appears when you click the PDF button. Then a PDF file isn't created on your hard drive; instead, your default email program (Mail or Outlook, for example) launches and creates a new email message that contains the PDF file, saving you several steps.

Save Time by Using the Share ➪ Email (as Attachment) Menu Item

We often finish working on a Word or Excel document and immediately email it to someone to edit or review or to do additional work on it. We could switch to the mail program, create a new, blank email message, and then drag the document onto it to add it as an attachment. But Office has an easier way.

To send a Word, Excel, or PowerPoint document to someone as an email attachment:

1. **Click the Share button in the upper-right of the ribbon.**

2. **Click Send a Copy.**

3. **From the Send As pop-up menu, choose Word Document, PDF, or HTML.**

4. **Click the share icon, and then select the email app you want to use from the list.**

   The icon looks like a box with an upward-pointing arrow.

When you do so, your email program (for example, Mail or Outlook) launches (if it's not already open) and creates a new email message that contains the document as an attachment. As with the PDF trick in the preceding section, this little shortcut can save you several steps.

This trick may not seem like much of a timesaver, but do it a few times a day and it soon adds up to true time savings.

Focus on the Task at Hand

As you can probably gather by our geeky diatribes, we use the computer as much as the next person, which means we've got a lot of apps and reminders and alarms and notifications vying for our limited attention.

Focus view to the rescue! Focus view (available only in Word) removes every element from screen except the page and the words you're typing. This sparse landscape makes it incredibly easy to concentrate on your words.

To engage focus view, click the focus icon at the very bottom of the current Word document window or choose View➪Focus from the menu. If you need to access a command from the menu or ribbon while in focus view, simply move your mouse cursor to the top of the screen and the menu and ribbon will temporarily pop into view, retreating out of view again once you've selected a command or moved your mouse cursor back down the page.

To exit focus view, press the Esc key or move your mouse cursor to the top of the screen and choose View➪Focus from the menu.

As in much of life, when it comes to using focus view in Word, sometimes less really is more.

Use the Open Recent Feature to Open Items from the Dock

Office has an easy way to open any document you've worked on recently: Right-click (or Control-click) the dock icon of any open Office app. When you do so, you see the Open Recent menu item, which lets you open any of the last ten documents you worked on in that app.

Get Help

You can find extensive help on the Help menu in each of the Office apps. Furthermore, if you can't find a topic in the built-in Help system, you might find it online by visiting `https://support.microsoft.com/en-us/office` in your favorite web browser. The point is that you don't have to stop working when you can't figure out how to accomplish a task. At least try the Help system or the online help before you throw in the towel.

Use Format Painter

We cover the Format Painter feature elsewhere in this book, but we want to mention it again in the context of enhancing your productivity. Format Painter lets you select any text and copy all its formatting. Then you can "paint" that formatting on other text by clicking and dragging.

By *formatting*, we mean *all* formatting attributes applied to the selected text — font, font size, bold, italic, line spacing, space before or after, color, and so on.

We promise that if you learn to use Format Painter, you will save yourself a lot of time and mouse clicks. In fact, after you get the hang of it, you rarely need to visit the Font or Paragraph dialogs (or palettes or toolboxes). When you know how Format Painter works, you can almost always change the appearance of a word, paragraph, or page with one or two clicks (or, better, keyboard shortcuts).

TIP

Format Painter does what the Copy and Paste and Match Formatting commands do. But unlike those commands, Format Painter is always right in front of your eyes on the ribbon's Home tab.

REMEMBER

Outlook doesn't offer Format Painter, but it is on the ribbon's Home tab in Word, Excel, and PowerPoint.

Speak Your Mind with Dictation

Most computers these days have a built-in microphone. But did you know that you can use that microphone to dictate your words in your Office apps?

We thought not.

Here's how to do it:

1. **In your document, place the cursor in the location you want your text to be.**

2. **Select Edit ⇨ Start Dictation (or press Fn+D) to open the Dictation window.**

3. **Your app begins listening immediately, so simply begin speaking your content.**

4. **Click the Done button when finished.**

You can also click the Dictate button on Word's Home tab (this isn't available in other apps) to open the Dictation window at the bottom of your document.

Don't forget to speak your punctuation! For example, when you're dictating your text and come to the end of a sentence, remember to enunciate the word "period" to place a period at the end of the sentence. The same goes for adding question marks, exclamation marks, and any other punctuation.

Fair warning — your computer's microphone can't discriminate between your voice and that of others, so make sure you're in a quiet environment to avoid any errors and to prevent words from being accidentally recorded.

Don't Forget Your Free OneDrive

Although our daily Office workflow has remained basically unchanged for years, our work habits and tools have changed a lot. These days, for example, we use a laptop computer much more, we have an iPhone and an iPad, and we take advantage of free Wi-Fi at Starbucks (and at many other places) almost every day.

We've already mentioned the browser-based Office for the Web apps and Microsoft's free OneDrive system, but we sometimes forget to use these great web-based tools — and you might forget too. So follow these tips to get the most benefit from the web-based Office components:

>> Remember to save files to your OneDrive (click the Share button in the upper-right of your current window and upload the file, or a copy of it, to OneDrive) in addition to saving them on your local hard drive. That way, you can edit them on any computer with a web browser.

>> Bookmark Office.com (at www.office.com/signin) in your browser's bookmarks bar. That way, you're reminded about it every time you look at your browser. From there you can access not only OneDrive but also other online Office apps.

>> You can download the OneDrive app on your iPhone, iPad, or Android device to access your stored files on them as well. Just go to the App Store on your device and search for *Microsoft OneDrive*, and then download the app.

» **Increasing screen real estate when you need it**

» **Customizing your keyboard shortcuts**

» **Taking advantage of templates**

» **Giving dark mode a try**

Chapter **23**

Ten Ways to Customize Office

You can customize Office for the Mac in many ways to make it suit your own needs. From toolbars to menus, you can easily put commands wherever they're handiest for the way you work.

In this chapter, we remind you of a hodgepodge of ways to customize your Office experience, ranging from modifying and creating toolbars and ribbon tabs to changing keyboard shortcuts and taking advantage of templates. Use this chapter as a motivator to maximize the efficiency of the apps you work with most often.

Modify the Quick Access Toolbar

Office's Quick Access toolbar, found at the top of every Office app window, is designed to deliver maximum utility in a minimum of space. So, it's not surprising that some commands you want to see on it aren't there and that others you never use are. Fortunately, you can easily add or remove commands from the Quick Access toolbar, if you like.

Here's an example. The Save command is already on the Quick Access toolbar by default, but we often use the Save As command when writing. Perhaps we want to make changes to a document but don't want to lose or modify some of what we've already written. We can use Save As to save a copy of the current document under a different name, allowing us to save the original as is and make any changes we like to the copy. Both versions of the document now coexist peacefully. Were it only that easy with other things in life!

We can thankfully add the Save As command — as well as a myriad of others — to the Quick Access toolbar, and can just as easily remove them, too. Here's how:

1. **Open the Preferences dialog in your app.**

2. **Click the Ribbon & Toolbar button.**

3. **Select the Quick Access Toolbar tab near the top of the dialog.**

4. **Select an item in the Choose commands from pop-up menu, scroll through the list of available commands, and then click to select the one you want to add to the Quick Access toolbar.**

5. **Click > in the middle of the dialog to add your desired command to the Customize Quick Access Toolbar commands list.**

TIP

To remove a command from the Quick Access toolbar, choose it in the Customize Quick Access Toolbar list and click < in the middle of the dialog.

6. **(Optional) Drag and drop commands in the order you would prefer them to appear on the Quick Access toolbar.**

7. **To save your changes, click the Save button in the lower right.**

Modify Existing Ribbon Tabs and Tab Groups

If you never use a certain command on a ribbon tab and you'd rather not have the command there to confuse you or clutter things, you can remove it. On the flip-side, you can also add commands to ribbon tabs and tab groups.

As described in earlier chapters, you can add or delete commands from any ribbon tab or tab groups. Simply follow these steps:

1. **Open the Preferences dialog in your app.**

2. **Click the Ribbon & Toolbar button.**

3. **Select the Ribbon tab near the top of the dialog.**

   You see two sections: Choose Commands From and Customize the Ribbon.

4. **Select an option in the Choose Commands From pop-up menu, scroll through the list of available commands, and then click the one you want to add to the ribbon.**

5. **Select an option in the Customize the Ribbon pop-up menu, and then click to select the tab and tab group to which you want to add the command you chose in Step 4.**

6. **Click > between the two sections to add the selected command to the desired ribbon tab.**

7. **Click the Save button in the lower right to save your changes.**

   Your new command is listed in the ribbon tab you chose.

To remove a command from a tab, click to select it in the Customize the Ribbon list and click the < button located between the dialog's two sections.

You may have noticed that the main tabs in the tabs list sometimes include tab groups, which are subcategories within the tab. Click > next to a tab group to expand its contents.

Show or hide ribbon tabs and tab groups by selecting or deselecting the check box to the left of their names.

There you have it: Customizing ribbon tabs and tab groups is easy and can make them easier to use and less confusing, too.

Create a New Ribbon Tab or Tab Group for Frequently Used Commands

You can create a brand-new ribbon tab from scratch for frequently used commands. (We find this option extremely useful.) Using a customized ribbon tab is an incredible timesaver compared to the other ways we might apply commands that aren't in the ribbon or are scattered among several ribbon tabs. Tab groups are also a good way to group commands into a single place so you can easily access them.

To do so:

1. **Open the Preferences dialog in your app.**

2. **Click the Ribbon & Toolbar button.**

3. **Select the Ribbon tab near the top of the dialog.**

4. **Click the + button at the bottom of the tabs list on the right and choose New Tab from the menu that appears.**

5. **Select the New Tab (Custom) that now appears in the tabs list.**

6. **Click the options icon (small circle with three dots) at the bottom of the tabs list and select Rename from the menu. Enter the name of your new tab in the Display Name field and then click the Save button.**

Add new tab groups to your new tabs in the same way, repeating Steps 4–6 but selecting New Group instead of New Tab in Step 4.

REMEMBER

Changes you make to menus and toolbars are saved in the app's Normal document template by default, which is automatically applied to new documents you create.

Focus with Full Screen

Focusing your attention on work can be tough with other distractions on your computer's screen. To help you concentrate on your documents, presentations, or spreadsheets, Office apps support full screen view, which lets the app take over your entire screen, crowding out any other items.

To enter full screen view from any Office app, choose View ⇨ Enter Full Screen.

When you're in full screen, the menu at top of the screen is hidden from view. You can make the menu reappear by moving your cursor to the top of the screen and holding it there for a second or so until the menu shows up.

To exit full screen, move your cursor to the top of the screen until the menu appears and select View ⇨ Exit Full Screen, or simply press the Esc key.

TIP

You can toggle between entering and exiting full screen view by pressing ⌘+Control+F.

Deal with Frequently Used Documents

If you work on the same document regularly, you can usually reopen it quickly by choosing File⇨ Open Recent. And, if you don't see the document on the Open Recent submenu, you can choose File⇨ Open Recent⇨ More to open the Project gallery, which shows you a longer list of recently used files.

Another way you can access the Project gallery is by clicking the Home button in the Quick Access toolbar. Clicking the Home button immediately opens the Project gallery to the Recent tab, where you can quickly peruse those previously open documents, spreadsheets, or presentations.

Remove Unused Keyboard Shortcuts

Sometimes, an Office app uses a keyboard shortcut that doesn't make sense to you. Or the keyboard shortcut conflicts with a keyboard shortcut from another program.

Fortunately, problems like these are easy to fix, at least in Word and Excel.

To remove a keyboard shortcut from a command, follow these steps:

1. **In Word or Excel, choose Tools ⇨ Customize Keyboard.**

2. **Select the menu or command category in the Categories list.**

TIP

If the command doesn't appear in the category you expect it to appear in, choose the All Commands category, which contains every single command in the app.

3. **Select the command in the Commands list.**

TIP

If you have difficulty finding the command, it may be because Microsoft gave the command a different name than the menu item that invokes it. Try typing the name of the command in the search field near the top of the Customize Keyboard window.

4. **Click the existing shortcut in the Current Keys field.**

5. **Click the Remove button.**

6. **Click the OK button.**

Change an Existing Keyboard Shortcut

A shortcut-related issue arises when you've memorized the shortcut for a particular command in another program you use and the Office app assigns a different shortcut to the command.

No problem — you can easily change the Office shortcut to match the one you've memorized. Follow these steps:

1. **In Word or Excel, choose Tools ⇨ Customize Keyboard.**
2. **Select the menu or command category in the Categories list.**
3. **Select the command in the Commands list.**
4. **Click the existing shortcut in the Current Keys field.**
5. **Click the Remove button.**
6. **Click in the Press New Keyboard Shortcut field.**
7. **Press the keys you want to use as the new shortcut.**
8. **Click the Assign button.**

TIP

If the shortcut you're trying to assign is already in use by another command, you see which command it's assigned to just below the shortcut you just typed. If you still prefer to use the shortcut with this new command, go ahead and click the Assign button.

9. **Click the OK button.**

Create a New Keyboard Shortcut

Sometimes, a command in Word or Excel doesn't have a keyboard shortcut but you wish it did. That's no problem. Follow these steps to add a keyboard shortcut to a command that doesn't already have one:

1. **In Word or Excel, choose Tools ⇨ Customize Keyboard.**
2. **Select the menu or command category in the Categories list.**
3. **Select the command in the Commands list.**
4. **Click in the Press New Keyboard Shortcut field.**
5. **Press the keys you want to use as the new shortcut.**

6. **Click the Assign button.**

7. **Click the OK button.**

Changes you make to keyboard shortcuts are saved in the Normal document template by default, which is automatically applied to new documents you create.

Create Your Own Templates

Creating your own templates for document types you use regularly is a powerful tool and one you should use as often as you can to save time and effort.

We cover Microsoft Word templates at length in Chapter 7 but mention them here to remind you that using them can save you much time and effort. You set them up once and can then use them repeatedly. The same idea applies to both Excel and PowerPoint: If you use a particular type of document regularly, for goodness' sake, create a template for it so that you don't have to keep repeating the same work.

After you've created and saved a template, you can use it easily. Choose File ⇨ New from Template, click the template you want to open from the gallery, and then click the Create button. That's all there is to it.

Experiment with Dark Mode

Dark mode is a dark color scheme that allows you to make distinctions more easily between some elements or figures on your screen, or in some cases enhance the perception of some graphics and images on the display.

Dark mode isn't built into Microsoft Office but is a feature of macOS. When you enable dark mode on your Mac, the dark color scheme is engaged system-wide, meaning every app and menu is affected by it (unless the app doesn't support the mode, which is increasingly rare).

To enable dark mode:

1. **Click the menu in the upper-left corner of your Mac's screen and select System Preferences.**

2. **Select General in the System Preferences dialog.**

3. **In the Appearance section of the General dialog, click Dark.**

What if you like dark mode in some but not all of your Office apps? Microsoft foresaw this possibility and made it easy to disable dark mode on an app-by-app basis. To disable dark mode for an individual Office app:

1. Open the Preferences dialog in your app.

2. Click the General button.

3. In the Personalize section of the General dialog, select the Turn Off Dark Mode radio button.

Index

Symbols and Numerics

About the Authors

Bob LeVitus, often referred to as "Dr. Mac," has written or co-written more than 90 popular computer books, with millions of copies sold worldwide. In addition to co-authoring 14 editions of *iPhone For Dummies,* he has written versions of *OS X For Dummies* and *macOS For Dummies* covering every cat- and California locale–named operating system Apple has released since System 7 (all for John Wiley & Sons, Inc., of course).

Bob has penned the popular Dr. Mac column for the *Houston Chronicle* since 1996 and the Dr. Mac's Rants & Raves column for *The Mac Observer* for almost as long. He has also written thousands of articles, reviews, and columns for dozens of newspapers and magazines over his 30+ year career.

Bob is known for his Apple expertise, trademark humorous style, and ability to translate techie jargon into usable and fun advice for regular folks. He has presented more than 100 workshops at Macworld Expos in the United States and abroad, given Macworld Expo keynote addresses in three countries, and offered his own Macintosh training seminars in many U.S. cities. (He also won the Macworld Expo MacJeopardy World Championship three times in a row before retiring.)

From 1986 to 1989 Bob served as editor-in-chief of the first desktop-published Mac magazine, *The MACazine.* From 1989 to 1997, he was a contributing editor and columnist for *MacUser* magazine, writing the Help Folder, Beating the System, Personal Best, and Game Room columns at various times.

Prior to giving his life over to computers, Bob worked in advertising at Kresser/Craig/D.I.K., a Los Angeles advertising agency and marketing consultancy, and its subsidiary, L & J Research. He holds a B.S. in marketing from California State University.

Dwight Spivey has been a technical author and editor for over a decade, but he's been a bona fide technophile for more than three of them. He's the author of *Apple Watch For Seniors For Dummies* (Wiley), *iPad For Seniors For Dummies,* 2022-2023 Edition (Wiley), *Idiot's Guide to Apple Watch* (Alpha), *Home Automation For Dummies* (Wiley), *How to Do Everything Pages, Keynote & Numbers* (McGraw-Hill), and many more books covering the tech gamut.

Dwight's technology experience is extensive, consisting of macOS, iOS, Android, Linux, and Windows operating systems in general, educational technology, learning management systems, desktop publishing software, laser printers and drivers, color and color management, and networking.

Dwight lives on the Gulf Coast of Alabama with his wife, Cindy, their four children, Victoria, Devyn, Emi, and Reid, and their pets Rocky, Penny, and Mirri.

Dedications

As always, this book is dedicated to my wife, Lisa, who has taught me pretty much everything I know about pretty much everything I know (except, perhaps, technology), and has put up with me for more than 30 years. And, as always, I dedicate this book also to my now-adult kids, Allison and Jacob, who love their iPhones almost as much as I love them (the kids, not the iPhones).

— Bob LeVitus

This one's for the newest member of our family, my adorable great-niece, Kamilla. With much love, sweetheart!

— Dwight Spivey

Authors' Acknowledgments

I'd like to thanks Dwight Spivey for doing the heavy lifting for this edition. You rocked it. Thanks again.

Thanks to Microsoft, for producing a product so convoluted, confusing, and lacking in documentation that this book will almost certainly become a bestseller. And, last but certainly not least, thanks to Susan Pink, my favorite editor of all time.

— Bob LeVitus

Carole Jelen, my wonderful agent, you are a godsend!

Bob, I cannot thank you enough for placing your trust in me to help you update and complete this edition of the book. It's been a pleasure and honor teaming up with someone of your stature in the world of Mac geekdom. ☺

Next, the awesome editors, designers, and other professionals at Wiley are absolutely critical to the completion of these books I'm so blessed to write. I hope every individual involved at every level knows that I'm truly grateful for their dedication, hard work, and patience in putting together this book. As always, extra-special gratitude to Susan Pink (you are absolutely indispensable and a joy to work with!), Steve Hayes (thanks so much for placing your trust in me), and Guy Hart-Davis (it's been so good working with you on another of many projects, my friend).

— Dwight Spivey

Publisher's Acknowledgments

Executive Editor: Steve Hayes
Project Editor: Susan Pink
Copy Editor: Susan Pink
Technical Editor: Guy Hart-Davis
Proofreader: Debbye Butler

Production Editor: Mohammed Zafar Ali
Cover Image: © Kaspars Grinvalds/Shutterstock